Georgia game
2017 —

For Kevin —
"thanks for your
support!"
Jim Ryan

D1600551

ON SOMEONE ELSE'S NICKEL

A LIFE IN TELEVISION, SPORTS, AND TRAVEL

TIM RYAN

radius book group

Distributed by Radius Book Group
An Imprint of Diversion Publishing Corp.
443 Park Avenue South, Suite 1008
New York, New York 10016
www.DiversionBooks.com

For more information, email info@diversionbooks.com.

First edition: September 2016
Hardcover ISBN: 978-1-68230-674-1
eBook ISBN: 978-1-68230-675-8

To Lee, the wife and mother who had the
best years of her life stolen from her—and us.

To Patricia, who came into our lives and brought my
family love they had lost, and joy newly found.

To Kimberley, Kevin, Jay, and Brendan of whom Dad is most proud.

To Patricia's children Celeste and John who joined
our family and welcomed us into theirs.

To our collective grandchildren who made our Sun Valley
Christmases special, and brighten every day we are together.

To my sisters: Cindy, like Lee taken too soon, Mary Jo
whose myriad interests and accomplishments are inspiring
and Kathleen whose zest for life is contagious.

To my late cousin Pat, who served as the brother I never had,
and as an uncle to my children who adored him.

PREFACE

Through the viewfinder of my brand new Minolta camera, the black rhino looked about the size of a Volkswagen bus.

When I pressed the autofocus and extended the zoom, the rhino's enormous ears, pricked up like a thoroughbred in the starting gate, filled the camera lens. His eyes seemed focused totally on me.

And it turned out they were. My companions here in the middle of the bush in southern Zimbabwe numbered three: The African tracker who had led us to the rhino's territory, a hired television cameraman, and Clive Stockil, owner of the private game ranch bordering the Sabi River.

Clive was the only one armed—a handgun on his hip—and he warned us that if and when we found a rhino, and if the rhino became a threat, he would not shoot the animal. In that scenario we were left to our own survival devices.

When the rhino had emerged from a thick patch of scrubby bush, the tracker had quickly nailed his skinny frame behind the only accessible tree in the clearing where we silently stood. The cameraman, with his camera anchored on his right shoulder—videotape rolling—jumped behind the tracker. Clive was out of my view, but a few steps behind and to the left of where I was standing, rigid, directly in front of and about thirty feet from the massive animal whose privacy we had interrupted.

The rhino clearly saw me as his target. I slowly lowered my camera, knowing there was no point in flight. Rhinos are surprisingly fast, and amazingly quick from a standing start—like a good NFL running back.

About ten seconds had passed from the time he had emerged from the brush and encountered his intruders in the small clearing. As he started his charge, my options were limited: dive left or right and hope the momentum of his enormous bulk would carry him past me—if I guessed correctly.

I went right. A shot rang out. As I rolled over my camera equipment in the dust of the terrain, I looked left to see the rhino, head low, horn protruding, catch Clive as he turned his body away. The impact pitched him through the air. Clive hit the ground about ten feet from where he had been standing, pistol in hand. The rhino rumbled away at full speed without breaking stride.

Fearful that the horn had caught Clive in the gut I scrambled to my feet, and with the others, ran to him.

"Clive, Clive where did he hit you," I shouted.

Struggling to his feet, dust still swirling around him, Clive muttered: "I'm okay, the bugger got me in the backside," as he swatted sand from his safari shorts. "I told you chaps I wouldn't shoot the animal."

Well, he hadn't. Clive had fired a shot into the ground to distract the rhino from his first target—me. As I dived right, I heard the shot and saw the rhino veer to my left—toward Clive. The rest of the ten seconds of drama had dissolved into a cloud of dust and shouting voices.

Clive had saved my life—and in fact his own. He and his men had translocated a few rhino to stock his game farm, and because rhinos in Southern Africa in the eighties and nineties had been under continual threat from poachers, one of many things being tried to save them was to shave off their valuable horns—the source of revenue for the poachers and their illegal traders.

While "our" rhino's horn had grown back to about six to eight inches in length, the normally needle-like point was rounded off and blunt. Still, had the beast hit Clive head-on, or trampled him, the damage from a rampaging, 2,500-pound animal at full speed could well have been fatal. Clive's bravery and quick wits left him with only a badly bruised butt and a broken wrist watch.

And what you may ask, was a TV sports announcer doing risking life and limb in the African bush? On this dangerous occasion it was to film a wildlife segment for a TV show on CBS Sports. In fact, it had been boxing—a sport I became identified with in the 1980s—which took me to Africa the first time, and opened the door for me to a career and lifestyle totally unique among my peers in the sports broadcasting business.

Fifty-three years later I still look back with wonder on a tapestry of experiences on six continents that my life as a television sports announcer has afforded me. It has been a life as much about seeing the world and its treasures, as describing athletic prowess to sports fans gathered in front of TV sets—a life learning about different cultures and cuisines, hearing different languages, exploring different landscapes.

Given the opportunity by three different television networks over the years, I chose a path less taken by most of my better-paid colleagues anchored to their desks in lavish TV studios far from the game-sites. I chose to be at the scenes of the action, especially if they were in exotic locales around the world.

It has been quite a ride from the wheat fields of Manitoba to the top of the Swiss Alps and the wild bush of Zimbabwe, from gritty hockey rinks to dazzling Olympics venues, from Holiday Inns in college football towns to five-star hotels in Paris and Rome.

Join me, as I reminisce about my unusual journey, and what I learned along the way—about the world, and about myself.

CHAPTER 1

Who Is This Guy Anyway?

The esteemed sports broadcaster Curt Gowdy, who was the top-gun announcer at NBC Sports early in my career, was once being interviewed by a journalist who asked where he was from. Curt's reply began: "Well I was originally born in… and then…"

Normally an articulate and grammatically informed announcer, Gowdy managed to imply that he was born twice, presumably in two different locations.

I recollect that I heard that story from an NBC stage manager, Jim O'Gorman, who worked with both Curt and me and others over many years. O'Gorman was a calm, reassuring presence in the broadcast booths of live events who could be counted on to not only give accurate counts on his fingers (albeit only from ten on down) but to have in his kit-bag everything an announcer could need while tethered to a microphone cable for three hours or more: hangover cures, Band-Aids®, Preparation H®, and Imodium®, among other creative necessities.

But I digress.

I was "originally born" in Winnipeg Manitoba, in 1939. My father Joe Ryan, son of a wheat farmer, met and married my mother Helen Killeen in Ironwood, Michigan where he had been working in the lumber business. After a brief time in Chicago, Joe and Helen moved to Winnipeg where my father— with a law school degree and an accounting background—took a job with the Manitoba Wheat Pool. A sports fan but not an athlete, he also managed minor-league sports teams in Winnipeg. His interest in sports landed him a job as a sportswriter, and then as a columnist with the Winnipeg Free Press.

When Winnipeg's first professional football team was being formed in

1933, he helped find investors and became the first general manager of the team when it joined Calgary and Regina as the western cities in the Canadian Rugby Union. The CRU later morphed into the Canadian Football League.

Joe went on to win three Grey Cup championships with Winnipeg in 1935, '39 and '41.

After the war years (during which he served in a civilian government job in Ottawa) he was the first general manager of the Montreal Alouettes. We moved there from Ottawa in 1946. The Alouettes won Dad's fourth Grey Cup in 1949.

After a ten-year hiatus from football when he was a stock-brokerage executive in Toronto, where we moved to in 1951, he returned to football as the GM of the Edmonton Eskimos and he finished his career there, as a famous sports figure in Canada.

During his tenure as a financier in Toronto, Joe remained well-known to football fans. He got special attention in favored cocktail lounges and even from cab drivers, whom he hired most days to take him to work downtown from our home in North Toronto.

We had a dog at the time—a Kerry Blue Terrier named Molly Dooley. While she had very good bloodlines, she had no serious training from the Ryans. A gregarious and inquisitive girl, she regularly took off on jaunts near and far. Most often someone smitten by her charms would rub her curly coat and check her collar for an ID. We would get a call and send a taxi to pick her up.

One morning Joe was on his way to his office. The cab driver opened the car door for him. "Oh I know who you are," he said, and Dad—pleased to be recognized—was about to ask if the driver was a football fan, when the cabbie added, "I drive your dog!"

For his exploits as a "Builder" in the CFL, Joe Ryan is in the Canada Sports Hall of Fame in Calgary, the Canadian Football Hall of Fame in Hamilton and the Manitoba Sports Hall of Fame in Winnipeg. Among his distinctions are hiring the first American coach in the league, Carl Cronin from Notre Dame, importing the first U.S. Player, halfback Fritzie Hanson from North Dakota State, serving as chairman of the CFL Rules Committee, and creating a revenue-sharing fiscal policy that enabled the smaller cities to compete with Toronto, Montreal, and Vancouver. He died in Victoria B.C. in 1979 at the age of seventy-seven.

My mother and father were married for fifty years. Helen became a minor celebrity in the Winnipeg area when the press made it known that after the Bombers games, Joe brought the muddy uniforms home and she washed them in her machine—readying them for the next game.

Helen, a schoolteacher, was a demanding parent, an accomplished tournament bridge player, an avid football fan and a political critic. She also raised three daughters—the eldest Mary Jo now lives in Ireland in retirement, an adopted sister Kathleen, who with her late husband Ron raised three girls in Toronto, and my youngest sister Cindy, a schoolteacher who died of melanoma at the age of 56, leaving her husband Terry and two grown children.

Obviously sports had a major influence on me as I grew up in Montreal and Toronto. I played all the sports through my high-school days at De la Salle "Oaklands" in Toronto, although with my father's skinny frame and a decided lack of talent—just making the teams was my greatest accomplishment as an athlete. I did have the distinction of being the smartest of three quarterbacks on my high-school team, which still left me third-string. Our starter, Paul Palmer, actually went on to play at the University of Michigan and then as a defensive back in the Canadian League at Hamilton.

Dad's journalism gene also had its influence. By my senior year in high school I decided that was what I wanted to pursue—on the news side. With the help of my student-advisor, Brother Stephen of the Christian Brothers, I applied to the top journalism schools in the U.S.: Missouri, Columbia, Fordham, and Northwestern, along with Canada's only reputed one, Western Ontario.

When my Father got wind of the plans (he was not a particularly hands-on dad) he said, "Why not Notre Dame?" This surprised me, until I remembered that he was a die-hard "subway alumnus" of ND, having worked in the States for several years during the Depression and fallen for the Fighting Irish.

So we sent an application there, and I was accepted. Having had my seventeenth birthday in May of 1956, I started as a freshman in South Bend in the fall.

CHAPTER 2

"Cheer, Cheer For Old…"

My college life began with a dispute between a cocky Canadian student (me) and an arrogant Holy Cross cleric (him).

I had arrived expecting to begin my sophomore year, having completed five years of high school in the Canadian system and believing, wrongly as it turned out, that my credits for Grade 13 would count for my Freshmen year at Notre Dame. It came as a big shock when Father Sheedy, Dean of Students, coldly informed me otherwise.

Unimpressed with my case for skipping freshmen year, and unsympathetic with my distress over the fact, Father Sheedy offered me a deal. Make the Dean's List my first semester—scoring an average of 88 on a scale of 100—and I could start my sophomore year in the spring.

Angry and upset, once back in my dorm in Breen-Phillips Hall, I threw up.

The hall rector sent me to the infirmary where I spent the next two days seriously considering taking the next train back to Toronto. Getting no encouragement whatsoever from my parents to do so, I got over my nausea and my teenage tantrum. I would stay at ND, determined to show the S.O.B. Sheedy that I could make his damn Dean's List.

I didn't. Well at least not the first semester. It was football season of course, and I was a wide-eyed freshman, immediately caught up in the atmosphere of the Fighting Irish. Terry Brennan was the coach, the team wasn't up to the standards of the Frank Leahy years, but it had the brilliant Paul Hornung.

Football Saturdays in South Bend sent an electric charge through campus that was palpable. Classes Monday through Friday that first semester were just about getting to Saturday, when thousands of families and fans poured onto the leafy grounds of the university to follow the marching band of the Irish from the quadrangle of residence halls to Notre Dame Stadium.

Swallowing my juvenile antipathy to Father Sheedy, I decided there was too much fun and excitement to miss with my head buried in the books. I would enjoy this freshman year in full.

Unfortunately, fans of the football team didn't have much to enjoy.

Despite Hornung's heroics, the Irish weren't very good. Alumni and media were screaming for Brennan's head. But the atmosphere and legendary spirit still made getting up early on Saturday mornings an easy thing to do. It was a two-minute walk to the venerable seniors' hall, Sorin, from my freshman hall and that's where the action was on football Saturdays. A makeshift band of student-musicians would assemble on the porch of the stately old building, a party would ensue—happily supplemented by the girls of St. Mary's College nearby. (ND was still an all-male student body in the fifties and sixties.)

Of course a party there didn't include alcohol in any form (except for a few surreptitious shots smuggled in discreetly), but still good times were had by all—until the games started!

The most fun I had with the football team was trying to recruit Hornung for the Canadian Football League. My father had contacted me on behalf of the team that was going to draft the Heisman quarterback, hoping he might consider the CFL over the NFL. The theory was that since the Irish had had such a poor season, he might have dropped down the ranks in the eyes of NFL teams. The CFL would give him the chance to use his triple-threat talents on the wider field where QBs who can run can thrive. Then if he showed his stuff in Canada as a rookie he would still attract NFL interest.

My job was to get friendly with him and cajole him into considering going to Canada.

I did my bit. I knocked on his door in his senior hall one day after the season, introduced myself, and told him why I was there. He didn't close the door—either on me or the CFL idea—and we became friends. But as the school year wore on, I had the sense that he believed he would go high in the NFL draft despite Notre Dame's 2 and 8 season—one of the worst ever for the Fighting Irish.

He was right, Green Bay picked him, and the rest as they say, is history.

As it turned out, our friendship was renewed years later at CBS when we were both football broadcasters on NFL and college games.

Meanwhile, I didn't make the Dean's List that first semester, but used my freshman writing class to create an opportunity to meet the legendary Notre Dame Coach Frank Leahy. There was a writing contest for freshmen, and I chose to write about the firing of Terry Brennan, in the context of Notre Dame's long history of renowned coaches. Through the Sports Information office I was able to make contact with Coach Leahy, explain what I was doing, and ask if I could get some comments from him.

To my surprise, he invited me to lunch at his home in nearby Michigan City! Mrs. Leahy prepared lunch, and Frank was friendly and helpful—while careful not to be too critical of Brennan. All the while I was nervously scribbling down notes, and left after lunch thrilled by the experience.

My classmates were mightily impressed that I had pulled off the interview—at Leahy's home no less!

I didn't win the contest.

Social life at ND was limited. It was after all a boys-only university until the 1970s. St. Mary's College is an all-girls school a twenty-minute walk across campus. Visiting restrictions were rigid at both Catholic schools, although there were frequent "mixers" and of course prom nights.

Some more adventurous guys risked suspension by sneaking a girl into their dorm room for overnight trysts, or organized sleepovers at houses of student friends who lived off-campus. But our hero was a classmate by the name of Jim Ausum, who in our senior year billeted his St. Mary's girlfriend in his room for a full week over the Easter Holidays, somehow managing to avoid scrutiny from the priest-rectors in Sorin Hall. I will spare you the details.

As for off-campus entertainment, occasional weekend trips to Chicago—ninety minutes away by train—could offer the chance to drink beer, hear some live jazz and maybe even see a strip show, pretty exciting stuff for a teenaged college kid. Many of the saloons were owned by the Chicago mob—at one of them one night, the star of the show was an amply endowed lady of some renown, Tempest Storm.

Joined at the bar by a couple of my classmates, I showed my fake ID and ordered a Budweiser as Ms. Storm's backup band warmed up the crowd.

(The drummer was Barrett Deems who had played with Louis Armstrong and was clearly down on his luck playing in a strip bar.)

"I'll have a Budweiser," I said to the bartender with authority.

"Fox Head," came the gruff reply.

"No, Budweiser," I said bravely.

"Fox Head, kid, that's what we serve here." And he slapped down a bottle of Fox Head in front me.

Even an ingenue like me could figure out that the mob owned the bar, *and* the beer distributorship for Fox Head, a beer I had never heard of before.

Meanwhile, Tempest, partially wrapped in a long fake-fur stole, strutted to the stage to a dramatic drum-roll by Barrett Deems and proceeded to mesmerize us with a strip routine that introduced me to the dazzling technique of twirling a tassel affixed on one glorious breast in one direction, and a tassel on the other in the *opposite* direction.

In the late fifties college kids out on the town were easily impressed.

CHAPTER 3

Finding the Path

Despite the worst four-year record for a Notre Dame Football team in its then history, I loved every minute of my time in South Bend. I majored in Communication Arts with the intention of becoming a news reporter after graduation. Summers I worked as a copy boy at Canadian Press in Toronto, then as a rewrite man on the overnight desk at the *Toronto Star*, where a young Ernest Hemingway had once toiled.

My highlights at the *Star* were having a Page One bylined story about a convention of Jehovah's Witnesses being held in Toronto; beating the police to a 3 a.m. crime scene and finding the body of a murder victim before the cops did; and convincing the entertainment editor to use me as his jazz critic.

My love of jazz has stayed with me over a lifetime and I have made many friends in that world. More on that later on.

Also in the summer, I began my career behind a microphone, although at the time it was just for fun. My sister Mary Jo had recommended me to the creators of a radio show that used high school kids on the air discussing teenage topics. I was one of the moderators. I enjoyed it, but my goal going off to college was still to be a newspaperman covering news. (I remain a news junkie to this day). I am proud to say that two of my classmates and friends carried our journalism banner very high after graduation: Terence Smith (son of famed *New York Times* sportswriter "Red" Smith) went on to become White House correspondent for the *Times* and later a news commentator for CBS News and PBS, and James Naughton (who, along with me and others founded the first intercollegiate jazz festival while at ND) became managing editor of the prestigious *Philadelphia Inquirer*.

At Notre Dame, the university had a campus radio station, run by

Calling basketball on Notre Dame campus radio.

students, as an extracurricular activity—no credits—to the Communication Arts program. I auditioned to be one of three or four sports reporters. At the time, I had no thought of that becoming my career.

Meanwhile, the summer following my freshman year I pitched an idea to CFRB radio in Toronto to let me have the two-hour slot they had given to the high-school show I had been on, with me as the disc-jockey playing the "new" music teenagers were listening to from across the border in Buffalo, N.Y., "rhythm and blues," soon to become appropriated by white folks as "rock 'n' roll."

Hosting "The Record Romp" with the latest "race music" on 78 rpm records provided from a local music shop gave me more of a taste of the microphone—not to mention the music!

Meanwhile, calling play-by-play of games of Notre Dame baseball,

(Carl Yastrzemski starred as a sophomore before turning pro with the Red Sox) and basketball—with a close friend and fellow student Mike Mullen as the "expert analyst"—on the campus radio station slowly had an effect on my future plans. A job at the *Star* as a news reporter was waiting for me in Toronto, but after a senior year as Sports Director of WSND, I did start to think about broadcasting as a career.

There were some other considerations in my graduation year of 1960.

Four years earlier, at a high-school "Shoe Shuffle" in Toronto, I had conjured up enough nerve to ask a pretty blonde girl to dance. Her name was Leona Muir; she was a senior at Loretto Abbey, a Catholic girls' school. I was likewise in Grade 13 at De La Salle "Oaklands," a Christian Brothers school nearby. We both lived in what was known as North Toronto.

Leona enrolled a St. Michael's College of Nursing in Toronto, when I was off to Notre Dame. We dated through the summers, to the point that my mother became convinced that we might marry before finishing college! Despite my assurances that we would not do so, it remained a worry on Helen's part.

Well, even though Leona, who became known to friends and family as Lee, made a few trips to Notre Dame for college events—including graduation (Dean's List, Cum Laude—take that Father Sheedy!) we promised not to marry until after I had a job and Lee was working as a Registered Nurse.

Graduation from ND in 1960 was quite a show. Outgoing President Dwight Eisenhower delivered the commencement address—Secret Service crawled around the campus for days prior. Cardinal Giovanni Montini, who was to become Pope Paul VI, said the Mass, my father Joe hugged me in pride and cried for the first time in my memory, and schoolmarm Helen was relieved to see that Lee and I had completed our education.

And I had a job waiting for me at the *Toronto Star*, with a wedding planned for a year later in May of 1961.

CHAPTER 4

"Lights, Camera..."

During my senior year at ND I learned that there would be a new television station going on the air in January of 1961. CFTO-TV would be the anchor station for a new Canadian television network called CTV, which, unlike the existing Canadian Broadcasting Network, CBC, would be a strictly commercial enterprise with no government funding.

CFTO's owners included John Bassett, who owned *The Telegram*, one of three Toronto newspapers. He was also a part owner of the Toronto Maple Leafs hockey team and the Toronto Argonauts of the Canadian Football League. Bassett planned to make sports a big part of CFTO's programming. He hired a well-known sportscaster from Western Canada, Johnny Esaw, as Sports Director. He set about acquiring football, hockey, and Triple-A baseball rights, and well-known sportscasters to cover sports on the daily news shows.

Why not apply for a job at CFTO, I asked myself. I was enjoying my role doing sports on the campus radio station and hosting interview shows with the ND coaches and Athletic Director Ed "Moose" Krause.

Yes, I loved being a newspaper newsman, I had the job at the *Star* waiting for me, but why not send a resume tape to Esaw and see what happens?

Came May and graduation, and in June I started at the *Star*. I felt the right thing to do was to tell Herb Manning, the man who had hired me, that I had sent an application to CFTO. He was very understanding, told me he would love for me to stay at the *Star*, but that if I got the TV job I should take it. And that if things didn't go well at CFTO, I was welcome back anytime to my newspaper job.

In September, still hoping for word from CFTO, I received an offer

Tim and Lee's wedding. Toronto, May 27, 1961.

from a producer friend of my sister Mary Jo to host a TV program aimed at teenagers, on the CBC local station CBLT. Mr. Manning was fine with it, since the schedule didn't interfere with my newspaper job. A month later came a call from Johnny Esaw: would I like to join CFTO as his assistant, with a chance to learn about the TV sports business both on and off-camera, and the promise that eventually I would get to be on-air.

Both Paddy Sampson, the CBC producer who gave me my TV start and Herb Manning of the *Star* wished me luck in my new career and on January 1, 1961 I stood in the brand-new studios of CFTO-TV as the huge color-cameras launched the beginning of Canada's television network CTV.

Lee and I were married on May 27, 1961 and like all newlyweds with high hopes and big dreams had no idea what lay ahead in our lives. Daughter Kimberley Ann was born in October of 1962, so Lee gave up her nursing duties at St. Michael's Hospital, where she had worked on the team assisting during one of Canada's first open-heart surgeries. Son Kevin Kennedy arrived on New Year's Eve of 1963, honored with the name of the U.S. president who had been gunned down two months before.

Johnny Esaw had delivered as promised—I was now doing the weekend sportscasts, hosting a weekly bowling show and calling Junior-A hockey on Sunday afternoons. By the time son Jay was born in 1965, I had gained valuable experience on-air and working on the production side of the NHL telecasts and Esaw's talk show, *The Sports Hot Seat.*

And working for a station owned by John Bassett had other rewards. He was a powerful political figure in Canada, and despite being a member of Canada's Conservative Party, he had struck up a relationship with the notably liberal U.S. Democrat Robert Kennedy.

In 1964 Kennedy was still serving as the attorney general of the United States, following the assassination of his brother the president in November of the preceding year.

Mr. Basset hosted a lavish banquet honoring Robert at an elegant Toronto hotel and with my being a rabid Kennedy fan since my days at Notre Dame, I was thrilled to be, with Lee, included as guests.

I had clipped a newspaper column by Nathan Cohen—my former boss during my days as the jazz reviewer at the *Toronto Star*—that had lauded President Kennedy's contributions to the arts during his time in office. I had kept it with the intention of including it with a note of sympathy to Mrs. Kennedy, to be mailed after a period of time in which I assumed she would be inundated with similar gestures. Now, I had a chance to hand it to Bobby and ask him to deliver it to Jackie! I would wait for an opportune time—at the coffee service perhaps, and just politely interrupt Mr. Bassett, explain that I would like to give an envelope to Mr. Kennedy and done deal!

Right.

As I stood up from our table to approach the dais, Lee gestured to me and pointed out a man who seemed to be approaching me. Yes, Secret Service—two of them actually. Little brass pins in their lapels and buds in their ears. Like in the movies.

"I'm sorry sir, you can't approach the dais."

Embarrassed, I quickly explained my intentions were pure, could they please ask Mr. Kennedy if it would be okay. They did so, I stopped shaking, Mr. Bassett waved me forward, introduced me to Mr. Kennedy who offered his hand with his famous smile and promised that he would personally give the envelope to Mrs. Kennedy.

Less than a month later, a letter dated May 5, 1964 on the letterhead of the Attorney General, Washington, came a thank-you note signed by hand, "Robert F. Kennedy." Framed, it hangs in my home office.

Meanwhile, things continued to go well at CFTO. We had made a second house-move, renting a bungalow in a Toronto suburb closer to the TV studios. Kim was our oldest child, but still pre-school at age four! With three little ones at home Lee had her hands full. But my work didn't yet involve travel, so I was able to help out, and in the summers, we enjoyed occasional weekends on Stoney Lake—about ninety minutes from Toronto—with friends who also had young children.

I was beginning to think longer term. The "ceiling" for TV jobs in Canada was low, with only four major markets: Toronto, Montreal, Ottawa (the nation's capital) and Vancouver. There were only two TV networks. Many top Canadian film and TV performers, directors, and writers were heading south for the bigger opportunities: newsmen Morley Safer, Peter Jennings, Barry Dunsmore, and Mark Phillips; film directors Norman Jewison, David Cronenberg; and actors Lorne Green, William Shatner, and many more.

When in 1966, the National Hockey League announced it would expand for the first time in 1967 from six to twelve teams, I saw my opportunity. Esaw assigned me to cover the awarding of the new franchises, and when I arrived at the venue with our film crew, I had under my arm six copies of my resume and six audiotapes of my hockey play-by-play. After each interview of the new owners, I would hand them my stuff and tell them I was their man to be their broadcaster and their public relations man, since it was unlikely in most of the new cities that there were people with my unique qualifications.

Bold and brassy, yes, but it worked. I was soon offered jobs by four of the six new franchises: Minnesota, Pittsburgh, Philadelphia, and San Francisco/Oakland. I had never been to the Bay Area and San Francisco sounded like the most romantic of the six new NHL locations.

"California Dreamin' " by the Mamas and the Papas became a gold record in 1966. Need I say more?

CHAPTER 5

Hockey With "Peanuts"

Hockey took me to the United States—boxing, tennis, and ski-racing took me around the world—usually on someone else's nickel. And in the later years Lee and the children were able to join parts of the odyssey.

When we left for California in the spring of 1967, three little kids in tow, our Toronto friends thought we were nuts—forging off into the great unknown. In the sixties, our generation hoped to get to college, get a job and get married, then settle down and make a life in our hometowns. None of our peers had given a thought to moving elsewhere.

It was a little tougher on Lee than me. My parents had moved West from Toronto several years earlier when Dad became the GM in Edmonton, and then retired to Victoria B.C. in 1966. Only one of my three sisters still lived in Toronto, and we saw each other only occasionally. But Lee's family was still intact in Toronto, and both her parents had chronic illnesses that restricted their activities and travel. Her sister Sandra was a nurse and her two brothers were still living at home with jobs in the area.

Still, Lee was a "gamer," and excited about the prospects of our new life in the U.S. We exited our house lease, packed up the kids, and flew to Victoria where the family would stay for a few weeks with the grandparents while I found us a place to live in Oakland.

With green card in hand, I joined the San Francisco Seals—playing their last minor league season in the Western Hockey League—at a road game in Seattle. I actually emigrated to the U.S. from Canada by boat—by ferry from Victoria—turning in my papers at Port Angeles, Washington. A few nights later I was staying at the Edgewater Hotel in Oakland, where the offices for the new NHL team would set up shop.

The hotel was across the Nimitz Freeway from the new Oakland Coliseum, known as the Jewel Box for its stylish design of glass and girders. It would be the home of the California Seals, and the new American Basketball Association Oakland Oaks.

I had made it to the San Francisco Bay on someone else's nickel—the team's principal owners, Barry and Mickey Van Gerbig—but the housing was on me. I found an almost-new ranch-style house with three bedrooms, in the hills above the Coliseum. Two hundred-fifty dollars a month. 1967. Wonder what it would be today! The team had a deal with the local car dealer, and so I had a free car. At $10,000 a year salary, all freebies were gratefully received.

The commute from our subdivision known as Sequoia Highlands, wound down through a forested area that encompassed the Knowland Park Zoo, and then opened onto the flats of south Oakland. The road passed through a modest neighborhood that was best known as the territory of Hell's Angels leader Sonny Barger. His house was easily identified by the number of Harleys and black-jacketed riders hanging out in front.

Sonny never became a hockey fan. But he did do some time in the penalty box—federal prison.

My two years with the Seals flew by. I was the radio broadcaster doing all the games home and away on a local Bay Area station, and was also the VP of Public Relations and Publicity. The latter was the tough part, but a great experience. Oakland sports fans never took to hockey. Our hope that the Seals fans from the San Francisco days would cross the Bay Bridge to watch the NHL version didn't happen in any numbers.

Despite drafting fairly well in the NHL's first-ever expansion draft, the Seals failed to make the playoffs. Our general manager, Rudy Pilous and coach, Bert Olmstead were not a match made in heaven. Pilous, under pressure from Olmstead, was fired before the first season began. Olmstead, a fiery former Montreal star, quit after a long winless road-trip east. Needless to say, I was tested early in my new career as a PR man.

Still, there were many upsides and many lasting friendships formed. Team president Frank Selke, from a famous Canadian hockey family, was a warm and patient man in a difficult role. Team captain Bobby Baun, a former Toronto all-star was a leader and a neighbor who also became a dear friend as did his wife Sally with Lee.

Our two most important sportswriters were Spence Conley of the

Oakland Tribune and the late Jack Fiske of the *San Francisco Chronicle*. I courted them constantly in my role as PR director, and days and nights on the road helped build close relationships.

Fiske, a Brooklyn-born transplant and knowledgeable boxing reporter, could be an acerbic critic of the Seals, but on the other hand, on a road trip to New York he introduced me to my first authentic kosher Jewish deli with a bagel-and-lox breakfast at Kaplan's in the Diamond District.

Conley and I became bar-pals after night games, and he wound up meeting his future wife one night in Boston at the bar of the Copley Plaza hotel where dozens were snowed in after a blizzard.

Another night on the road, in Montreal, I paid a stern price for my effort to entertain the media for dinner at the famous Ruby Foo's restaurant. Encouraging Fiske, Conley, and Fran Tuckwiler of the *San Jose Mercury*, to let me order something special—Fondue Boeuf Bourguignon—I condescendingly instructed them on the safety precautions required.

"Place your fondue fork with the pieces of beef on them into the sizzling hot oil fondue pot, and when ready, be sure to move the beef from the fondue fork to a separate fork, before putting it into your mouth," I directed.

Heads nodded knowingly.

Conversation ensued—led by me as usual—a dissertation on the history and excellence of Ruby Foo's, interrupted by a howl from my voice that startled tables around and brought a rush of wait staff to ours. Yes, I had put the fondue fork into my mouth, literally peeling skin from my lips.

Gasps of horror from my tablemates turned to laughter as the embarrassed host sucked on ice-cubes—mouth shut—for the rest of the evening.

My efforts of getting butts into the seats at the Coliseum didn't produce much more success than my efforts to impress the media on the road. The local press and broadcasters were more than fair in their coverage. The fact was that there were simply not enough sports fans in the Bay Area who were willing to give hockey a try, or if they did come once, they didn't necessarily come back.

Our most loyal fan turned to be our most famous—Charles Schulz, creator of the *Peanuts* comic strip. He owned season tickets and drove to every home game with his family from Santa Rosa, more than an hour away. Born and raised in hockey country—Minnesota—he was a knowledgeable

LEFT: Oakland Coliseum: Introducing Charles Schulz and John Ferguson.
RIGHT: Tim with Seals investor, singer/actor Bing Crosby.

and devoted supporter. Having the Seals to cheer for, he even built his own hockey arena near his home/studio, so that he could start a senior men's league and begin a kid's hockey program as well. We became very good friends, and a trip to his property, which he called the "Coffee Grounds," was a treat for Lee, me, and our children.

"Sparky," as he was called by friends, even agreed to be a cover-boy on our Seals program. The world-famous cartoonist had frequently included Montreal tough-guy John Ferguson in Snoopy's fantasies of playing hockey, and so I asked him if he would be willing to present an original panel to Ferguson when the Canadiens came to play the Seals. Sparky, excited at the very idea of meeting Ferguson in person, replied "Yes, of course!"

I secretly arranged with the hockey player known as Fergie to present his number 22 jersey to Sparky when Schulz gave him the cartoon panel at center ice of the Coliseum. I'm not sure which man was most thrilled, but Sparky swore that he slept in that jersey and wore it when he played in his "seniors" games in Santa Rosa!

But even the creator and voice of the great athlete Charlie Brown couldn't save the Seals.

With low ticket sales and little advertising income, the Van Gerbig brothers were forced to send out capital calls to all of their original minor investors—an oversized group with deep pockets which included prominent golf executive Sandy Tatum, singer/actor Bing Crosby, investor Tony Boalt, along with some other nickel-ante dilettantes. Few were forthcoming with new funds.

Giving up on Oakland, the Van Gerbigs tried to move the franchise to Vancouver, but were rebuffed by NHL owners. The team went up for sale in its second season, 1968–69. Two groups attempted to buy at a fire-sale price, one led by a minor-league radio station owner Woody Erdmann, (whose glamour "partners" were football star Pat Summerall and baseball great Whitey Ford), and the other, the new owners of the Harlem Globetrotters— Potter Palmer of the hotel family, John O'Neil, a wealthy businessman, and young George Gillett, a Wisconsin investor. (Gillett went on to be a TV station-group owner, head of Vail Resorts and of several sports franchises— including, many years later, the Montreal Canadiens). Unfortunately for the Van Gerbigs, the first group went bankrupt and the second one never came up with the money.

With the handwriting on the wall, and the ugly prospect of being jobless with a wife and four children, I started looking for work as a full-time sportscaster. Baseball character Charlie Finley eventually bought the Seals, but within a few years they wound up in Cleveland as the Barons, and ultimately they sank, un-seal-like, into NHL oblivion.

CHAPTER 6

High Anxiety

The summer of 1969 was scary. Shortly after the hockey season ended in May, my salary stopped. Barry Van Gerbig arranged for me to continue to have use of the freebie Plymouth for a few more months, but my meager bank balance was being stretched to pay the rent on the house and feed my family. There were the proverbial sleepless nights as my mind whirled trying to figure out what to do next.

Lee was her usual supportive self, confident that I would soon find a job. Kimberley, our oldest was just seven, the boys, Kevin and Jay were six and four. All three had been born in Toronto. Now we were about to have our first American-born, due in mid-July. I had hoped to land a job at the only Oakland TV station—one I had pitched (without success) to carry some of the Seals games. For a time the general manager had shown more interest in having me on his station than having the Seals games. But his interest had waned, and there was nothing open in San Francisco—TV or radio.

I started sending resumes around the country—any place where I had contacts of any kind. Weeks went by. The baby arrived, a healthy boy, on July 12: Brendan Patrick, born on "King Billy's Day," the day honoring the hated (by Irish Republicans!) King William of Orange—a mythic figure in the history of British-owned Northern Ireland.

Brendan's birth-date didn't seem like a good omen for his out-of-work father, an Irish Catholic whose forebears came from County Tipperary in the South. But we were thrilled, mainly because for the first time I was permitted to be in the delivery room to see our new son enter the world, for which Lee and I were grateful to the staff of Oakland's Merritt Hospital.

But perhaps it was Brendan's birth that did bring good luck, just as the

Ryan coffers were close to empty. Two contacts, one in New York and another in Philadelphia arranged interviews for me. One was for a sportscasting slot on the local news on WCBS-TV, New York. My friend, a fellow Canadian from Toronto who was in Sales at the station, had been told there was an opening and I was to see the news director.

I pushed the limits of my credit card for airfare, found a cheap hotel and with resume-tape in hand went to the famous CBS "Black Rock" building on West 52nd Street.

"What are you here for?" was the greeting received as the door to the news director's office opened. I am sure I gulped and stammered.

"Well, uh, uh, uh… for the sportscaster job opening?"

You guessed it, there wasn't a job open; the less-than-courteous news director didn't know why I had an appointment with him; and I was out the door in minutes.

I was devastated, not to mention virtually broke. I called my Toronto friend—he was totally mystified, apologetic, and embarrassed. I was still very much out of work. The next day I took a train to Philadelphia for my second appointment, a slim chance at a similar job at the ABC affiliate there. This time, courtesy, but no cigar. "We'll call you if anything opens up…"

Back in New York, I called home and gave the distressing news to Lee. I couldn't afford to stay in New York any more than another day. I would try another couple of names I had on my contact list. One was a man named Jack Price, who ran a company that produced closed-circuit telecasts of major boxing matches—this being the era before cable-TV and Pay-per View.

We arranged to meet that evening for a drink. Jack told me he knew that WPIX-TV, an independent TV station in New York, (owned by the New York *Daily News*), was looking for a news anchor who could also do the sports results. He offered to make an appointment for me the next day with his friend Don Carney, who produced the Yankees games on WPIX.

Now this is where luck and timing kicked in again: yes, WPIX was looking for a news anchor who could also read the sports news with some authority, thus saving another salary on the *WPIX 10 O'Clock News*. Carney was not involved in that program, but walked me into the news director's office, told him that I was a sports announcer who had news experience, and might be a good fit for the job. Of course my news experience, except for a handful of noontime news reports at CFTO in Toronto, had been in print—at the *Canadian Press* and the *Toronto Star.*

I headed to the airport feeling I had made a good impression, but knowing this was a total long-shot. Surely they would choose a more experienced news anchor to join their incumbent, Lee Nelson, in their two-anchor format.

CHAPTER 7

Helluva Town

About two weeks after my return to Oakland, and with no other immediate job prospects, my optimism was waning. Baby Brendan was now about a month old; Kimberley, Kevin and Jay were blissfully unaware that Dad was scrambling for his life to pay the rent. Lee remained calm and encouraging. But despite promising that they would let me know quickly—one way or another—WPIX hadn't called. Yet.

Then they did.

Could I be in New York, on the air September 15th, when they would launch their new format: Lee Nelson and Tim Ryan as co-anchors, on a brand new set, with guest commentators like famed columnist Jimmy Breslin? They would offer me a two-year contract for $26,000 a year.

It was one month before the start date. Could I possibly deal with our Oakland landlord, find a place to live in the New York area, check out school districts, pack up our belongings and move Lee and the four kids—and still be ready to (gulp!) start a new career as a news anchor… in New York City?

Of course I could!

The news director said, "Come as soon as you can." They would put me up in a hotel near the WPIX studios in the *Daily News* building on 42nd Street while I went house hunting in the mornings and attended meetings in the afternoons with the news staff. They were determined to be ready to go September 15. Airline tickets were arranged.

Lee was ecstatic. We hugged and kissed and danced—until reality set in. She would be in Oakland alone with our four kids including a one-month old baby for at least a month and maybe longer. I would be alone in New

York, choosing housing without Lee's input, and trying to adjust to the idea of becoming a TV news anchor in NEW YORK!

My temporary home in Manhattan was the Shelton Towers Hotel on Lexington Avenue in the East 40s—walking distance to the Daily News Building.

Some fast research helped me decide that living in the city with four young children was a no-go on all fronts, and Westchester County was a better commute than Long Island or New Jersey. So every morning in the weeks before D-day on Channel 11, I rode the Metro North train lines, meeting real estate agents to look for affordable rental houses. I found one in a leafy town called Larchmont with a five-minute walk to the train station and a 30-minute train ride to Grand Central Station, two blocks from WPIX.

With much relief, I telephoned Lee and said I would soon be on my way back to make the big move to the Big Apple. I don't remember much about the actual move (we had been through that exercise five times already in seven years of marriage), but I know it included a Siamese cat named Thai, which our Oakland landlord had insisted was part of our lease when he and his family had moved to Australia for business. Since they were not returning to the U.S. anytime soon to reclaim the creature, they asked me to adopt Thai. Only the children were thrilled to have the cat come with us to New York, although I must admit, Thai and I had become pretty close friends.

It was finally sinking in. After nearly four months with no income, a small severance from the Seals, and little savings here we were, on our way to New York for a TV job that I had only dreamed about. All of this just three short years after taking the big leap of faith from the security of Toronto to the unknown future in the Bay Area of California.

In 1944, a Broadway show titled, "On the Town" introduced a song with a lyric that would become a classic, "New York, New York—it's a helluva town."

In 1969, it certainly was. And I would get to be part of it.

CHAPTER 8

Artistic Athletes
and an Artist of Sport

WPIX-TV Channel 11 was one of three independent or non-network affiliated stations in 1969 New York. The other two were Westinghouse-owned WNEW, and WOR-TV, owned at the time by a merger of General Tire and RKO Pictures. WPIX and WNEW had 10 o'clock nightly news shows. So we were not competing head to head with the early-evening network news programs. Still, it was kind of cool, if not daunting, that Lee Nelson and I were presenting the same news each day as NBC's Huntley-Brinkley and Walter Cronkite at CBS, who were just a few blocks away.

The year 1969 was a magic year of news and sports in New York. A noisy and bitter mayoral election battle between the elegant aristocrat John Lindsay and the combative working-class favorite, Mario Procaccino dominated news coverage in print and on the airways. It was an improbable year for New York sports fans: the lowly National League Mets had become the "Amazins" enroute to a World Series victory, the basketball Knicks, led by determined leader Willis Reed won the NBA title for the 1969–70 season, the hockey Rangers made the NHL playoffs, and "Broadway Joe" Namath brashly predicted a Super Bowl victory for the football Jets—and then delivered.

In my news-anchor role, I had quickly boned-up on New York politics, and while Nelson handled the heavy lifting in our nightly coverage, I frequently did interviews with political pundits and important figures in the campaigns. *Daily News* columnist Jimmy Breslin—already a newspaper legend—was a

LEFT: On WPIX news set with co-anchor Lee Nelson.
RIGHT: Tim with artist LeRoy Neiman.

regular contributor (remember, the *Daily News* owned WPIX). Lindsay won the November election, although he proved to be a largely unpopular mayor.

Of course as the sports guy, I got to cover all of the wondrous exploits of the 1969 New York teams, but missed most of the evening home games since I had to be in the studio in ample time for the 10 p.m. program. Still, Madison Square Garden and Shea Stadium were my second homes. I met and made many great friends in those "homes," including the artist LeRoy Neiman, who loved sketching and painting athletes of all skills, and attended all of the big sports events—leather-bound sketchbook in hand.

LeRoy had gained early fame as the resident artist for *Playboy Magazine*, and concentrated his skills on the "beautiful people " at beautiful events—all over the world. I thought he would make a good feature piece on the WPIX news—a New York art icon who exuded style and glamour.

We did the shoot at his studio in the elegant Hotel des Artistes on Manhattan's Upper West Side. It was a thrill for me to see his workplace and be surrounded by finished and unfinished canvases on all sides. He was working on something as we set up lights and the camera. I had been chatting with his wife Janet who had graciously poured me a drink, and turned to start the interview. LeRoy, with a palette of pencils and chalk, had drawn a large-size rendering of me, glass in hand! It was the beginning of a life-long friendship—ended in June of 2012 when LeRoy died at ninety-one after a long illness. Needless to say that drawing went home with me, and I came to own several of his works over the years. And I am grateful that I was able to visit with him and Janet at the their apartment-studio just a few weeks before he died. Leroy was bright and witty to the end.

As for the real home in Larchmont, I was learning to deal with the TV hours—a train into the city around noon, a train back to Larchmont that arrived close to midnight. Not conducive to great family life. Somehow Lee managed to get Kim, Kevin, and Jay to elementary school each day, and baby Brendan was of course still at home. We treasured weekends when we could all be together. That would change soon enough.

To make things more interesting in our home life, the nice house we had first found turned out to be very temporary. The landlords, from Spain, suddenly were returning and begged us to break the lease and let them back in after only a couple of months. Nice guys that we are, we did so, but only after we were able to find another, but less desirable rental in Larchmont.

That one we were in for less than a year, since I was now able to afford mortgage payments and with the help of my old college friend Dick Corbett who loaned me the $10,000 down, we bought our first house.

That made our *eighth* move in eight years.

Price, the closed-circuit maven who got me in the door at WPIX, called one day to tell me that he was now the vice president of broadcasting at Madison Square Garden, and that there was an opening for the play-by-play job on the Rangers road telecasts on WOR-TV. Rangers General Manager Emile Francis knew who I was, and liked the idea of an experienced hockey guy taking the job.

The question was whether WPIX would allow me to take the job with games that appeared on a rival station, and would they allow me to continue as their co-news anchor. (There would not be enough money from the Rangers games alone). I explained this to Francis and said I would make my pitch to WPIX. Much to my surprise, they agreed to the idea. So suddenly I was back in hockey—and was able to continue my newer career in TV news.

I was also back on the road, but for only about a dozen games a year that were scheduled for TV on WOR. Rangers fans of a certain age will remember that those were the days of stars like Rod Gilbert, Jean Ratelle, Vic Hadfield and a young Brad Park.

I worked the Rangers telecasts on WOR for two seasons, while continuing at WPIX in my dual news/sports role. In 1971, PIX hired a new News boss, Bill Brown, who came from California. He had already hired a new anchorman, Doug Ramsey, who had been on-air in New Orleans. He would replace Lee Nelson. Brown, a big bear of a man, affable in nature, called me into his office to tell me about the change.

"Mr. Ryan, you are doing an excellent job as a news anchor here. But I plan to go with only one and that will be Mr. Ramsey. I have been watching your sports segments, have seen your Rangers telecasts, and as much as you love news, I think your heart is really in sports."

It was "gulp" time again. Was he going to let me go from WPIX?

No, he wanted me to stay, but to do just the sports segment. He had no problem with me continuing to do the Rangers games on WOR.

Relief.

So I stayed, and at the same salary. Brown was a great guy and Doug Ramsey and I remain close friends to this day, although he is retired from TV news and lives back in his home state of Washington. Doug and I shared a mutual love for jazz, and he and I spent more than a few late nights at jazz clubs from Harlem to Greenwich Village. Doug was already a prominent jazz writer and critic, and continues to write a jazz column.

And then, once again Jack Price started another chapter in my career: boxing.

CHAPTER 9

Boxing's Bad Bedfellows and "The Fight of the Century"

I was still at WPIX when Jack Price called out of the blue. "How's it going? Those guys treating you all right? Francis is happy with your Rangers work, want to do some boxing? Let's have a drink."

We had a drink. Jack told me that Mutual Radio Network was starting a monthly boxing series, covering live fights, needed a blow-by-blow announcer, was I interested?

Of course I was. But apart from reading results of big fights on WPIX sports reports on the evening news, my only boxing broadcast experience was calling the Bengal Bouts on the Notre Dame student station WSND. The Bengals matched students who liked to box and were willing to train for a few weeks to compete in an annual event in the old Fieldhouse on the campus. Ticket proceeds went to Holy Cross missions in Asia.

So I had called some boxing on the radio. Jack thought that was fine, he would recommend me to Ed Little, the boss at Mutual.

I got the job, did about a half-dozen live calls—mainly from Madison Square Garden—and had two particularly memorable experiences in the process. The Mutual fights didn't unduly interfere with my WPIX nightly news obligations, and ultimately launched me into a major part of my career, and my life of travel and adventure. They also led me into a $3 million lawsuit and a horribly frightening night for Lee.

I was calling a Mutual Radio fight September 15, 1970 at the Garden between former Heavyweight champion Floyd Patterson and Charlie Green. Two years and a day before the fight, Patterson had lost his WBA title to fellow American Jimmy Ellis on a much-disputed decision. That fight took place in Stockholm, Sweden where the judging was done only by the referee. The referee was also an American, New Yorker Harold Valan. The fight went the distance. Valan scored the decision for Ellis. The heavy consensus of boxing media at ringside and watching on TV back in the U.S. scored it for Patterson.

In my broadcast lead-up to the Patterson-Green fight, I commented that, "many observers of the Ellis fight felt that Patterson had been 'jobbed' by referee Harold Valan." There had been many press accounts using that very expression. I simply reported that fact. This was Patterson's first fight since his loss in Stockholm. He was attempting a comeback with the hope of a second chance at Muhammad Ali, to whom he had previously lost in a try for the title. The disputed decision in Stockholm was a big part of the story of his fight against Green—his chance to prove that he was still championship material.

Valan sued me and Mutual Radio. He found an ambulance-chasing lawyer in New York who took his case on a contingency basis, claiming that his client had been libeled and slandered. Weeks had passed since the fight (Patterson won with a 10th round K.O.). I was in Montreal calling a Rangers game against the Canadiens on WOR-TV. Lee was home in Larchmont with our four children. The phone rang in my hotel room a little after midnight. It was Lee, distraught.

A drunken man had arrived at our house, rang the bell, banged on the door. Lee naturally, was reluctant to open it. The man yelled at her from outside saying he was from the sheriff's office and it was "about her husband." With the safety chain still on its lock, she pulled the door ajar. She could see he was drunk—waving a piece of paper at her and saying her husband was being served with a summons. Lee was petrified, having no knowledge of what the summons could be, and physically afraid of a drunk at her door at midnight, with four young children in their beds. She slammed the door shut and called me in Montreal.

I called the Larchmont police immediately. Of course the man had disappeared before their arrival to the house. It turned out that he was a process-server delivering notice of Valan's libel lawsuit. Needless to say, I reported him to his boss, the county sheriff, who apologized profusely and the man was fired. Of course that didn't alleviate the fright Lee suffered that night, nor my guilt for not being there.

The lawsuit—demanding $3,000,000—was ludicrous. Neither Valan, nor his lawyer, had any chance of making a dime from it. Apparently some friend of his had heard my broadcast and told him he should sue, so he did. But Valan probably gained some satisfaction from learning—if he did— about the drunken process-server frightening Lee, and also that he cost me thousands of dollars in legal fees to see the lawsuit dissolve without ever reaching a courtroom. Mutual Radio effectively said to me, "you're on your own," and did not offer to cover my legal costs. Their in-house attorneys also scared off Valan's bullshit guy.

I remained very angry with Valan—more because of the summons incident that scared the wits out of Lee, than of his bogus attempt to make a chunk of money in a courtroom. I figured I would run into him some time, and sure enough I did—but that's a story for a later chapter.

The Mutual Radio series was short-lived, but included another memorable incident in 1973. Mutual president Ed Little asked me to come to their headquarters in Washington D.C., where I would call the Joe Frazier-Joe Bugner fight which was being held in London. I was joined by Floyd Patterson as my expert commentator. The fight was on closed-circuit television back to the U.S. and Little had organized a cocktail party at the Mutual Studios for some clients and VIP guests to watch the fight via a special video feed, with the audio on Mutual Radio. Patterson and I were to be in a broadcast booth at the studios, calling the fight from the incoming TV pictures.

Mr. Little asked us to come early to attend the party and mingle with the guests. Naturally, the popular former heavyweight champ was an attraction, but not nearly as big an attraction as was a guest who happened to come to the party directly from testifying at the Watergate hearings! His name was John Ehrlichman, a high-level White House staff member in the administration of Richard Nixon. For those of you dear readers too young to remember, he and Bob Haldemann served eighteen months in jail for their roles in the scandal that led to Nixon's resignation as president.

In any event, it was a startling occurrence to see Ehrlichman—headed for the hoosegow—being introduced around as a celebrity by his friend Little, and posing for photos, along with Patterson of course, with the other guests. A press photographer from New York, whom I knew from seeing him frequently at sports events, was snapping away furiously. His name, believe it or not was, and is, as far as I know, Bermuda Schwartz. Little steered Ehrlichman over to the photog, introduced him to me, and Bermuda captured the reluctant handshake (at least on my part) for history.

I was furious. As soon as Ehrlichman had been moved along by Little, I grabbed Schwartz by his camera-arm. "I don't want to see that in the *Daily News* tomorrow—my mother hates that creep," I said, "and so do I. Promise me you will send me the negative."

He didn't, but nor did he sell the photo (I think Floyd and the soon-to-be Watergate convict did make the papers) and Bermuda did send me a print that hangs on the wall in my rogues gallery right next to the *Newsweek* cover of Nixon with his quote, "I Am Not A Crook."

Frazier beat Bugner in twelve…

Between those two eventful boxing matches I called for Mutual Radio came the biggest thrill of my young career—and forty-five years later, I remember every minute of the excitement: Ali-Frazier 1, Madison Square Garden, 1971.

Once again, my great now long-departed friend Jack Price got me the shot. In his role as the director of broadcasting at the Garden, Jack was handling all of the closed-circuit setup for the telecast, working with the fight promoters, cable-TV titans Jack Kent Cooke and Jerry Perenchio. Price was also in charge of all of the international radio broadcast arrangements. Many countries had sent announcers to provide radio descriptions of the highly anticipated matchup between Muhammad Ali and Smokin' Joe Frazier. But anywhere the closed-circuit TV was being broadcast into movie theaters, stadiums, arenas, and makeshift sites worldwide, there would be no radio broadcast allowed. That was of course to ensure that fight fans in those locations would pay for tickets to watch the live telecast.

Most of the English-speaking world, at least in the major cities, had TV venues. So did many of the U.S. military bases.

Jack called me two days before the fight and asked if I would like to be the radio broadcaster for the New Zealand public radio network. They were latecomers to the international coverage and could not afford to send an announcer from the other side of the globe. There was no other English-speaking radio broadcast going out that they could link to. The only English-speaking announcer was the esteemed Don Dunphy who would call the live TV version with Archie Moore and actor Burt Lancaster as his expert analysts. (Don't ask.) That feed was not available to any radio broadcast.

Of course I said yes to Jack and couldn't believe my luck—I was actually going to call one of the biggest heavyweight championship fights of all time. The fact that my voice was only going to New Zealand, and no friends or family would hear me didn't matter at all. I was going to be part of what was sure to be an incredible spectacle at the Garden, and get paid to be there!

The morning of the fight Jack called again. I could hear the tension in his voice. "Have you seen *The New York Times*," he asked.

"Not yet," was my reply.

"Well do you have any problem if your call goes to the Armed Forces Radio Network around the world? You are the only English-language radio announcer doing the fight. It's too late for them to make other arrangements. They would be very grateful. There's no money."

Page one of the *Times* told the story of the fact that for the first time in memory, The Armed Forces Radio Network would not be receiving a broadcast of a heavyweight championship fight. It had been a long-standing tradition that servicemen and -women would gather around radios at U.S. military bases around the world to listen to the big fight. But this time, the promoters were not providing the traditional radio-feed to the troops.

Embarrassed by the reaction to their plan, Cooke and Perenchio quickly capitulated, allowing a radio broadcast to be carried on the AFR global network—MY radio broadcast!

"You'll hear from some general in a few minutes," Jack said, "stay by your phone…and thanks, Tim."

I did. The general called from Army headquarters in Washington D.C, profusely thanked me for allowing my call of the fight to be on the Armed Forces Network, sorry they had no money allocated for this, what else could he do for me to express his gratitude?

"Not a thing," I replied, "It's a huge honor and privilege to have my call be heard by servicemen around the world, and I will happily do it for free. But if it's possible, could you record it for me and send me the audiotape? I'd love to save it for my kids."

I still have that quarter-inch reel-to reel recording, which of course by now, has also been dubbed into a CD.

(Years later, Jack Kent Cooke who by then had become the owner of the Washington Redskins, reminisced about the promoters' faux-pas while the two of us were watching a Redskins Friday practice for a Sunday game in D.C. which I would be broadcasting for CBS. I think he blamed his partner Perenchio…)

Ah yes, "The Fight." A scene out of a movie—indeed the scene at Madison Square Garden that March evening in 1971 was replicated in feature films more than once in later years. It had the mix of a sporting event, a Broadway opening, and Oscar night, drawing people from every walk of life: film stars, mobsters, politicians, show-girls, millionaires, working stiffs, hookers, drug dealers, clergymen.

"Look there's Sinatra! Diana Ross! The Mayor! The Cardinal!"—a parade of dressed-up humanity creating a buzz of excitement that hasn't been matched at a boxing match since.

I can't actually recall, but WPIX either gave me the night off so I could do the fight broadcast, or perhaps I did a stand-up report for our 10 o'clock news before the Main Event took place. There was certainly plenty to talk about, and just pointing a TV camera at the spectators coming into the Garden dressing in everything from ermine and mink (even on some of the men), tuxedos and floor-length gowns to leather-jackets and jeans, gave a sense that tonight was something special: "The Fight of the Century."

What I do remember was the near-panic I felt when fifteen seconds before round one, we had not established a radio connection with New Zealand!

I was sandwiched in among several dozen foreign-language announcers crammed into the hockey press-box, midway up from the Garden floor to the bleacher seats high up in the rafters—a long way from ringside where the TV announcers were, but still with a good view of the ring.

Technicians had been feverishly checking each broadcast location to make sure lines to countries receiving only radio coverage or non-English TV coverage were all functioning in the minutes before the fight began.

"Hello New Zealand, Hello New Zealand," I repeated over and over again as the clock wound down to the start time and I could see the ring announcer about to introduce the fighters. Finally, a voice from Down Under came into my headset. "We hear you Tim, thanks for doing this, stand by and wait for our cue!"

"Ladies and Gentlemen," came the sound of the ring announcer, and off we went, describing the action of one of the most historic sports events ever, sending the blow-by-blow account to New Zealand (where it was already Tuesday) and to countless U.S. military bases around the world linked to the Armed Forces Radio Network.

A knockdown in the tenth round from one of Frazier's fearsome left hooks broke open a very close fight, and Frazier became the undisputed heavyweight champion with a 15-round decision.

It was well after midnight when I caught a late train home to Larchmont. Lee was awake, waiting for a report.

"It was terrific in every way," I said. "The broadcast went fine, and what a fight! An unforgettable night."

CHAPTER 10

Big Breaks In The Big Apple

Despite my euphoria after the Ali-Frazier fight at the Garden, I had no idea what role boxing would play in my career over the next twenty-plus years. Or how it would be the sport that truly brought the blessings of world travel on someone else's nickel.

Hockey was still the focus of my play-by-play road, and that road made quite a turn not long after the thrill of the "Fight of the Century." I was in the second year of doing the Ranger games on WOR—working this season of '71–72 with hockey writer Norm McLean—and still working on the *WPIX 10 O'Clock News*. In the spring of 1972, the NHL's television rights changed hands—from CBS to NBC. One day I received a call from an executive at NBC Sports, Scotty Connal.

I had had correspondence with Scotty back in 1967, just after I had taken the job in Oakland. NBC had been bidding against CBS for the NHL rights, and I had contacted both networks to see if they would be hiring new announcers for the games. CBS won the bid and kept the announcers they had, but Scotty had sent me a nice letter saying he had liked the tape I had sent, and would look me up in Oakland when he came to the Bay Area for other sports coverage.

In my reply to him I had said, "You never know, we may wind up on the same team yet!" Well, five years later, that happened when I received that phone call at WPIX from Connal.

"I have been watching your work on the Rangers games, and you may have heard we have acquired the rights to the NHL *Game of the Week*. Would you be interested in joining us?"

It was a short conversation. Of course I was thrilled to get a network shot—but a hockey season on its own wasn't going to pay my mortgage. And I was still under contract to WPIX. Could these things be worked out?

Connal said he was aware of my circumstances, and would offer me the chance to join the New York NBC station, WNBC, to be the sports guy on their 11 o'clock news, with news anchor Jim Hartz and weatherman Dr. Frank Field. He would also add some other sports on the network as we moved along after the hockey season. Could I get out of the WPIX and WOR deals?

At that point I did not have an agent. I was using a lawyer/accountant to look over my contracts and prepare my tax returns. But fortunately, both the WPIX and WOR folks were cooperative—understanding that this would be a great opportunity for me. No hard feelings, go for it!

And so we did. Lee and I were on cloud nine, even though the NBC job would mean later nights getting home on the trains to Larchmont, in addition to weekly travel for the NHL games over the seven-month seasons. But we were now in the big leagues, with more money and a chance to expand our horizons. Kim, Kevin, and Jay were in elementary school—only our three-year-old, Brenden was still at home all day. It was going to be hectic for a few years, but we could look forward to summer weekends at the Apawamis Club in Rye, and some travel times together.

As I took the commuter train into New York for my first night on the WNBC late news program, I couldn't help but remember humming the same tune as I had walking from my hotel to WPIX for the first time three years earlier. "If you can make it there, you'll make it anywhere—it's up to you, *New York, New York.*"

There I was at 30 Rockefeller Plaza, home of the peacock of network broadcasting, NBC. I had a desk in the local news offices, shared the makeup room with the network stars like John Chancellor, Barbara Walters, and Tom Brokaw, and shared the WNBC studio set with two veterans of local news, Hartz and Field who couldn't have been more helpful and welcoming. The days were long. Frequently I would need to be in the city by noon to attend press conferences, public relations events or do interviews at the Garden, Yankee Stadium, or Shea Stadium. If I rushed from the set when we were off the air at 11:30, I could make a train that got me home by 12:30.

That schedule definitely had its downsides. My hope was that it wouldn't be too long before I got to do the early, 6 p.m. news program—or better yet, have enough network assignments that I could give up local news shows and have more evenings at home.

For better or worse, and there definitely was some of each, doing the 11 o'clock news opened a bunch of new doors in the Big Apple.

In my two years at WPIX, I had often gone out from the studios for a quick dinner at nearby restaurants—a plate of pasta at pizza joints; sushi or noodles at modest Asian spots; an occasional steak at the Pen and Pencil; or a burger and beer at an Irish pub named John Barleycorn, (rumored to be a gathering spot for Irish-American supporters of the IRA). But it was another Irish establishment that became my favorite hangout—P.J. Clarke's. And in the years that followed during my time at NBC, and later CBS, the saloon on 3rd Avenue at East 55th was the scene of many happy and interesting times. And too many very late nights!

There had been a P.J. in the early 1900s version of Clarke's, and his nephew Charlie stayed on for years as a bartender working for Danny Lavezzo who had become the new owner. The glory days of the sixties to the eighties saw Danny presiding at a large round table, just inside the door of the back dining room. At the entrance, the most powerful maitre'd in New York, Frankie Ribando ruled the roost, sorting out the Who's Who of locals and out-of-towners wanting to see and be seen while downing Clarke's famous "Cadillac" burgers and spinach salad.

Clarke's was a mecca for New Yorkers in the entertainment and sports worlds. Danny loved both of those enterprises, right behind betting on the horses. An invitation to join him at his table was tougher to get than a ticket to a Knicks or Rangers game. Every night, an eclectic group of his favorites would assemble, several of whom would have been there the night before— and the night before that! The actor Martin Gabel and his TV personality wife Arlene Francis, sportswriters Dan Jenkins and Pete Axthelm, Broadway columnist Jack O'Brian, sportscaster Jack Whitaker were among the regulars, and Danny's fellow horse-racing maven, Jimmie Martin was an enduring presence. So was my friend Jack Price, who, naturally, got me the entree to this heady world.

Other tables were decorated with the likes of film stars, famous athletes, socialites and politicos; Sinatra was a regular when in town, New York Governor Hugh Carey as well. Composer Johnny Mercer wrote the saloon anthem, "One for the Road" while schmoozing with bartending legend

Tommy Joyce up front; Jackie Kennedy brought her children to Sunday brunch. Jake LaMotta, "The Raging Bull" had a regular bar stool.

One night there, *I* was the raging bull. Seated at a table just in front of the exclusive and famous Back Room was Harold Valan—the boxing referee who had sued me those many months ago and caused Lee a very traumatic few days. Valan was sitting with three or four other men, including the former middleweight champion and colorful character, Rocky Graziano.

My blood boiled at the very sight of Valan and ignoring Rocky's cheerful greeting, I got right into Valan's face with a series of expletives. Valan started to get up, the others at the table restrained him. Rocky meanwhile tried to distract me with one of his usual barroom lines: "Hey—didn't I fight you in Cleveland one time?"

Fortunately, I calmed down before punches were thrown. On the other hand....

On another late night at Clarke's, fisticuffs did take place, albeit briefly, between two of the saloon's regulars when they were in town—the actors Jason Robards and George C. Scott. Apparently they were close friends, but that night, well into the sauce, they came to disagree over something or another. Suddenly they were on their feet at their table in the middle of the back room, voices rising. I don't remember who threw the first punch, but it was a short-lived affair as Franke Ribando sailed from his post at the doorway to get between them before any damage was done—to themselves or the patrons at nearby tables.

The fracas ended with a hug and a few embarrassed laughs. The audience applauded.

Just as I was settling in to the late news routine at WNBC Channel 4, and eagerly anticipating my first season of the NHL *Game of the Week* on the network, it was a night at Clarke's that expanded my horizon. NFL commissioner Pete Rozelle was an occasional patron of Clarke's, often in the company of network sports executives who carried NFL games, including then CBS Sports president Bill McPhail.

McPhail was a revered figure in the business—a thorough gentleman, soft-spoken and witty. I was introduced to him, along with Rozelle and some other NFL and CBS execs. A few weeks later, McPhail contacted me and asked if I could be available to be a post-game interviewer on CBS NFL coverage during the coming season. *Football!* My first chance to be involved in the sport that was my heritage. Of course the offer was complicated by the fact that I was now an NBC contract player, and it would require NBC allowing me to take on the CBS deal, which was just six games.

Scotty Connal, a good friend of McPhail's (as was most everyone in the TV sports business) said he had no problem with me doing the CBS gig, but the station manager of the local station, WNBC, was not keen on the idea that his sportscaster on Channel 4 would be seen on rival Channel 2, WCBS.

I had told McPhail of Connal's positive response, now I had to call him back to say Channel 4 wouldn't go along. Gracious as always, McPhail said he understood, and that maybe sometime in the future, I would come to work for CBS full-time. How prescient that was!

• • •

P.J. Clarke's was sold after Danny Lavezzo died. His son Danny Jr.—a very nice man like his dad, operated it for a few years, but ultimately gave it up. Fortunately, the new owners respected it enough to keep the look and decor while upgrading the kitchen and the menu—most importantly they left the most famous urinals in New York in the men's room. There are only two of them, made of well-used porcelain, but they are about four feet high and a foot wide. Even after two many beers, they are hard to miss.

Two other dining establishments in New York banked a lot of my money, Elaine's way uptown on the East Side attracted night owls from the arts, journalism, politics, and sports. It wasn't for the food—which Elaine herself staunchly defended but rarely found supporters—it was for the cachet of drinking with kindred spirits at late hours. Elaine Kaufman (now no doubt operating a similar saloon in the Great Beyond) could sit her considerable self at Table One—near the cash register—with the likes of famous writers, actors, playwrights, musicians, athletes—all the while keeping an eye who was coming through the door.

One night I was there at a table up front, with Elaine perched on a bar stool at the cash-register. The place was packed. Tourists had read about Elaine's in magazines and newspapers as a place to spot celebrities, and they squeezed in from the street to the bar area hoping to order a drink and be part of the scene. This night, a man in a loud, big-checked sport jacket, his wife following meekly behind, had managed to work his way from the door to where Elaine—garbed as usual in yards of Italian silk—stopped him in his tracks.

"You won't like it here," she yelled over the din of the bar crowd. She had clearly sized him-up as being from Iowa or Idaho and with her saloon already full of paying customers who passed her muster, this otherwise seemingly nice couple was being told to get lost.

On another late, late night I was sitting in the dining area beyond the bar. It was a quiet night at Elaine's, partly because it was after 1 a.m. I was sitting with the brilliant jazz musician Paul Desmond, who was a regular there when in town. We were at the coffee stage, when suddenly the only other two people left in the back room—obviously inebriated and profane, got up from their table and started to fight. A couple of waiters were in the room, clearing tables. Neither made any effort to intervene. I yelled at the guys to break-it-up, as cutlery and glassware were being strewn everywhere. The waiters disappeared. A minute later, into the back room came an enraged Elaine—a sizeable and frightening sight. With the two waiters cowering on the sidelines, she grabbed each of the protagonists by their necks and marched them out of the restaurant to Second Avenue. When she returned, with eyes blazing, she fired the two waiters on the spot.

Don't mess with Elaine. Nobody did.

• • •

The famous 21 Club, a former speakeasy in Midtown with a clientele whose commonality was mainly money, provided other entertaining evenings when I could afford the bill. One evening back in the eighties Lee and I were having drinks with friends at a table near the door of the downstairs bar area. I had in front of me a tall gin and tonic.

On his way out of the room was the well-known—if not always well-regarded—comedian Milton Berle. I did not know him nor was I interested in meeting him. But one of our friends at the table greeted him and introduced us. Berle leaned over the table proffering his hand, and with his other hand, put his fingers into my glass of gin and tonic, and with that shit-eating grin of his said, "Nice to meet you."

A really classy guy. I was wishing it had happened at Elaine's so I could watch her give the jerk the bum's rush.

CHAPTER 11

Entering the Golden Age
of Sports TV

Life was good at NBC. The 1972–73 hockey season was approaching and I was beginning to appreciate what turned out to be—for the next twenty years, the Golden Age of TV Sports. Scotty Connal hired former Red Wings star Ted Lindsay to be our expert analyst, fellow Canadian Brian McFarlane—a regular on Hockey Night in Canada telecasts—as our intermission host and assembled a hand-picked production and technical crew, including renowned director Ted Nathanson. And of course, there was Peter Puck!

While Ted, Brian, and I were at first skeptical that a cartoon character (created by the Hanna-Barbera Company, animators of *The Flintstones*), could add anything to a hockey telecast, we were quickly proved wrong.

Peter Puck became a bigger star than most of the players on the ice! He appeared during the intermissions between periods of the game, presenting a primer on hockey: the rules, the equipment, the terminology, and the history of the game. While our run on NBC only lasted three seasons, years later I would be stopped by fans at football or basketball games, demanding to know, "Where's Peter Puck?" Unfortunately, we didn't make enough of those fans to keep us on the air longer.

But the three years we were on with the NHL *Game of the Week* were the best years of my young working life. First of all, the NBC Sports management group was superb. President Carl Lindemann, Vice President Chet Simmons, and Executive Producer Scotty Connal led a department that was committed, competitive, generous, and fun to be a part of. I was just thirty-three years old and getting a chance to play in the "Big Time" with some of the most talented people in the business. Not to mention some pretty nice perks, the first of which came from our title sponsor, the Chrysler Corporation. They offered—no insisted—that Ted, Brian, and I drive one of their cars. Not just around the block—but for the length of the three-year TV contract with NBC! We got to choose our model of Chrysler and it was delivered to our doors.

I chose the Chrysler Imperial, which in 1972 was not only the top of their line, but was about the size of an Onassis yacht. Lee was totally embarrassed to see it parked in front of the house. But it wouldn't fit into the garage! Each year, a Chrysler dealer would arrive with the new model, and take away the old one.

The kids, of course, thought this was a perfectly acceptable way to have a family automobile. All four could fit into it quite comfortably. And, "Besides Dad, no one else on the street has such a fancy car."

Over the three-year run, we became part of NHL history. After the perennial champion Montreal Canadiens won yet another Stanley Cup in our first season, beating the Chicago Black Hawks four games to two, the Philadelphia Flyers became the first expansion team to win a cup in '74–75. Unfortunately, even though the Flyers brought a new energy to the sport, not enough folks in the United States tuned in to *NHL Game of the Week* to make the series profitable for Chrysler. It would be many years later before the NHL returned to network television.

There was another thing that attracted attention to hockey in those three years, and it became another part of the joys of being a part of the NBC crew. Ted Lindsay, long-retired from his playing days, came up with the idea of bringing our skates along each week to the game sites and playing a little pick-up hockey the mornings of the afternoon telecasts. When we would go to the rinks to watch the teams have their morning skates for the late-afternoon games (4 p.m. Eastern on NBC), "rink rats" as they were known—ice maintenance guys, arena staff, some team office workers, would take to the ice when the teams were finished.

Ted said, "Why don't we join them—we'll form an NBC team from our crew and take on these guys around the league." So we did.

At first it was fairly rag-tag. Ted, Brian, and I got on the ice and shot pucks into empty nets, invited some of the rink rats to join us, no keeping score, no pads—just a friendly skate. Frankly I was surprised that Scotty

Tim with NBC line-mates Brian McFarlane and Ted Lindsay.

Connal, who was producing our games and was the big boss, allowed us to even get onto the ice. But it didn't take him long to bring his skates and join in. Scotty had played some minor league pro hockey in his time, as did one of our cameramen, Ray Figelski. That gave us a forward line and two defensemen.

Then Ted prevailed upon "the other Ted," our director Ted Nathanson to become our goalie. Nathanson had never played hockey, could barely skate, and had no clue how to even put on all the pads, but he was brave, or crazy, or both.

And so the NBC team was born—and by the second season we were bringing shin-pads and hockey gloves and Lindsay had organized to have NBC jerseys made—with numbers on the back of course. The word got out to rink rats around the league, and so each week we had opponents waiting to take us on—and have the thrill of playing against Hall-of-Famer Ted Lindsay, Brian McFarlane—college star at St. Lawrence University, and Tim Ryan, who barely made his high school team in Toronto.

As you might expect things occasionally got out of hand. Rink rats soon invited friends and family to come and watch. Inevitably there would be some character who ignored our rules—firmly stated by Ted Lindsay before each game.

No fighting, no body-checking, keep the sticks down.

Those who ignored the rules paid a heavy price: dealing with Lindsay. Ted had been a feared player in his NHL days—not an enforcer, but a highly skilled goal-scorer and fierce back-checker who did not hesitate to, as he put it, "lay the wood on him." A few times in our NBC team's games, a few guys had the poor judgment to test Teddy—forgetting his nickname was "Terrible Ted." They would take home a souvenir of a bruise here and there, or perhaps a cut lip or bloody nose.

Ted was now in his fifties, but he worked out every day at the Red Wings training facility and his body was a piece of steel. A total gentleman off the ice, but on it....

As the games went on, the competition became stiffer, and lineups deeper. We had to recruit Scotty Connal's sons, two of whom were good high-school players in Greenwich, Connecticut. We now had two lines, which certainly helped our legs over the hour we spent on the ice. Two memories stand out from that glorious time.

One was when our telecast was in Minnesota. The North Stars management had heard about our tour and we had a call from them saying they had a team that wanted to play us, but it would be in St. Paul, not in Bloomington where the North Stars played. It turned out that then-Governor Wendell Anderson was an avid fan and former college player at the University of Minnesota and had played on the 1956 U.S. Olympic team that won a silver medal. He still played regularly in a local senior's league and was challenging us to a game against his team.

I think they beat us, but the best thing was that Gov. Anderson insisted on taking us all to his favorite hamburger joint after our game, and his special choice of burger was sensational. A good time was had by all, except by the North Stars who lost their game later that day!

The other unforgettable time was when we were covering a game in Chicago. There were no rink rats to play that day, but we suited up anyway and waited for the Blackhawks to finish their game-day practice. When most of their players had left the ice, we skated on and chatted with a couple of the Hawks who were lingering around shooting pucks. Our goalie, Ted Nathanson took his place in the nets, but without noticing that Lindsay was chatting with Dennis Hull, who owned the biggest slap-shot in the NHL— bigger than his better-known brother Bobby.

While we were taking shots at Nathanson—who had actually improved considerably and could now also slide from one pipe to the other without falling—Lindsay was asking Hull to let one of his high hard ones go at our goalie.

Ted saw him coming just in time to realize that it was Dennis Hull bearing down on him. Hull let fly from the blue-line. The puck hit Ted in the shoulder and knocked him back into the net. But the puck stayed out! Nathanson had a bruise for weeks, but what a badge of honor! And he had stopped Dennis Hull.

All these years later, I still can't believe we were allowed to risk injury while playing the morning of those NHL telecasts on NBC! My wife Lee would say each week as I headed to the airport, "What happens if you get a black eye, or a cut, or worse, and you can't go on the air to do the telecast?" Fortunately, I never had to answer the question—nor did the rest of our crazy group. How Scotty ever convinced his bosses, Carl Lindemann and Chet Simmons to let us do it, I'll never know.

Maybe he just didn't ask them.

The NHL *Game of the Week* series ended in 1975. When we had worked our final game, Scotty Connal gathered the entire crew around the production trailers, and gave us a farewell speech. All the men were choked up. He had kept virtually the entire team, of production personnel, videotape operators, camera people, audio and video technicians, maintenance folks, cable pullers together for the past three years.

Ted Lindsay asked to speak on behalf of the announcers—he knew them all by name, because he had made it a point to. When he finished telling them that it had been the greatest experience of his hockey career to work with them in television on NBC, there was not a dry eye to be seen.

Those three years, with that NBC crew, remain the best years of my working life—and I had thirty-eight more years still ahead of me, filled with great times and great people.

CHAPTER 12

Lord Stanley's Cups

While my NBC network focus was now on NFL football, hockey was not off my plate. When the NHL had expanded for the second time in 1972, it added the Atlanta Flames and the New York Islanders, creating a crosstown rivalry with the Rangers.

In the months before I made the switch to Channel 4 in New York, I had covered the expansion story for WPIX. The Islanders owner, garment-company entrepreneur Roy Boe, who in 1969 had bought the New York Nets of the American Basketball Association, was a huge basketball fan, but knew nothing about hockey. After my interview with him, he asked if I had any suggestions as to whom he should hire as his General Manager of his new hockey team. As we kicked around some names he had been given, I suggested Bill Torrey, whom I knew was looking for another NHL job after the collapse of the California Golden Seals.

Torrey had been briefly with the Seals between the Van Gerbig years and the takeover by Charlie Finley. He had impressed me with his hockey knowledge, his business sense, and his likeable personality. As luck would have it, I was able to put Boe and Torrey together.

Boe soon sold the team to some wealthy local investors and within just seven years, Torrey and his coach Al Arbour had led the team to its first of four consecutive Stanley Cup Championships. In the modern era, only the Montreal Canadiens had won four cups in a row, having won five in a row in the mid-fifties when the NHL was still just a six-team league, and four in the years prior to the Islanders feat.

As soon as the NHL *Game of the Week* was dropped by NBC, Torrey called me to ask if I would like to take over the Islanders local telecasts

1980: With Lee and the Islanders Stanley Cup.

on WOR starting with the 1975–76 season—a limited schedule similar to my previous one with the Rangers. I had left the WNBC Channel 4 news programs after a dispute with the news director Earl Ubell, and so I had no conflicts during the weeknights.

That opportunity gave me the chance to be part of the incredible success story of the Islanders. Working with former Islander Ed Westfall, and for one season with then-radio disc-jockey George Michael, I broadcast the road telecasts for seven seasons, including the first two of their Stanley Cups.

I have two Stanley Cup rings for those wins in the 1979–80, and 1980–81 seasons, but I have never, and will not ever, wear them. Torrey had insisted I be included with the players and team personnel who had received them. I protested, on principle, that even though I was paid by the Islanders to call the games, I didn't believe team announcers should receive championship rings—in any sport. After all we don't contribute to the victories in any way; we just describe to fans what happens on the ice. I have always been bothered by seeing other of my colleagues flashing those rocks.

Nevertheless, Torrey had my name engraved on rings each time, even though he never asked me to be a "homer" on my commentary, knowing I would not agree to that either! I took pride in my being objective with my calls—unafraid to be critical of team or individual performance. Islander fans, and often the players themselves, weren't always happy about that! In fact, during my Ranger broadcast days, I was once physically threatened by Ranger star Vic Hadfield in the team locker room after a home game.

I had been critical of Hadfield during a previous game for one thing or another, and his wife, listening to the telecast, had reported me to Vic. When I came into the locker room after the next game Vic saw me, and pushed me into a toilet stall, complaining about my comments. "My wife told me you were on my case the other night."

As a couple of teammates pulled him away, I said to him, "Vic, does she ever report all the good things I say about you when you play well?" No reply!

Vic and I remained friends. I never met his wife.

The Islander Stanley Cup rings? I put them in a bank safe-deposit box for a number of years, but later on had them mounted in a Lucite box so hockey fans visiting our home could enjoy seeing them up close.

Meanwhile, Chet Simmons and Scotty Connal were advancing my NBC sports network career, starting with a new studio show in 1975 they titled, "Grandstand." I made a few studio appearances that first year, giving halftime scores of NFL games. But I also got to start my NFL play-by-play life, which lasted twenty-two football seasons. In those days, NBC had the rights to the American Conference, CBS the National Conference. ABC had just one game each weekend, (Monday Night Football which had debuted in 1970), and was the premier college football network. There was no FOX, no ESPN—cable TV networks did not yet exist. There were only twenty-six teams, meaning each network got to televise six or seven games each Sunday. To be one of the six announcers who worked every weekend on NBC or CBS NFL games put an announcer in very special company.

NBC's star announcer was Curt Gowdy and he would be assigned to the top games each week; Jim Simpson was number two. I was the rookie who didn't get a game every week, but was thrilled to be in the company of the handful of men who were NFL announcers. I worked with former Denver players Floyd Little and Mike Haffner, and Lionel Aldridge of Green Bay.

Even though road life had been first-class doing the NHL *Game of the Week*, NFL life was another level. Remember, this was the "Golden Age of TV Sports"! So even a young guy got the perks—on someone else's nickel! We traveled first class, we stayed in the best hotels, we had generous expense accounts—which meant the best restaurants—and limousines from home to the airports, and our limos had police escorts from the stadiums to the airports.

Let's face it, we were spoiled rotten!

CHAPTER 13

A Love Affair With Europe

"The Hockey Years," which ended in 1981 after the second Islander Stanley Cup win, had been great years for our kids—well the boys, anyway! When I started doing the Islander games, Kevin was twelve and Jay ten, Brendan four. Kim didn't care much about hockey. So the two older boys got to go to Islander home games, and I would try to take each one individually to a road game or two each season. By the time the Isles had won their second Stanley Cup the boys were all teenagers, and Kim was off to Georgetown University. But in 1977, Dad's working life was changing again and all of the Ryans would be affected.

When I had signed with NBC in 1972, an agent who represented Joe Garagiola, the network's star personality on its Major League Baseball telecasts (and later on the *Today Show*), contacted me to ask if he could represent me. His name was Felix Shagan. He was an independent with just a few clients, but they included NBC's film critic Gene Shalit of *Today* and David Hartman, the host of ABC's rival morning show.

I was flattered of course, and signed on. He handled my second NBC deal and would tell me that I was the logical successor to Gowdy and we would both make good money when that came to pass. I wasn't so sure of that happening, but so far so good. But just as we were negotiating a new contract in 1977, Shagan heard from Barry Frank, the Vice President of Sports for CBS.

Frank told Felix he knew my deal was up, that he would like me to come over to CBS. He was offering NFL play-by-play, NBA basketball, a role in U.S. Open tennis, and… boxing!

The year before, at the 1976 Summer Olympics, the U.S. boxing team had done surprisingly well. Several medalists emerged from the team: heavyweight Leon Spinks, his brother Michael, a light-heavyweight, welterweight Sugar Ray Leonard, and lightweight Howard Davis, Jr.

Frank saw an opportunity to return boxing to the networks—it had been a long time since popular Gillette *Friday Night Fights* ("to look sharp…"). He had seen me calling a boxing card on NBC not long before my contract was to expire—a show from Paris, featuring heavyweight Earnie Shavers.

That assignment for NBC was my first taste of international travel on "someone else's nickel." Lee and I had made our first trip to Europe a year earlier, during vacation time in 1975. The children were now old enough to be left with a babysitter, and I was making enough money to afford a trip. It was our first real "getaway" since our wedding in 1961. All of our other vacation trips had included the kids. We went to London, where we visited my former boss in Oakland, Barry Van Gerbig, whose wife Victoria was the daughter of the famous actor Douglas Fairbanks Jr. Of course we had tea at the Fairbanks house—quite a treat—saw the London sights, and then flew on to Madrid.

In Spain we were joined by Jeffrey Lyons, my friend from my WPIX days when he was the theater/film critic on our newscast. His father, former Broadway columnist Leonard Lyons, had been a close friend of Ernest Hemingway. Jeffrey, through that connection, had become a bullfight aficionado, having spent a summer at the bull ranch of legendary matador Antonio Ordonez.

We obtained excellent tickets to the huge Plaza de Toros in Madrid through a friend of mine, and went to the bullfights with Jeffrey who talked us through various stages of the "corrida." I wasn't sure how we would respond to what we were watching for the first time, but Lee was quite intrigued and caught up in the artistry of the spectacle. In fact, we went again the following day when the matador and bulls moved down to the village of Aranjuez for the traditional corrida there as part of the "Festival of San Isidro."

(A footnote: Aranjuez was the summer home of the Bourbon Kings of Spain, and is celebrated in the Spanish musical composition *Concierto de Aranjuez*, by Joaquin Rodrigo.)

While we had been high up on the *sombre* side of the stadium in Madrid, here we were in the sunny first row of a tiny arena, protected from the bulls only by what appeared to be very flimsy, very old wooden fences! Several times, bulls charged into them adding some unwelcome excitement.

Back in Madrid, we treated ourselves to drinks at one of Hemingway's haunts, El Gran Cafe Gijon and the roast suckling pig at the famous Casa Botin. Lee and I continued our journey through Spain to Portugal with stops along the way to Merida, where we watched archaeologists excavating Roman ruins, and the charming village of Trujillo, named for the conquistador explorer.

In Trujillo, we poked our heads into a very old church, part of a convent occupied by nuns who had taken vows of silence that last for several years. A nun greeted us when we entered the empty church and seemed very eager to give us a guided tour. She chattered away in Spanish. And we were able to deduce that she had just then finished her silent time and was now eagerly able to speak. The tour lasted longer than planned, but the least we could do for this charming woman, was to let her talk!

We dropped our rental car in Lisbon and flew to Faro on the Algarve coast. We had read in the papers that a peaceful coup by the Portuguese military had just taken place, but life was going on as normal, and the resort hotels were still open. When we landed, there were armed soldiers directing us to immigration and customs. It was a little unnerving and more than a little inconvenient since the entire airport personnel had disappeared and the soldiers weren't offering to transport baggage out to the taxi area. But we made it to our hotel without incident, and while its staff had also seen some defections, we had a delightful few days enjoying beach time, grilled sardines, and vinho verde during the day, and sightseeing in the nearby fishing village of Portimao.

Two years had passed since that first foray into Europe, but this time my trip to France was at NBC's expense. I promised Lee we would get to Paris together some time, which we did a few years later.

There were two fights scheduled for NBC—Shavers, a top-10er who could punch, against Henry Clark, whose claims to fame were holding the California title and also having a remarkable physical resemblance to Muhammad Ali. The main event featured world middleweight champion Rodrigo Valdez from Colombia, defending his title against the French champion, Max Cohen.

NBC Sports Vice President Chet Simmons wanted to make sure we established the glamorous French capital as the venue for the first boxing telecast in many years on NBC. My colleague, prominent sports journalist Larry Merchant and I were sent out with the four boxers, to four different locations in and near Paris.

I went with Clark and our camera crew to the Palace of Versailles, and with Cohen to his own popular bistro, named Chez Max (what else?). Clark not only looked a lot like Ali, he fancied himself a big personality. He displayed it with a swank wardrobe, and an elegant, silver-topped walking stick. Henry was well-educated, bright and a very pleasant guy. He was excited to be going to Versailles for his bit in the promotion. In the car ride out he wanted to know about the palace, which kings had lived there and when. I gave him my best CliffsNotes® rundown on Louis Quatorze, told him he was known as the Sun King, that he was even more foppish than Henry was, and that he liked mirrors so much, he had a whole ballroom walled with them.

When we arrived, our producer decided we should shoot the piece on the grand terrace leading to the expansive royal gardens. Clark soaked in all the beauty, clearly impressed with the opulent surroundings.

"Now Henry, we have only time for a few lines here. We'll walk across the terrace, I will ask you what you think of Louis the fourteenth, and you answer me with just a brief impression of what you are seeing here in Versailles, okay?"

"I am ready," replied Henry, and I was hoping that meant ready for his fight as well, where he was a heavy underdog. But he was clearly in his fantasy milieu here.

"Now, we can do a few takes," said the producer. "Just keep your answer short Henry."

"Rolling!" shouted the cameraman.

Tim: "So Henry—a long way from your home in San Francisco, here we are at the magnificent Palace of Versailles, which was home to the Sun King. What do you think of it?"

Henry: "Tim, (pause as he gestures grandly) "that Louis the fourteenth… was a king-and-a-half!"

"Cut," said the producer, and then burst into laughter with the rest of us.

"Was that enough?" asked Henry. It was merely… perfect.

Nessim "Max" Cohen lacked Clark's wit. And his Chez Max was no Versailles. It was a run-of-the-mill bar/bistro in a run-of-the-mill *arrondissement.* It featured lots of smoke and fight photos. Scenic it was not, but our producer had taken Shavers and Valdes to other obvious Paris landmarks, so Cohen's saloon served up the gritty side of the City of Light. His boxing pictures on the wall featured himself of course, and the late Marcel Cerdan who even in death is one of France's great sporting heroes. (His grave, next to the love of his life, Edith Piaf, in the Cimetière du Père Lachaise still attracts lines of tourists.)

Max's brief interview with me was matched only by his brevity in the ring against Valdes. After being pummeled by Valdes for three rounds, Cohen failed to come out for the fourth, quitting on his stool. That was a huge disappointment to a sellout crowd of boxing-mad Parisians who reacted with boos and whistles. Actor Jean-Paul Belmondo, a friend of Cohen's, buried his face in his hands. NBC was in panic mode—we had a lot of time to fill and no back-up programming.

"Get in the ring Tim, do some interviews."

Gil Clancy, who was training Valdes, lengthened his answers for me, and then offered to call up the actor Omar Sharif, an avid boxing fan. During a commercial we got Sharif in the ring. Like Belmondo he was embarrassed by Cohen's bailout.

On camera, I asked Sharif what he thought this shabby performance would mean to Cohen and his bistro Chez Max.

"Tim... I think no one will go to Chez Max anymore!"

For his part, Henry Clark's wit turned out to be sharper than his punches, but he managed to go the distance against the slugger Shavers, losing by decision.

It was the first and last boxing coverage I did for NBC, but the "sweet science" continued to be a linchpin in the rest of what lay ahead for me in TV sports. Paris was just the *amuse bouche*—an opening act for a lifetime of travel to exotic locales, covering sports I love in very nice places... well, most of them were nice!

CHAPTER 14

CBS and the Eighties

The 1980s turned out to be the most satisfying decade of my working career, and my personal life. The variety of sports I had hoped for, the chance to see the world on someone else's nickel, the thrill of covering big events, and the opportunity for Lee and I to have some quality time together despite a hectic schedule—all came together during those years.

It began with the end of my hockey life—but what a finish! Two Stanley Cup wins by the Islanders capped my broadcasting of hockey (they went on to win two more to make it four in a row); then came the chance to move up through the NFL announcer ranks, being anointed CBS's winter sports guy covering alpine ski-racing, figure skating, bobsleds, speed-skating, cross country, ski-jumping, and free-style skiing. I continued to be a part of CBS coverage of the prestigious NCAA basketball tournament; hosted the *CBS Sports Spectacular* series; called matches and co-hosted the late-night highlights show at the U.S. Open tennis championships; and began what turned out to be the best-ever network coverage of championship boxing.

And it was boxing that provided Lee and me a life-changing experience in the African bush. More on how that came about and its significance in our lives a little later in this narrative.

Today's anchors on the myriad sports-talk shows are always asking their experts to "break down" the story of the upcoming game. So let's do that sport-by-sport with this special ten-year run in the eighties at CBS.

• • •

TOP: Tim with NFL partner Terry Bradshaw.
MIDDLE: Tim with NFL partner Matt Millen, and stats crew Dick Bossung and Terry Kane.
BOTTOM: Tim with John Madden.

While NBC had given me my first taste of boxing on network television, Scotty Connal—my hockey maven—had also given me the chance to do NFL play-by-play which was to become a major part of my schedule of events at CBS. Over the next twenty-one years while I was exclusive to CBS sports, I worked a full schedule of NFL games, and a few seasons of college football as well. My broadcast partners included some of the biggest names in their sport: quarterbacks Johnny Unitas of the Colts, Roman Gabriel of the Rams, Joe Theismann and Sonny Jurgensen of the Redskins, John Brodie of the 49ers, Terry Bradshaw of the Steelers, linebackers Nick Buoniconti of the Dolphins, and Matt Millen of the Raiders, running back Tom Matte of the Colts, wide receiver Johnny Morris of the Bears, offensive linemen Randy Cross of the 49ers and Dan Jiggetts of the Bears, defensive end Fred Dryer of the Rams, and defensive back Irv Cross of the Eagles.

The NFL networks had several teams of announcers, adding them as the league expanded, which provided more games each Sunday. There remains an obvious pecking order of announcer teams—an inevitable changing of partnerships. Some of the analysts just don't have the natural skills or the work ethic to make it at the network level. The same can be said, but less so, of the professional play-by-play announcers. In the eighties, with two of the then three major networks carrying the Sunday NFL games, there were only six to eight positions available for each role.

The top partnerships got the big games each week—at CBS, when I joined the group in 1977, Pat Summerall (working with Tom Brookshier) and Vin Scully (working with a variety of NFLers) were the top two teams. I started down in the seventh spot, and made it to number two for one season in 1987, when Joe Theismann was a highly touted rookie. Joe did so well, he left after one season for more money at ESPN!

Over time, I became known as a good tutor for rookie analysts, and had success breaking in Theisman, Buoniconti, Jiggetts, Dryer, and Randy Cross. I also took pride in rejuvenating a few who had rocky starts with other play-by-play men—most prominently Terry Bradshaw who had lost confidence and even some of his ebullient personality in his two seasons as a booth analyst. After our stint together Terry went on to thrive as an analyst and then became a major star of the NFL studio shows, both at CBS and later at FOX.

A sidebar to my time with Bradshaw. One time in the off-football season, Gil Clancy and I were in San Francisco covering a fight. I was jogging in Golden Gate Park where I saw a sign saying Mikhail Baryshnikov was appearing with the San Francisco Ballet that evening. I was a big fan of his, so I stopped at the Opera House hoping I could get a last-minute ticket, and I did.

Telling Clancy I was going to the ballet was tantamount to my covering a polo match (which I actually did once for CBS and suffered Gil's derision for years after). I told him I would meet him at a joint called Tosca in North Beach after the ballet performance.

I had a cheap seat high in the Opera House but still with a good view of the magnificent dancing by Baryshnikov. At intermission I was scanning the balcony box seats and recognized the bald head of Terry Bradshaw.

I made my way down to where he was seated with his then-wife, figure skater JoJo Starbuck, and Terry and I agreed that the Russian dancer was a terrific athlete. But Terry acknowledged that going to the ballet was JoJo's idea! (Sometime later, our chance meeting at the Opera House became a column item in the *Chicago Tribune*.) But for me the evening got even better.

When I got to Tosca to join Gil, I learned from the bartender that Baryshnikov had been coming in most nights after his performances. Sugar Ray Leonard was working our TV fight with Gil and me, and I had arranged for an old college friend, Guinness McFadden (now a successful vintner in California) to join us for breakfast the next morning—his chance to meet Sugar Ray. I was eager to go back to Tosca that night, so while Ray passed on that, Gil, Guinness, and I went for drinks after dinner.

Once there, a guy at the bar recognized us and introduced himself as a big fight fan. His name was Boz Scaggs, a popular singer who lived in San Francisco. I told him we had heard that Baryshnikov might be in Tosca and, sure enough, after we had been talking for some time, the ballet star appeared. Boz made the introduction. That gave me the chance to meet Misha and briefly discuss with him an idea I had long nurtured.

I wanted to make a documentary film to be shot in Zimbabwe, following a herd of impala—the prettiest and most graceful of the African antelope—through the four seasons of a year. (More on the "why" of this idea later.) My plan was to have a soundtrack of ballet music and have it choreographed and hosted by Baryshnikov, whom I had heard was a lover of African wildlife. He took an immediate interest in the project and we corresponded several times.

However, he ultimately turned me down because of his ballet commitments during the year I had in mind to shoot the film. I regret I never did get that documentary made—but I had no regrets about going to the ballet that night in San Francisco! Bradshaw, Boz, and Baryshnikov made for quite a trifecta.

Unlike Terry Bradshaw, many famous ex-players were short-lived in the broadcast booth. Johnny Unitas and Bart Starr were good examples of great players who didn't make the cut. Neither seemed to understand they had to prepare for a telecast just as they did when they were players. They seemed to think that just by being who they were and showing up, the fans would enjoy their comments about the game on the field. In their view, learning the numbers of the players, or studying videotape for game-plans was either beneath them or simply unnecessary.

My favorites as partner? Roman Gabriel, a perfect gentleman and a hard worker; Joe Theismann, for his enthusiasm and desire to be good in his new role; Johnny Morris, a former star with Mike Ditka on the Bears, with whom I worked parts of eight seasons (my longest run with the same analyst) which meant lots of Bears games during their run to the '85 Super Bowl; and Matt Millen, the most willing learner, a fine human being with a great sense of humor, and a respect for all the support-folks around him in the booth.

While I never worked with now-retired John Madden, I take a tiny bit of credit for his well-earned rise to the top. When CBS hired him after he left coaching the Oakland Raiders, he attended the seminar in New York (gathering all of the announcers and production people) which the networks hold each year before the season begins. After the meetings, a group of us including John, retired to my favorite watering hole, P.J. Clarke's.

In the back room, Madden sat down at a table of CBSers including me. He immediately peppered me with a bunch of questions about what he had heard at the meetings, wanted to know everything about communication in the booth, how the replays worked, how would he know when to speak— were there signals between him and the play-by-play guy, did the producer and director talk to him during the game—everything, including whether you got a hot dog at halftime.

I had never met another rookie broadcaster who was so seriously curious about how it all worked, and wanted to get answers *right now!* It was clear he was going to be a very well-prepared analyst, just as he had been a coach. Despite the socializing going on around him that night at Clarke's, he was intently taking in all of the information I could give him on his first day at the office.

Of course John went on to a multi-Emmy Award-winning career with the late Pat Summerall—and deservedly so.

It's been well reported that Madden had an admitted fear of flying, and made a deal with Greyhound to travel to games in his own customized bus. The rest of us poor souls made do traveling by air, first class, staying in 5-star-hotels (well, at least in the 5-star cities), dining in the top restaurants and having police-escorted limos to the airports from the stadiums. After one Detroit Lions game ran long, and it appeared we would miss our flights home, CBS ordered up a helicopter to fly us from the stadium parking lot to the airport! Ah, yes those were the days my friends!

Still, the most fun and satisfaction came from being at the game venues, calling the play-by-play, always trying for the perfect broadcast while knowing this is virtually impossible working "live" for four hours at a time. For most of my football life I had a terrific support crew in the booth—spotter Terry Kane and statistician Dick Bossung. Announcers rely on those folks to be quick and accurate in pointing to the charts identifying runners, tacklers and receivers and providing the right yardage and pertinent stats. I always went with my own view of the play, but knowing Terry would be there—finger on the team's chart—if I wasn't sure of my call. Dick would be quick with downs and distance, length of punts, and pass plays.

Preparation for NFL football began on the Mondays for next Sunday's game: Viewing tape of your game—finding flaws and errors. Tuesdays were for screening game tapes of the two upcoming opponents, Wednesdays going over information, lineups, and stats for each team, Thursdays preparing your spotting "boards," often having conference calls with team PR men and sometimes traveling to the game site. Fridays were for meetings with the home team's players and coaches after watching practice. Saturdays were spent at the visiting team's "walk-through" and then talking with players and coaches, followed by a production meeting with our crew.

I had the good fortune to work with some of TV's top sports producers during the eighties—David Michaels, Mike Burks, Bob Mansbach and Richie Zyontz among them. They came to the game fully prepared with the storylines and were well-liked and respected by their technical and production crews.

NFL games provided opportunity for fine dining as well! In the Golden

Age expense allowances were generous—and most Friday nights and some Saturdays were spent in top restaurants with excellent wine lists!

Favorite restaurants? Well some have gone to cuisine heaven by now, but in the eighties La Maisonnette in Cincinnati was a favored French; Gene & Georgetti's in Chicago for steak and "garbage salad"; a family-owned spot on the shore of Green Bay for fresh Walleye pike; The Rex for abalone on Balboa Bay when in Orange County for L.A. Rams games; Berns Steakhouse in Tampa; Washington Square Cafe (later Moose's) owned by the late, great Ed Moose in San Francisco; Loon Cafe in Minneapolis for wild-rice soup; Ray's Boathouse in Seattle for Pacific salmon, L'Osteria in south Philly for Italian, (Orange-flavored pasta!); in Detroit a restaurant in Greektown for a plate of tiny lamb-chops grilled with oil, garlic, and lemon squeeze; Obrycki's in Baltimore (when the Colts were still there!) for blue-crabs served on paper with wooden mallets to break them open; Joe's Stone Crab in Miami; The Mansion in Dallas; Paul Maguire's Buffalo-wings saloon in Tonawanda, N.Y.

Friday nights were usually group nights out for dinner, but Saturdays most guys would want to do room-service and work on game notes.

What did we get from meetings with players and coaches? Maybe a good personal story or two from the players, but rarely any good information related to the game. Only a few players are memorable to me—again not for sharing anything about a game plan I could use on the telecast, but for great stories about heritage, family, and college life. Three were quarterbacks—two from the deep south: Bobby Hebert of the Saints, Brett Favre of the Packers and Jim McMahon of the Bears. Hebert from the bayous of Mississippi and Favre from farm country in Louisiana, told colorful stories about grandparents and local characters with wit and charm. McMahon told colorful stories of being an Irish Catholic breaking all the rules at a Mormon school, BYU.

As for coaches, well therein lies a tale! For the next chapter.

CHAPTER 15

More Football—
Coaches and Characters

Football coaches are a strange breed.

It's understandable. They are among the least job-secure employees in any business. Knowing that more wins than losses is the only criterion for further employment explains why many get up at 4 a.m. to watch game videos and stay through supper-time for daily meetings with their assistants. Their constant insecurity also explains why in some cases paranoia sets in. No one outside their inner circle is to be trusted. A victory is at stake every Sunday. Their job depends on winning more than the other coaches do.

Loose lips sink ships. A game-plan is top secret. Playbooks are to be kept under lock and key. And God forbid that anyone in the organization should let slip any information to anyone outside the organization—especially to the dreaded media, and most especially to those damn TV announcers!

Now, there was, and I assume still is, an NFL league rule that requires head coaches to give interview time to the network announcers at a time to be agreed upon—usually after Friday practice, or Saturday around noon. Visiting team coaches meet the TV folks when they arrive with their teams on Saturdays—mid to late afternoon.

In the eighties only a handful of NFL head coaches talked to the TV guys willingly. I am sure that hasn't changed with the newer crop of coaches. Most regard it as worse than sucking lemons, or shopping with their wives. That group, forced to do so, were determined to say as little as possible in the shortest possible time.

There were exceptions to that attitude, but I am hard-pressed to think of more than a handful. The greatest in the good-guy category was John McKay, then coach of the Tampa Bay Buccaneers, who, during his tenure, were better described as the Florida Doormats. Following a distinguished career as the coach at the University of Southern California, he was the first coach of the expansion Bucs, and needed all of his skill and all of his great sense of humor to try and turn rookies and castoffs into a viable NFL team.

But McKay, despite the travails of his bottom-feeding squad, understood the need for cooperation with the media since Tampa was trying to build a fan base. Unlike his NFL coaching colleagues, he didn't have a distrust of the TV guys, or a fear that they might spill his game-plan to his opponents. (Of course McKay might think it wouldn't affect the likely outcome even if they did!)

He was a delight to spend time with, answered every question from the announcers and producers with wit and wisdom, and would draw up his opening series of plays on the blackboard for us. He understood we were doing our job as he and his staff had done theirs during the week—preparing to "play our best game" while describing his team's effort to do the same.

Others of that time who were in the good-guy category—or at least gave us needed time and useful information for our jobs—included another former USC coach, gregarious and always honest John Robinson of the Rams, Bud Grant of the Vikings (despite his taciturn demeanor), Jerry Glanville of the Falcons who loved country music and was sure Elvis was still alive, Wayne Fontes of the Lions who always smiled through consistent adversity, and Dick Vermiel of the Eagles who always wore his heart on his sleeve.

Then there were the difficult ones.

Notice I said difficult, not to say they weren't mainly polite, businesslike, and professional. Sometimes they even smiled. But they made it clear that meeting with the TV guys wasn't fun—it was part of the job they knew they had to do. They didn't have to like it.

Some memorable examples: Chuck Noll, imperious coach of the very successful Pittsburgh Steelers. Chuck made it clear that he would be telling you nothing that would be very useful in bringing some insight into your telecast for the benefit of the viewers. Asked about injuries to his players, the answer would be "day-to-day" as to their recoveries. Asked about strategy for the game in question, "Why I would tell you that?" Asked about new wrinkles in the offense, "If there are any, you'll see them in the game." Defense? "We do what we do." The opponents? "They are a good football team."

Thanks, Chuck.

Noll treated coaching in the NFL as though he were employed by the CIA—sworn to secrecy, and suspicious of any foreigners asking questions.

"Let's talk about your wine cellar." Now that would bring a smile. Noll was a knowledgeable wine collector, and I imagined him enjoying a sip or two of a fine wine on a terrace at his home—but keeping a sharp eye for anyone trying to read the vintage on the label of his Lafite.

Don Shula of the Dolphins—the man who led them to a still-record unbeaten season of seventeen games and a Super Bowl win in 1972—could be gregarious and welcoming to the TV guys when they arrived at the Miami practice facility. But he could also keep us waiting well beyond our scheduled meeting time. And like his counterpart Chuck Noll, he would offer only generalities—nothing that would add to our coverage of the game.

Again there was the prevailing sense of mistrust—"these guys might take information I give them and take it to the other coach tomorrow." But unlike Noll, Shula would try to disguise his impatience with a dose of bonhomie.

Then there was Sam Wyche of the Bengals. One season when he was in Chicago to play the Bears, his team arrived at a hotel in the city at around 4 p.m. My broadcast group and I were waiting at the appointed time. An hour went by, players came and went, but no Sam. Another hour passed. We were getting a little annoyed. Just as I was suggesting we bail on Wyche, in he came saying he didn't have much time to give us.

My cold reply was to the effect that we had arrived in time for our meeting, he had not. That we showed respect for him by waiting, but he had shown none for us. Needless to say it was a long wait for a short meeting—that produced nothing of value.

Interestingly, Wyche's coaching career ended not long after, and what do you know? He became a TV guy.

Mike Ditka was another case altogether. He would greet us gruffly (even though my then partner was Johnny Morris who had been a teammate of Big Mike on the Bears), announce the amount of time he would spend with us, and then proceed to be entertaining—his way of avoiding answering any questions which might have dented that armor.

I couldn't help liking him (and still do), but I determined that the best way to get him to pay attention to us—instead of lighting and relighting his stogey—was to call him out. One Saturday we met with him at his chosen time, noon. As soon as we entered his office at Halas Hall, Ditka announced; "Fifteen minutes men, I have a golf tee time at 1 o'clock."

"Wait a minute Mike," I replied, "you'll have to push it back. We're doing our job here in order to make the best telecast of your game possible. And you have an obligation to give us some time and material that will be helpful to us." Johnny was silently dumbfounded. He had never seen anyone get into Ditka's grill.

Big Mike took a pull on his cigar and smiled broadly, "Okay, just don't make me too late—what do you want?"

We never had a problem with Ditka after that incident. And in the march to the Super Bowl in 1985, he gave us lots of good stuff to use on air.

The most infuriating coach was Monte Clark, one of a quick succession of losing Detroit Lions head coaches. A quiet, seemingly very nice man, Clark was the most paranoid, humorless, and uncooperative coach I ever dealt with. He had the nerve to tell our producers that Johnny Morris was not welcome at our TV meetings when the Lions were playing the Bears. He evidently truly believed that Johnny would report back to Ditka with anything that Clark said that might be useful to the Bears.

It was an unforgivable insult. The very idea that he would be concerned that Morris would be so unprofessional as to pass Clark's comments to us on to another coach—any coach—was preposterous. As I pointed out to Clark, why would any coach welcome information about his game from a TV announcer, without assuming we were giving *his* information to another coach another week?

To be fair, not *all* coaches fit the "strange breed" profile. When we get to the nineties in this odyssey, I'll tell you about some who were in, my view, of a special breed—fine coaches and fine men.

CHAPTER 16

Basketball—NBA And NCAA

The CBS years were crammed with assignments forty-four to forty-eight of every fifty-two weeks. Football was the most demanding, and so the perks on someone else's nickel were much appreciated. My first couple of years at CBS included doing a handful of NBA basketball games. My partners were Celtics great John Havlicek, Keith Erickson who had been a star with the Los Angeles Lakers, and Jon McGlocklin, a former Milwaukee Buck.

Basketball was clearly not my strength. I had played a little in high-school in Toronto—in Phys Ed classes. But from the beginning of my career what I hoped to do was learn about and cover a big variety of sports—and not be locked into or identified with only one or two. The whole landscape of competition appealed to me—especially those sports that were truly international. I enviously watched the early days of *Wide World of Sports* on ABC and hoped that one day I would get to cover sports in other countries. But the NBA experience set me up for a sixteen-year-run doing the NCAA basketball tournament, which CBS had acquired in 1982.

Over that NCAA time in the eighties I worked with several announcers, but mainly with the delightful and insightful Dan Bonner and the unique and colorful Bill Raftery until 1992 when CBS Executive Producer Rick Gentile paired me with the great Al McGuire—former Marquette coach and quirky raconteur—for my last seven years of covering the tournament. Al's former partners in a three-man-booth had been Billy Packer, with Dick Enberg as the play-by-play man when all three were at NBC during its NCAA tournament years.

I knew Al slightly during that NBC era, had in fact interviewed him at his office during his coaching days at Marquette, and in 1975 he and I had

NCAA tournament with Al McGuire and CBS colleagues
Cathy Barretto and Steve Scheer.

hosted an NBC Final Four studio show. But working with him calling games on CBS was a great treat and a great experience.

Al was a unique and special person. One of the best people I have ever known. His most famous moment while working with me was an impromptu dance he did after a thrilling tournament win by the Syracuse Orangemen. While we were doing the post-match on-camera interviews with the excited winners, the college band playing in the background and fans still cheering, Al—mic in hand—suddenly became an Irish step-dancer, much to the delight of the players—and the viewers!

CBS used the video clip for several years as a Tournament promo.

Al made "Holy mackerel!" an identifiable exclamation after a great play, along with a number of McGuire-only expressions describing the action in a game—many of which were indecipherable—except to Al!

His off-court life was exceptional too. During his coaching years, he would take off to New Zealand after the season, rent a motorcycle and ride around the scenic islands on his own—a vagabond winding down from the rigors of wins and losses at Marquette.

He loved tin soldiers, and almost secretly, built up one of the most important and valuable collections in the U.S.

In our final season working together, 1998, it was obvious Al was ill. He wouldn't acknowledge the severity of his illness, but he knew it was leukemia, and after a brief reunion the following season with Packer and Dick Enberg (who had joined CBS), he gave up working the sport he loved so much.

I called him at his Milwaukee home a few days before he died, or as he referred to it in his Irish way, "Going to the other side of the grass." He asked me to give my home address to his son, Allie—he had something he wanted to send me. It turned out to be one of his beloved tin soldiers. A Canadian Mountie, for a Canadian-born friend. Signed carefully in gold on the tiny base, "For Tim from Al."

Even with Al McGuire as my partner, I never got to do a men's Final Four. Al, God bless him, did many in his NBC days with Packer and Enberg. But I did get to do a Final Four—in the Women's NCAA Tournament. My partner was a wonderful woman and great athlete, Ann Meyers Drysdale.

She had been a star player at UCLA and was married to the great baseball pitcher Don Drysdale of the Dodgers until his untimely death in 1993 while on a road trip as a broadcaster for the Dodgers.

We covered the North Carolina victory over Louisiana Tech in the 1994 Final in Richmond, Virginia. One of the stars of the Tar Heels winning team was Marion Jones, who went on to Olympic infamy as a gold medal sprinter who was later stripped of her medals for doping violations.

But I am ahead of myself. Working as an announcer during March Madness in the eighties was always a treat. Announce-teams would set a goal, as the college basketball teams did, of getting through as many rounds as possible. By the end of the decade I was a regular into the "Elite Eight," then I could relax and watch Jim Nantz and Billy Packer handle the Final Four.

CHAPTER 17

Tennis: All About Love

In many ways, tennis was my first love (after Lee of course!). I had played some as a teenager in Toronto and had a brief career in college as a freshman walk-on to the Notre Dame tennis team. I didn't belong at that level, and the coach and I discovered that at about the same time. The team led by Max Brown and the Heinbecker brothers, Bill and Pete, turned out to be one of the best ND squads of that era. After graduation I settled for following friends of mine who were top players in Canada, Don Fontana, John Bassett Jr., and Carmen Bolton. (Bassett's daughter Carling became a highly ranked player on the women's tour.)

Getting a chance to cover big-time tennis on TV was all about luck and timing. And it turned into a nearly thirty-year run on six different networks!

CBS held the rights to the U.S. Open in 1978, and I was assigned to be one of the play-by-play announcers, calling some outside-court matches from a monitor in a cramped trailer-space in the TV compound. My partners were Billie Jean King on women's matches and John Newcombe on the men's. As a rookie tennis announcer, I was thrilled to sit alongside such superstars of the sport, and over the years both have become great friends of mine.

As the CBS coverage expanded to covering two "show" courts, I was passed over as the number two behind Pat Summerall, and asked to host the nightly highlights show. Van Gordon Sauter was in his brief tenure as head of CBS Sports, and when I pleaded my case, he listened courteously, and held his ground. "Well, Mr. Ryan, I admire your work, I know you love tennis, but I would like you to do the late night show. If you prefer not to, then I'm afraid you will not be working the Open."

I preferred not to (stubborn Irish) and so was off the Open for the next

TOP: Calling U.S. Open tennis with Tony Trabert and Mary Carillo.

RIGHT: Jimmy Connor's 34th birthday in the CBS studio.

BOTTOM: At the U.S. Open with John Newcombe and Walter Cronkite.

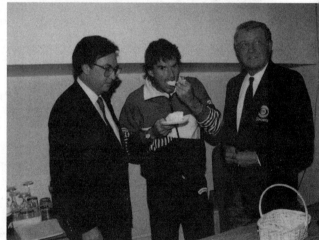

two years. When I returned, new management offered a compromise—host the highlights show (with Mary Carillo), anchor the studio daytime segments on the weekends, and also do some play-by-play. I was happy to come back to a sport I loved. I held the dual role until 1994 when Pat Summerall moved from CBS to FOX and then-CBS boss Neal Pilson gave me the top spot as the number one anchor on Center Court, the Louis Armstrong Stadium court.

The eighties saw the great battles between McEnroe and Conners, the dominance at the Open by Ivan Lendl and Martina Navratilova, and the emergence of Steffi Graf. The Open was becoming the hottest sports ticket in New York. For celebrities, Flushing Meadows, Queens, despite its unattractive name, was the place to see and be seen.

Some A-listers were genuine tennis fans and club players, comedians Alan King and Bill Cosby among them. CBS producer for the Open was a man who didn't even like the sport. Frank Chirkinian was best known as the man who got and kept the Masters Golf tournament for CBS by cultivating a cozy rapport with Augusta's poobahs. He played and loved golf, and produced all of the PGA Tour events on CBS. A cocky, likeable man with an acerbic sense of humor, he got the tennis job because CBS needed to amortize his hefty contract over more events in the course of a year.

Frank was CBS's Pearl Mesta (New York's legendary socialite hostess) in the studio office area in the deep corridors of Louis Armstrong Stadium. Cronies of his, CBS executives, visiting pro-golfers, politicians, and show biz types sifted in and out of Frank's office where his favorites could share a drink from a hidden bar in one the desks. Jimmy Connors celebrated his birthdays there, and an occasional tennis production meeting was actually held.

A thin wall separated the office from our studio with the anchor desk from which I provided updates and conducted interviews. The one door to it was guarded by the usual red light and by our stage manager, Chuck Will. When Chirkinian was on hand entertaining his guests, Chuck was a busy man, constantly reminding the visitors that next door we were actually on the air when the red light was on.

Most of the big names in tennis during the eighties came through that door for interviews, and the late-night shows when I was joined by the irrepressible Mary Carillo were always fun—and often we were covering live action from late-running matches featuring top players in late-night dramas.

But one of the most dramatic episodes that took place in the studio didn't involve tennis at all.

September 11, 1987 was a Friday. I was anchoring the studio portions of the CBS coverage. The second of the women's semifinals was being played: The German star Steffi Graf against the American Lori McNeil, who had upset fellow U.S. player Chris Evert in the quarters. McNeil won the first 6-4, Graf won the second and so it was going three sets, and heading beyond the time scheduled for tennis that day on CBS.

Meanwhile in Miami, news anchor Dan Rather was preparing for his usual 6:30 p.m. *Evening News* program. The program was in Miami instead of New York because Rather was covering the U.S. tour of Pope John Paul II.

In our studio I was being warned to go quickly to CBS News when we signed off the air following the match. It was 6:38 p.m., Graf had won the third set to advance to the final (which she would lose to Martina Navratilova). On camera I gave the final score and said, "We now join the *CBS Evening News* with Dan Rather."

It had been a long day, watching two matches on the studio monitors. There was no more tennis that day—I had the evening off. Lee and I planned dinner in New York. I quickly left the studio. In the next-door office, someone said, "Where's Rather?"

The picture on the TV monitors was black.

Chuck Will, still with his headset on—connected to our production truck—yelled, "Get back on set, back on set!"

Our producer was yelling as well as I put my earpiece back in and took my place at the desk. "Vamp! Fill—we'll get some highlights up!"

Six minutes had elapsed from the time Rather walked from his on-air desk in Miami in a fit of pique over the tennis match running into his newscast.

When he reappeared, I was given the cue to say goodbye from New York—again—and "throw it to Dan Rather in Miami."

It was Page One the next day: Dan took a lot of heat for his angry decision to abandon his ship in Miami, but as things turned out, it was just one of several brouhaha's during his career.

I have another story involving Dan in a much different light, as you will see soon.

And more tennis—in more places—in the following twenty years.

CHAPTER 18

Boxing: A Life Changer

I've noted that hockey was the sport that brought me to the U.S., and boxing was the sport that took me around the world. Well, the trip to Paris in the late seventies for the boxing card on NBC was just an hors d'oeuvre.

By 1978, the star-filled U.S. Olympic team from the 1976 Games in Atlanta had galvanized CBS to sign several of the now-fledgling pros to exclusive contracts for a series of fights. The group included Olympic champions Howard Davis Jr., and the Spinks brothers, Leon and Michael. (Sugar Ray Leonard's clever manager Mike Trainer kept his man non-exclusive). But CBS built an ad hoc relationship with promoter Bob Arum and his Top Rank Company. Arum, a Harvard-educated lawyer had worked in the U.S. Attorney's office before becoming aligned with Muhammad Ali and promoting several of his fights in the late sixties—before Ali's three-and-a-half-year layoff for refusing to be drafted. Bob had been building a stable of entertaining fighters of all weights. Several became regulars on CBS where they became stars and champions: Ray "Boom-Boom" Mancini, Alexis Arguello, Tommy Hearns, Marvin Hagler, Hector Camacho, Aaron Pryor, Yacqui Lopez, and many more.

Boxing was on CBS every weekend year-round—sometimes on both Saturday and Sunday afternoons as part of the series *CBS Sports Spectacular* which paired the fights with other events, including the Tour de France. As noted earlier, it was a renaissance of a sport that had been ignored by the networks since Gillette's *Friday Night Fights* in the early days of television.

It didn't take long for Arum to line up partnerships with European promoters who had quality boxers in several weight divisions. Matches taking

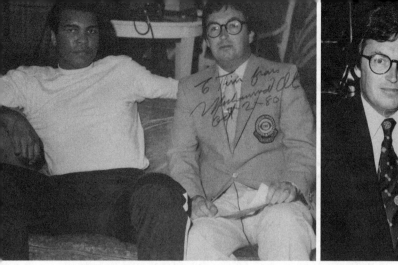

LEFT: Tim interviewing Muhammad Ali, who autographed the photo!
RIGHT: With boxing promoter Bob Arum.

place at night in Europe played perfectly into afternoon time slots on CBS—and perfectly into my hopes of seeing the world on someone else's nickel.

And so began what turned out to be a twenty-two-year run of covering boxing, and of being paired with one of the greatest broadcast partners anyone in our business could ask for. Not to mention one of the greatest people. Gil Clancy and I became lifelong friends, although he left me behind a few years ago, at the age of 88. Together we covered more than three hundred championship fights—most of them on CBS between 1980 to mid-nineties and then several more on pay-per-view for Top Rank.

The foreign locales stretched from Europe to South America to Asia, the Caribbean and South Africa. It was a geographic and cultural banquet. And some of the fights were pretty good too! In Europe over the years we made stops in France: Paris, Bordeaux, Grenoble and the beach resorts of St. Tropez and Le Touquet. In Italy: Rome, Milano, Torino, San Remo, and Campione d'Italia. In then-Yugoslavia: Belgrade and Split. In Hungary, Budapest. In England, London. In Monaco, Monte Carlo. In Northern Ireland, Belfast.

In Asia: Japan, Tokyo. In the Caribbean: Puerto Rico, Trinidad. In South America: Argentina, Buenos Aires. In Africa: South Africa, Mmabatho, Sun City, and Johannesburg.

All of the fight locations brought their own charms and delights and each have provided memories—some, of course more indelible than others. And some, life-changing.

In 1979, Bob Arum was approached by South African businessman Sol Kerzner to stage a fight in a village near Johannesburg. A bit of historical background is necessary here. South Africa was still run by the apartheid government of the National Party. Under threat of sanctions from many other countries, it had created territorial " homelands" for each of the major tribes, and declared them independent of South Africa. Each homeland had its own president, in most cases a local chieftain, often friendly with the real government. It was a blatant public relations move by the South African administration, and it was scorned by democratic countries around the world.

But Kerzner saw an opportunity that could help create economies for the tribes, and a chance for him to expand the hotel business to include gambling casinos—prohibited in South Africa by the governing party.

The government, influenced by descendants of the Dutch Reformed Church, frowned on drinking, inter-marriage, and certainly gambling. But many of the Afrikaner men were not so religiously inclined as to skip all the pleasures of the flesh.

Kerzner made a deal with the "president" of Bophuthatswana, homeland of the Tswana people, which allowed him to build a hotel/casino in a small village about an hour's drive from Johannesburg, called Mmabatho. It was a test case to see if wealthy South Africans would come to gamble—and gambol. Sol had been an amateur boxer and loved the sport. He thought staging a championship fight in Mmabatho—televised internationally— could also lure foreigners to come to South Africa to vacation. A win for both the National Party government and for the tribal peoples in the homelands.

So, improbably, there we were: Top Rank and CBS, Tim Ryan, and Gil Clancy in a rickety old soccer stadium in Mmabatho to televise a WBA heavyweight championship fight between African-American John Tate and an Afrikaner policeman named Kallie Knoetzee. Guess who the virtually all-black audience assembled in the bleacher seats was cheering for?

Tate didn't disappoint, scoring a knockout win over the cop.

Meanwhile, Kerzner's attractive hotel/casino received a ton of publicity and led him to expand his interests in Bophuthatswana with the construction of Sun City and the Palace Resort, right on the doorsteps of Johannesburg.

We returned there a year later for the heavyweight title fight between Mike Weaver and Gerry Coetzee, and Sun City's arena was sold out—to mixed-race audience, which Arum described as the first time such a thing had ever occurred in South Africa. Weaver won the fight. The sanctions were still on, apartheid still prevailed, but another amateur boxer imprisoned on an island near Cape Town would change all that.

His name was Nelson Mandela.

Several months before Gerry Coetzee's heavyweight championship fight with Mike Weaver in the fall of 1980, the South African stopped an American Journeyman Mike Koranicki in the first round at Rand Stadium in Johannesburg.

Since CBS was to carry the upcoming title fight, Arum convinced us to do the warm-up as well. It was my second trip to South Africa, and with the fight in the city where much of the apartheid turmoil had taken place— particularly in the black township of Soweto—I was eager to see and learn more about the civil rights issues.

As it turned out, a CBS news correspondent in Jo'burg contacted our boxing producer offering his services at the fight. We hired him to assist at ringside, and I asked him a million questions about the racial struggle in South Africa, and if it was possible to tour through Soweto.

He told me foreign whites were discouraged from going there. Had he been there? Well yes, but only as an accredited reporter, and there were many restrictions on those. "Can we go for a look?" I asked. "I'll take the risk if it doesn't put you in jeopardy."

Off we went, the afternoon before the fight.

"Stay in the back seat, out of view until I tell you it is clear," were his instructions.

When we arrived at the village with no white cops in evidence, he said, "Okay, you can have a look around. I'll drive by Bishop Desmond Tutu's house." The township—as these black-populated villages are known, was a shamble of mud-bricked shanties, corrugated tin roofs slapped on, no electrical wires to be seen, and villagers carrying buckets of water from a communal pump.

We were looked at with suspicion by the locals—my guide saying they would assume we were plain-clothes police.

Tutu, the feisty Anglican bishop and civil rights activist whose influence was feared by the apartheid government, had the best house in town—a small, but neat brick house with a proper roof and a small fenced garden. Children played on the dusty road in front.

"The people love him and the white cops leave him alone," my guide told me.

As we slowly moved through the village to the outskirts, school-children appeared, smiling and giggling as we drove by. They were clearly curious as to who these two white men must be, driving slowly through Soweto on a weekday afternoon.

A little farther on we came across two teenage girls, dressed in school uniforms, carrying their book bags.

I asked if we could take a chance and stop and tell them we were TV people from America, and could we talk to them—maybe offer them a lift to their homes?

"They will probably say no—they will be afraid."

"I'm sure, but can we try?"

"Okay."

"Hello… we are from the U.S. We are here for the big boxing match with Gerry Coetzee. Do you speak English?"

Big smiles.

"Yes, we do, a little," answered one of them. "Do you speak Afrikaans?"

"No," I replied. "Although my friend knows a little. Are you walking home from school? We can give you a ride along this road, although we know we are not supposed to be here."

Giggles. "Okay, you can take us a little way."

We stopped, I moved into the front seat, and the two girls climbed into the back.

They wanted to know everything about America—where did we live? Are there big stores there? Did blue jeans cost a lot? Do people there know about South Africa? Will more people from America come to Soweto? Could we go to school there?

They were not afraid, but I was—for them, and what could happen to them and their families if they were seen with two white men in Soweto.

"Do you have far to go from here?" I asked, "I think you better walk the rest of the way."

They got out of the car. "Thank you so much, thank you!" They exclaimed, waving to us as we pulled away.

I could feel the beads of sweat on my brow.

"That was dodgy," said the newsman, "but I am glad you could meet some of the young people of Soweto."

We returned to my hotel without incident. The memory of the experience stays with me to this day.

CHAPTER 19

Arum's Fistic Follies

Of course I remember some great fights we covered as we traveled the world televising Top Rank-promoted matches on CBS through the eighties and into the nineties. But the fact is the best memories of those days had to do with experiencing the foreign locales, and frequently, the antics of Arum. Bob says he is not interested in writing a memoir, (a shame, it's a great story), so I feel it's my duty to share *some* of the times we had together over the years.

Paris is… well, Paris! But Grenoble, the mountain town that hosted the 1968 Winter Olympics, is best remembered by me for a short trip with Arum and Clancy from the city up to the cloistered monastery of the Carthusian monks who make the delectable herbal liqueur, Chartreuse—named for the village where it is made.

Over a couple of glasses of wine a few days before the fight, Clancy and I explained to our Jewish friend, Arum, that the monks had taken vows of silence, and while visitors could view the monastery from the outside, the monks would not converse with them. Bob was convinced he could get one to talk with us. He was willing to make a bet to that effect.

Up the winding road from Grenoble to Chartreuse we went, with me driving a rental car. There was no sign of life at the monastery. We circled the main building, until we found what appeared to be the entrance. There was no welcome sign. The door had a small sliding mailbox-size slot, reminiscent of a 1920s speakeasy.

"Let's knock," insisted Arum, determined to win his bet. After two or three attempts to get some attention, the wooden slat slowly opened. Behind it appeared the face of a monk, his index finger over his tightly closed mouth. He slowly shook his head once, and closed the slat. For once, Arum was speechless.

But then, as we had told him, so was the monk.

Another Arum episode occurred in Bordeaux, at the end of a welterweight title fight. A basketball game was scheduled on CBS following the boxing show. Our producer George Veras had warned us that if the fight went the distance we had to get off the air very quickly. There would be no time for a post-fight interview. Arum, trying to be helpful, had come to our ringside broadcast position and put a headset on that would allow him to hear our producer, as he was communicating with Gil and me and also the production coordinator in New York.

Sure enough, the fight went the distance, and was close. Ring announcer Michael Buffer, he of "Let's Get Ready to Rumble" fame, was waiting for the score-cards to be handed to him and there was a delay.

Veras, watching the second's ticking off to sign-off time, started yelling, "Get the decision, get the decision!!"

Buffer finally got the cards, and then with Arum frantically waving his arms at him to start his announcement, Buffer calmly began, "Mesdames et Messieurs, le décision est official..." (Buffer prided himself on giving his announcements in the local languages before repeating them in English for the TV audience.) "Fifteen seconds to off-air," Veras screamed into the headsets. Gil Clancy and I sat there helplessly. Arum, sitting right next to us, was red-faced with rage at Buffer.

"Forget the fuckin' French, forget the fuckin' French!" he yelled, loud enough for his orders to Buffer to be heard over our open microphones, and thus to millions of viewers watching CBS. It was a triple-alliteration for the ages.

Buffer finally got the decision announced in English, I gave a quick goodbye from Bordeaux, and the basketball game we were joining, was joined late.

That was Bob's debut as a broadcaster, but he had become familiar to fight fans as a presence in the ring after winning performances by his boxer-clients. Unlike arch-rival promoter Don King, he didn't try to hog the spotlight and expect to be interviewed on TV. But his sheepish grin and a bear-hug for his victorious gladiator became a regular part of the post-fight scene in the ring.

But Arum's best TV-appearance took place, on-camera, in Red Star Stadium in Belgrade, Yugoslavia. Belgrade is the capital of restored-to-nation-status-Serbia. But in June of 1978, it was the capital of Yugoslavia, a conglomerate of seven countries and a stew-pot of languages, dialects and religions, all stirred by dictator Marshal Josip Broz Tito.

Tito was languishing in his palatial estate (he would die less than two years later) when Top Rank and the CBS crew arrived to televise the first-ever live event from the Eastern Bloc to the United States. Mate Parlov was making the first defense of his WBC Light-Heavyweight title against Englishman John Conteh. Some enterprising Serbian promoter had convinced Arum that this would make for a great fight, an historic telecast and a big payday—all things very appealing to Bob, who also appreciated the romance of being in such an exotic venue. His Yugo-partner assured him there would be a huge crowd in the enormous soccer stadium to support the Yugoslav champion, and promised a spectacular post-fight party aboard a yacht on the Danube River.

In fact, there was a sizable crowd in the cavernous Red Star stadium, although the overly large ringside section of seats stretched from goal-line to goal-line and sideline to sideline, meaning that unless you were seated in the first ten rows or so, you would need binoculars to see the fight, as was the case with most of the spectators in the grandstands.

Nevertheless…

The local language in Belgrade was Serbo-Croatian, and since none of our group spoke or understood it, the import of the distinction between the two nationalities was lost on us. But not on the crowd in the stadium, who seemed strangely split in their support of Parlov and his British opponent. Well, it turned out that Parlov, born in a seaside town called Split, was Croatian and had no Serbian-cred with the fight fans in attendance. Still he was a Yugoslav, and the majority of the sizable crowd was backing him.

For his part, Conteh expected no support. A talented boxer and an affable guy, he also had a good business sense. Long before prizefighters sported local and national advertising on their trunks, Conteh, knowing the fight would be shown on British TV had picked up a few extra quid by selling some ads to British sponsors. This despite CBS reminding Arum that no ads in the ring or on the boxer's apparel were to be allowed. Most importantly, cigarette advertising had been banned from TV advertising.

So Bob made sure to warn both boxers and their managers: no ads on their clothing, and certainly no cigarette ads.

But Conteh, a bit of a rogue, had affixed several patches on his trunks and even on his shoes which weren't seen by anyone until he removed his robe in the ring, seconds before the bell rang for Round One. Several of them were for Marlboro cigarettes!

Arum, sitting just behind me in the first row was enraged. He leapt out of his seat and climbed up the steps to Conteh's corner and reached through the ropes—tearing off the advertising patches just as Conteh was about to go to the center of the ring for the referee's instructions.

Parlov was nonplussed. The referee was stunned. Conteh was laughing as Arum clawed at the patches until they came free. Furious, he stumbled back down the steps clutching the offending ads.

It was all captured live on worldwide television, with me providing play-by-play of Bob's impressive speed afoot, and manual dexterity in tearing off the patches. Years later, when reminded by me in a telephone conversation of that incident, Conteh said he didn't remember all the details, but showing he hasn't lost his wit, said of Arum's actions: "I think I got ripped off!" Fortunately, his trunks had stayed on.

Oh yes, the fight. It was actually very good, although it ended unsatisfactorily for Conteh who lost on a split decision. Gil, Angelo and I, and others thought he had won a close one, and Parlov looked very much the worse for wear. In fact the winner and still champion went directly to the hospital after the decision was announced. Conteh wiped his bloodied face, was gracious in our post-fight interview, and an hour later was on the party boat on the Danube.

The local promoter had hired a sizeable yacht, with enough deck space on the stern for a small bandstand, a bar, and tables full of food. The musical group featured a woman who was apparently the most famous pop-folk singer in Yugoslavia. She was quite good. Government officials, Belgrade TV people, State news media, Top Rank and CBS folks, Parlov's training staff, (but not Parlov who apparently spent the night in hospital)—all were aboard as the boat pulled away from the dock after midnight for a cruise down the Danube.

Oh yes, and Conteh and his camp, which included his wife and other family members. In fact, after a drink or two, he became the life of the party!

Arum meanwhile kept looking warily around him as the music wafted into the late night and the party boat cruised smoothly down the river with the lights of Belgrade fading in the distance. Jokingly or not, as the evening and the drinking had worn on, members of Conteh's family were threatening to throw Bob into the Danube. The boxer's mother—well "into her cups" was urging her family to toss Arum overboard, apparently blaming Bob for her son's loss to Parlov. And in fact there were security people on board and police boats following us at a less-than-discreet distance.

Lee had not made this trip with me, although she made many others over the decade of the eighties to follow. But as I stood on the bow of the boat with the band playing a romantic-sounding song, I wished out loud that she was standing next to me, under a star-filled sky, sailing down the Blue Danube. It was 5 a.m. before the boat got back to Belgrade.

Arum was safe—and dry.

CHAPTER 20

Difficult and Delicate Decisions

Two truly memorable experiences came out of the jaunt to Belgrade for that colorful event. Three hours after the boat returned to Belgrade I was on a small commuter airliner en route to Dubrovnik, the ancient walled city on the shore of the Adriatic in what is now, again, Croatia.

Then-CBS executive producer Mike Pearl had made the trip to Yugoslavia for the fight, and during the boat ride said since we were so close we should make a quick trip to see Dubrovnik before returning to the U.S. (changing return flights was not the expensive hassle it has since become). I agreed, and made a booking for one night at the Imperial Hotel, and found a 6 a.m. flight.

But when we got back to Belgrade in the middle of the night, Pearl decided sleep was more important than a taste of Croatian history and bailed out. I went ahead with the plan.

Groggily arriving in Dubrovnik, I was hoping the hotel would have a room available for early check-in. They did not. Ten-thirty was the best they could do. It was about 7:30 a.m. Where did they suggest I could go nearby to pass the time? I had had virtually no sleep. The front desk manager suggested taking a ferry boat from a dock close by to an island popular with fishermen and sunbathers. Leaving my luggage and taking a lightweight windbreaker to use as a pillow, I planned to find a beach and sleep for as long as I could and then return to the hotel.

The ferry boat was no more than a large outboard with benches along the gunwales. A handful of fishermen, poles in hand, were my fellow passengers at this early hour. When we reached the island about ten minutes away, I followed them up a well-worn path until a sign in Serbo-Croatian showed arrows pointing in opposite directions. The fishermen turned right, I assumed the bathing beaches were to the left.

A short walk led me to a deserted beach. There was no sand, just a sheet of flat, smooth rock descending from the path to the water. Dead-tired, I lay down on the rock-surface—nicely warming in the early-morning sun—folded my windbreaker under my head and fell asleep.

I was awakened sometime later by the sound of voices nearby. Sleepily, I looked at my watch…it was 9:30. I could soon get a ferry back and get into a real bed at the hotel. I rolled over to my right side and found my glazed eyes coming into focus on two naked people, two very attractive young adults, and the man applying sun-lotion to the woman's body. All of it.

I reluctantly shut my eyes, feigning sleep. I rolled over onto my left-side and peeked out from under my windbreaker-pillow. More naked bodies. Many more. Sitting, standing, walking, talking, swimming. Old people, young people, men, women, a few children.

"Omigod," I muttered to myself, "a nude beach!"

Now what do I do? Pretend to be asleep? Take my clothes off? Was there a protocol for this situation? Whose beach was it anyway? I wasn't sure what to do.

I nervously decided to leave my clothes on, get up casually, and walk quickly away to the ferry dock.

It was my first experience at a nude beach and as the boat took me back to the dock near the hotel, I had reached a conclusion that with the exception of the first couple I described, a nude beach is a place where you wish most people would keep their clothes on.

P.S. Dubrovnik was worth the trip despite my exhaustion and my awkward experience… beautiful coastline, pedestrian-friendly narrow streets with interesting shops, great fresh seafood, decent wine, and friendly people. I hope to go back some day.

I will skip the beach.

Eighteen months after the excitement in Belgrade, we had another educational experience in Yugoslavia. Mate Parlov was now fighting as a cruiserweight (a new weight class between light-heavyweight and heavyweight at 190 pounds) and Arum and his Yugoslav partner had him meeting an American, Marvin Camel for the vacant WBC title in Parlov's hometown of Split.

Like its neighbor Dubrovnik to the south along the Dalmatian coast of the Adriatic, Split is an ancient and revered city in Croatian history. It is the home of Diocletian's Palace, named for the Roman emperor and built at the end of the 4th century. Split is a university city, full of art and culture. I had been fascinated by Yugoslavia on my first trip, and insisted Lee join me for the second one. We had neighbors next door in Larchmont who were from Split, and they encouraged her to go.

During the fight week in Belgrade, the entire CBS group felt pretty sure that some of the local TV people assisting us there were actually government security types, making sure we didn't get answers to all of our questions, making suggestions as to where we should go to sightsee, and advising where we couldn't go. Tito-land was to be presented in its best light on American TV.

In Split, it became quickly apparent we had watchers and minders again, although this time it was more subtly disguised. Shortly after our arrival, a charming and friendly man arrived at our hotel and introduced himself to Gil Clancy and me as our "guide" during the time we were in Split. He was allegedly a professor of Fine Arts at the world renowned university of Split and said he would happily take us on a tour of the Palace, explain its history, show us all the great artworks around the city and at the University, recommend the best restaurants and generally keep us busy as tourists—not as curious television people from a U.S. network.

Well it turned out our minder was indeed an art professor, his name was Vladimir Sunko, and later in the week preceding the fight and after a few cocktails (Clancy introduced him to the "very, very, very" dry martini), he acknowledged that indeed, he had been assigned by the government to keep an eye on us. We promised to keep this secret amongst us, and proceeded to have a delightful and expertly guided tour of the wonderful place, in fact, in the public parks I saw statues by Ivan Mestrovic, who had taught sculpture at Notre Dame when I was there. Learning this, the professor beamed, and said Mestrovic's family home—now a museum—was not far away in the village of Trogir and he would take us there!

Gil took a pass on that, but Lee and I had a special experience with the professor. It became even more special when the day we were to leave, our new friend came to our hotel to say goodbye, and asked for our addresses in the U.S. About a month later a package arrived from Split—it was a landscape painting of that beautiful little city, painted by professor Sunko, an artist himself, and signed to us.

Meanwhile, Parlov and Camel boxed their way to fifteen-round draw in a less than compelling fight for the title.

A few months later, in the spring of 1980 Tito died. Even more difficult years lay ahead for Croats, Serbs, and the other nationalities that had made up the conglomerate of Yugoslavia.

The fights televised from Yugoslavia led to an encore in the Eastern Bloc. Some Hungarian entrepreneur with relatives in the U.S. convinced Arum that Hungary was ready for primetime, despite its struggling economy following the end of its communist pogrom. Arum, ever the one to boost business in a nascent democratic country, said "Why not?" So there we were back on the Danube, but this time, not in Belgrade but in beautiful Budapest, "The City of Baths."

I don't recall that the boxing card in Budapest was a big success—in fact, I don't recall who was in the fight. What I do remember—vividly—is the excursion that Clancy, and Rick Gentile, then part of our CBS boxing production team, and I took to the Turkish baths. We were encouraged to do so by the local Hungarian promoter who assured us it was an experience not to be missed. It was a centuries-old tradition, that was sanitary—despite being communal—though not co-ed!

There are many of the ancient Budapest bath buildings still extant. The one we were directed to had an imposing exterior in an old palatial kind of way. The interior was, well, cold—more of a relic of the recent communist era. Concrete walls, yellowed paint. A stern, white-clad woman—hair pulled back in a severe bun—took our money, handed each of us a towel no bigger than a hankie and without a word, pointed to a door down a tile-floored corridor. There were no guides, and no English on the sparse signs.

We found ourselves whispering to each other as we pushed through the first door into another unsigned hallway. There were no happy-sounding splashes to help us find the water. A somber, overweight chap wearing a towel appeared out of the gloom and in answer to our English "Where do we go for the bath," scowled and pointed to a door that turned out to be the changing room.

Now our whispers were enhanced with giggles. We stashed our clothes in old wooden lockers (no keys) and sat and looked at each other with a "what now?" expression. Clancy, bothered by an arthritic hip, needed help tying his loincloth. Rick gamely assisted. Another unpleasant naked guy appeared, and hearing our English, asked something that sounded like "cold or hot," pointing to two more doors. We chose hot. When we opened the door to "hot" (in Hungarian), the steam met us in our faces. It was so thick we couldn't see the pool. Making our way carefully, clutching our towels modestly, trying not to laugh too loudly, we edged into the pool. I think it was Rick who uttered the first, "Holy shit, it's HOT!"

After a few minutes of poaching ourselves until we were red enough, we stumbled single-file through the steam, one hand holding up our towels, one hand holding onto the towel of the guy in front. Another personable guy pointed us to the cold bath, which was as advertised. Being as there were no sounds from the several men soaking in it, we assumed they were all frozen solid, so we did not dally there.

By this point we were laughing and swearing uncontrollably—Rick wisecracking, Clancy bitching, and me taking the blame for insisting we couldn't be in Budapest without a bath.

CHAPTER 21

From the Nile to the Thames

Our children were now self-sufficient teenagers—in fact Kimberley was at Georgetown University and Kevin was a freshman at Boston College, which made it possible for Lee to travel more with me. In 1981, a good price for airfare and a Hilton hotel cruise-boat down the Nile gave us an exotic week in Egypt. We sailed from Cairo to Luxor with stops along the way to see the temples and tombs of the pharaohs. At the end of the cruise, we stayed two nights at the Mena House Hotel in Giza, across from the pyramids and took the obligatory camel ride into the desert.

Camels are not comfortable. Our private guide told us each camel had a name. Mine, for reasons unexplained at the time, was called Telephone. After twenty minutes or so of jolting along the hard-packed sand, Telephone decided to take the rest of the day off. Without warning, he bucked like a rodeo mustang and threw me off the saddle—a good two feet in the air.

Camels are tall. My flight path from blue sky to ground was about ten feet. I landed on my back.

Lee, on a more placid dromedary, could not help but laugh. "Well his name is Telephone... hello, goodbye!"

"Bring him back to me," I yelled, "I want to get back on." I am still not sure I meant that. But I was consigned to the guide's horse for the rest of the jaunt while he rode Telephone.

I spent two hours in a tub of hot water at the hotel, and my back was sore for a week. Still, we managed a trip into Cairo for cocktails at the iconic Shepheard's Hotel, jostled our way through a crowded souk, took a tour of the mummies at the Egyptian Museum and had dinner at a nightclub featuring belly-dancers.

Lee with Paul Levesque en route to Ascot.

For glamour and excess, it's hard to beat what the Brits call, The Season—the springtime each year for a social calendar that begins with the horse-race "meeting" at Royal Ascot in mid-June, followed by the Henley Regatta and concluding with Wimbledon for The Championships. In 1984, my old pal Paul Levesque organized for us to join him and some of his London friends to go to Ascot for Ladies Day. Through his connections with the Canadian government, he had acquired passes to the Royal Enclosure that would allow us to enter a seated area immediately below the box seats where the royals were seated to watch the racing.

On Ladies Day, the women dress up in their best summer frocks, and hats—as bizarre as one wishes—are de rigueur. The men with Royal Enclosure credentials are required to wear morning suits with tailcoats. Top hats or bowlers are optional. Our morning began at a pub in Eaton Square with champagne and Bloody Marys. A huge old Daimler limo arrived to take us to Ascot. As we approached the racetrack, traffic was stopped. It turned out that our timing had been exquisite. The Royal Family's gilded coach was just arriving from Windsor. People were lined up along the roadway to catch a glimpse of the Queen Mother, Queen Elizabeth and her son Prince Charles.

Lee was ecstatic. Our limo was stopped about 100 yards from the crossing. She leaped out, and sprinted along the roadside, one hand holding her wide-brimmed hat in place. We could see the carriage crossing our road just as she arrived there. When she returned to our car—all smiles—she exclaimed, "I saw him up close! I called out, 'Hi Charley!' and he looked right at me with a big smile and a wave."

She was sure he would recognize her when we were in the Royal Enclosure!

While we were shamelessly playing our parts in this scene out of *My Fair Lady*, it was hard to not remember that Britain at the time was literally sinking in debt. But that didn't stop the "toffs" and their ladies from pretending that the Empire was still afloat—well, at least here in the shadow of Windsor Castle. At the end of this sunny day, the champagne and Pimm's imbibers gathered around Ascot's bandstand to join in with the military musicians in a rousing version of "Rule Britannia."

And yes, we continued The Season with cocktails and lunch along the shores of the Thames for the Royal Henley Regatta, thanks to our dear friends Lorne and Margie Duguid, at a spot where very few of the spectators actually watch the boat-races. And of course, with good seats and hospitality in a sponsor's marquee at Wimbledon, thanks to my now agents, International Management Group. A few years later I would fulfill one of my career dreams: calling tennis matches at The Championships.

CHAPTER 22

Bordeaux and Bikes

On the boxing tour, Lee had been with me in Lugano, Switzerland where we stayed while covering a fight in nearby Campione d'Italia. That offered us a chance for a cruise on Lake Lugano to the famous chateau and art museum of the Thyssen-Bornemisza family, and a romantic night alone together for dinner at Villa d'Este on Lake Como. And Lee came with me to Bueno Aires for a middleweight title fight, which gave us a chance for an overnight at the Copacabana Palace Hotel in Rio enroute, and several nights in the sumptuous Argentine capital.

Lee was also with me for the boxing matches in Bordeaux and the following week in St. Tropez. It was July, 1987. We had brought along our youngest son Brendan on that trip—he had just graduated from prep school in Connecticut en route to Bowdoin College in Maine. It turned out to be an adventure for all three of us.

In addition to doing the boxing commentary, I was hosting the *CBS Sports Spectacular* series, which, in its time slot, included other sports as well as the fights—in this case CBS coverage of the Tour de France. I would do a live opening from wherever we were—in this case a location in France—and then throw it to the Tour commentary team, and after their segment was concluded, it would come back to me for the boxing.

The bonus for me on this trip—and for Lee and Brendan—was that we could drive through France the week between the two fights, and then have another week in Paris waiting to do a live on-camera open and close for the Tour's final stage down the Champs Elysees. It was the ultimate experience on someone else's nickel.

Rick Gentile helped me convince the bosses at CBS Sports that we needed to have a proper scene leading up to the fight in Bordeaux showing and telling our audience where we were—in this case, the most famous wine-producing region in the world. Being a bit of an oenophile, I was thrilled to be in the temple of red wine, and I had the good fortune of having some connections in the U.S., who could arrange for us to take a camera crew to several famous vineyards.

Michael Aaron, owner of wine retailer Sherry-Lehman in New York, set us up at Chateau Haut-Brion, Chateau Margaux and Chateau Prieure-Lichine. My afore-mentioned friend Paul Levesque, founder of the annual hockey dinner for the Canadian Society of New York, was working for the Rothschild's financial operation in New York at the time, and he arranged dinner at Chateau Lafite and an interview with the Baron Eric de Rothschild.

Son Brendan got to travel with our video crew to each of the locations, and Lee and I were guests for dinner with Jean Delmas, the Wine Director at Chateau Mission Haut-Brion and with Paul and a few more guests at Lafite. Needless to say it was an unforgettable few days.

The interview with the Baron, seated on his lawn above the vines of Lafite was unique for both of us.

"Well Mr. Ryan," said the Baron in his opening line, "this is the first time I have been interviewed by a sports announcer!" It was, of course, the first time I had interviewed a baron!

Dinner in the Chateau, which included a look at the family's private wine-cellar with bottles dating back to the 1700s, was spectacular. Several different vintages of Lafite complemented a simple wine-friendly menu. The guests included a writer from *Town and Country* magazine, and the famous photographer Horst. I was seated to the right of the Baroness Maria-Beatrice, who was most charming, with her legs folded under her colorful caftan. Lee was next to the Baron Eric, who was casually resplendent in a dark velvet smoking jacket, and somewhat tattered velvet slippers. Wine-waiters stood behind each guest, vigilantly pouring the Sauvignon Blanc from the neighboring Chateau Margaux, and the magnificent reds from Lafite. The Baron's newly produced cognac followed dinner, served in the chateau's intimate, green-velvet-walled library.

We used only a brief clip of the interview on the air, but the visuals from the magnificent estate certainly showed the environment of the Bordeaux wine country to boxing fans across America!

Our opening at the fight from an arena in the city of Bordeaux was unique for a sports event, to say the least. When Gil and I came on camera after the title graphics, we were seated in the balcony of the arena, at a bistro table covered with a checkered cloth, a bottle of Bordeaux and two wine glasses! I led to our little video scene-set from the famous vineyards and then threw it to our Tour de France crew. The boxing followed that day's stage of the Tour—it was the fight recounted earlier in our story when Bob Arum made air by loudly ordering the ring announcer Michael Buffer to hurry up with announcing the decision.

The next day, Lee, Brendan, and I drove a rental car into the Rhone valley of France, stopping overnight in Auch, home of Alexandre Dumas, author of *The Three Musketeers* and home to the liqueur Armagnac and desserts featuring prunes. A nice combination. We made a brief stop in Nimes—which features one of the best preserved Roman arenas—and then made our way to the famous Byblos Hotel on the French Riviera.

The plan was that as host of the *CBS Sports Spectacular*, I would join our crew covering the the Tour de France to do a short, taped, on-camera at the finish line of the Tour stage that ends atop Mount Ventoux, and then drive the tape back down the mountain to St. Tropez, the site of our fight that evening, a lightweight title bout between Jose Luis Ramirez and American Terrence Alli.

It was a bit of risky business: a three-hour drive, starting mid-afternoon from the mountain-top, hoping to arrive at least two hours before being on live at 10 p.m. to start the show in St. Tropez. But I couldn't have predicted what would make it even more risky. Lee and I had driven to the top of Ventoux well before the riders were on the course. We visited with the CBS production crew, and got some good advice as to how best to get quickly down the mountain when the stage was over. It was explained to us that my car would not be allowed to leave before the riders had all pushed off to cruise back down the track they had just labored up. Then the team cars, and officials and credentialed media cars like ours were to leave immediately before any of the spectators were allowed on the road.

We had been told to drive bumper-to-bumper all the way down, at whatever the pace was. No passing, but no dawdling. About halfway down to the valley below I checked my gas gauge. "Oh my god, I'm almost out of gas!" I wasn't sure how much farther it was to get to the bottom where everyone would disperse. And I had no idea if there was a village with a gas station on the way down, and whether I would be able to turn out of the caravan. And it was a Sunday! I was frankly starting to panic. Lee was gripping onto the videotape with one hand and her seat belt with the other.

Within a minute or two of my anguish we came to a village and I spotted a gas station. The caravan of cars and vans was moving swiftly, at about sixty miles per hour. In my rearview mirror I could see the car behind right on top of me. I put my signal on, and pulled the steering wheel to the right. Horns honked, tires screeched, but there was no contact. After gassing up, the question would now be, how do I get back into the line?

Well we did, without mishap but with a lot of fist shaking and angry glares aimed our way. Once clear of the caravan, we got back onto the main highway and even stopped in Aix-en-Provence for an omelet. With our boxing producer George Veras nervously waiting for our arrival in St. Tropez, we made it with time to spare for him to edit the Mt. Ventoux tape, rehearse our opening and get ready for the fight.

CHAPTER 23

Boxing and Bikinis

Boxing in St. Tropez, you may be wondering. Well it's not all babes in bikinis you know! Okay, so the French Riviera is not exactly a familiar venue for the Sweet Science, but once again Bob Arum had put a deal together with his usual "why not?" attitude. His local promoter was a woman nightclub entrepreneur who well before Madonna used only her first name: Regine. She owned and hosted the most popular restaurant-disco in nearby Monte Carlo, called Jimmy'z. She was a boxing fan and had a vacation house in St. Tropez. With a chance to stage a championship fight and promote her nightclub, she talked the village fathers into letting her take over an oceanside parking lot, turned it into an outdoor boxing arena complete with a special "champagne" section for the high rollers and VIPs.

Regine drew an enthusiastic sellout crowd, albeit not a huge one, into the parking lot to see what turned out to be a close and exciting fight with the decision going to Ramirez. For reasons still unexplained, since there wasn't a French fighter involved, after the decision was announced, people flooded into the ring, pushing and shoving to get to the fighters. Probably they were unhappy bettors who had backed Ali. One of our young production assistants who was gamely trying to steer the winner to me for a post-fight interview in the ring, discovered to his chagrin that among the interlopers was a pickpocket! (The next day he got his wallet back—sans le monnaie!)

The most fun for me—and our crew—came a few days before the fight, when our producer George Veras decided to capture some of the Cote-D'Azur scene at a nearby beach called "La Voile Rouge."

Our male camera crew loved the assignment—topless waitresses serving us lunch while a new band introduced by the famous singer Charles Aznavour entertained. The band was so good, Regine's husband Roger signed them to a promotional contract that very day and "The Gipsy Kings" were on their way to stardom! Aznavour joined us at our table for an interview with me, but the topless parts of the waitresses didn't make air.

Over the next few years we did several more fights on the French and Italian Rivieras including one in Monte Carlo with Prince Rainier at ringside to watch Tommy Hearns successfully defend his welterweight title.

Regine and her husband became good friends of ours, and Lee and I visited with them frequently at their restaurants in Paris and New York. When I became the anchor announcer at the U.S. Open championships in 1994, Regine hosted a celebratory bash at her Park Avenue establishment. She is one of a kind!

CHAPTER 24

Two Micks Visit the Old Sod

Lee's mother, Mina O'Gorman, was a Catholic from Northern Ireland. Two sisters had emigrated to Canada with Mina, but Lee still had many cousins in her mother's home town of Omagh, in County Tyrone. So thanks to a lightweight boxer named Barry McGuigan, and to Bob Arum's teaming up with Irish promoter Barney Eastwood, we found ourselves going to Belfast with a chance for Lee to visit her roots.

It was 1984. Our daughter Kimberley had just graduated from Georgetown University, and so as a graduation gift, she joined us on the trip to Ireland. It was a chance for her to learn about her heritage on her mother's side. Lee and I had had a vacation trip to Ireland a few years before, but this was our first trip to the British North. Gil Clancy was of course working the fight with me and his wife Nancy, who was from Limerick, also came along.

McGuigan was a Catholic, from Clones, a small village in County Monaghan in the Republic of Ireland, just south of the UK border. These were still the years of "the Troubles," the conflict between the Loyalists of British Northern Ireland, which remains predominantly Protestant, and the militants from the Catholic South, the Irish Republican Army. For the IRA—outlawed by its own Irish government—it had been a violent, quixotic effort to force Great Britain to give back the land of Northern Ireland to the Republic. For the minority Catholic population in the North, it had been not just a religious conflict, but an economic one as well. In the eighties, many remained supporters of the IRA.

Belfast was a powder-keg, but as often happens, sport, and music as well, bring combatants together in peaceful appreciation of artists. In the case of Barry McGuigan it was a little of both. Barry was a Catholic, an all-

1984: With boxing partner Gil Clancy and Chris Dundee.

Ireland amateur champion, an Olympian at the 1980 Moscow Games, and professional European featherweight champ who had fought most of his fights in Belfast and London. He was married to a Protestant. His father Pat was a singer, good enough to win the Eurovision Music Contest. When Barry became a boxing star, neither the British nor the Irish anthems were played before his fights. Instead, a dove-of-peace flag was carried into the ring, where his father Pat sang "Danny Boy," long accepted as an anti-war ballad.

A few days before the fight against American Paul DeVorce, who had lost just once in twenty-three fights, we drove to Clones to watch McGuigan in his final training sessions. In his modest family home, Pat had a boxing ring installed in the cramped basement, and friends and family gathered around our camera crew as we interviewed Barry and his father.

Lee and Kimberley and Gil's wife Nancy had come along, and all got a taste of Irish hospitality, as the McGuigans provided drinks and snacks.

In contrast, there was an inescapable tension in Belfast. Our hotel was on the outskirts, in a country setting. But we were asked by Eastwood to travel only with his driver when we were going in and out of Belfast. We asked the driver to show us where the Catholic part of town was in the Falls Road neighborhood. There was literally a wall along it separating the Catholics from the Protestants on Shankill Road.

Fortunately, there were no violent incidents during the week we were there, and in a remarkable similarity to my experience in South Africa a few years before when blacks and whites sat together to cheer on their favorites, at the King's Hall in Belfast, Catholics and Protestants set aside their differences to cheer together for their man McGuigan. It was an emotionally charged moment when the peace-flag was solemnly carried into the ring by a young woman, and with a crowd united by their Irish pride in Barry, there was hardly a dry eye as Pat McGuigan's tenor voice rang out, "Oh Danny Boy, the pipes, the pipes are calling…" There were certainly no dry eyes among the CBS announce team of Timothy Ryan and Gilbert Clancy!

McGuigan, a talented and sharp-punching banger, stopped DeVorce in five rounds—and became an instant hit in the U.S. Arum immediately signed a deal with Eastman to make more fights for McGuigan on U.S. television.

Lee, Kimberley, and I stayed an extra day to visit with the Irish relatives. Barney Eastwood kindly offered his driver to take us to County Tyrone where Lee's cousins, the McGirr family had a sand-and-gravel business. They had organized with other family members to gather for lunch in the town of Omagh (fourteen years later, the site of one of the IRA's worst terrorist attacks when a car-bomb killed twenty-nine people and injured dozens of others). They were all excited to meet us and talk about life in the U.S. Later, we went to the graveyard in a small village where Lee's mother's parents were buried.

For us, gaining insight about Catholic life in the Protestant north of Ireland was a valuable moment, and a reminder that religions more often divide peoples than bring them together.

A year later, Clancy and I were back in Belfast, without our wives, to cover the fight between McGuigan and another American, Juan Laporte. We had the same driver assigned to us by Barney Eastwood, and this time we talked him into getting us into the Catholic neighborhood, behind the walls with the virulent posters and graffiti scrawls promoting violence on both sides.

He volunteered to take us to a Catholic social hall—guarded by the IRA. He could do this, because it turned out, he was an ex-IRA soldier himself! I am still not sure there is something called an "ex" IRA member, but we took him at his word!

It was dusk as we drove slowly along the Falls Road, pulling up alongside a building with a small courtyard, protected by huge boulders placed along the curb—obviously to prevent car-bombers. There were no signs, and little light. The driver asked us to wait in the car until he signaled us to to come out. We saw him knock gently at the door, then a glimmer of light as a peep-hole opened, brief words were exchanged with someone on the other side, and he turned to wave us in.

As the door opened for us, we were greeted by sounds of Irish music played by a live band in a large, open room, well-lit and crammed with large tables filled with families having an evening meal. The Guinness was flowing, young people were dancing and our driver—obviously well-known there, introduced us to some of the apparent organizers of the affair. We were seated with a group of young people with their parents, and when the teenagers were told we were from the U.S., they wanted to know about the costs of blue-jeans, CDs, and all about rock stars and movie actors. We could have been at any community event in the U.S.—middle class families gathered together to celebrate or fundraise or whatever. Except for the presence of guards at the doors, with bulges under their coats.

CHAPTER 25

Trinidad, Toilets, and Rahway

For Clancy and me, our twenty-two years together were about fun and friendship. When we started out at CBS in 1977, Gil was still training some fighters—full- or part-time. But he quickly became the best boxing analyst television has ever seen. He watched every fight available on TV, he'd talk with the matchmakers about up-and-comers, and he followed the amateurs in the U.S. by doing the Golden Gloves fights each year at Madison Square Garden. He had the rare ability to watch *both* fighters equally on our telecasts and so was able to accurately describe the progress of a match, and always seemed to recognize the turning point in a fight, which he would explain calmly and clearly. When he got excited, you knew you were watching a great fight!

He had great respect for all boxers and most trainers. He had done both—boxed and trained—and he knew how much hard work and desire, not to mention guts and determination went into becoming a professional fighter.

Off the air, his Irish sense of humor made him popular with everyone who got to know him. He was friendly with the boxing crowd, with fans, with hotel personnel, bartenders, and waitresses. He was a great kidder. Over the years we developed a predictable routine: sniping at each other at breakfast because I would buy the morning paper, get up to get the orange juice or whatever, and he would be reading it when I returned. This would result in a shouting match over whose paper it was, etc. Anyone nearby assumed we didn't get along very well. Newcomers to the CBS production crew were convinced that was the case. Frequently we had to allay their fears that this was all an act—yes we argued over anything, that's just Irish, don't worry when the bell goes we will be friends again on the air!

He and Nancy had seven children. They all lived close to the family home in Malverne, New York. They were the center of his life. He loved his fighters, particularly the great Emile Griffith, whom he helped financially in Emile's later years. You could take Gil to the bank—he was solid gold.

We had a terrific time together and covered some great fights and saw the world together on someone else's nickel. And we sure had plenty of laughs—often at our own expense—as you have read in our episodes in Belgrade, and Budapest, Grenoble and Bordeaux, and in less glamorous locales like Trinidad and Atlantic City. I frankly can't remember which fight we were covering in Trinidad and Tobago but that island country in the Caribbean had a useful lightweight named Claude Noel who fought for world titles more than once.

What I do remember about the fight was that it was outdoors in Port of Spain, and our on-camera position was high up on a platform held up by rusty scaffolding and reachable only by a rickety ladder.

Clancy, then in his sixties, was apoplectic. "We're going to climb up there? Are you kidding me?"

Creative directors at CBS had had us up on rooftops, on hotel balconies, theater stages—but this was by far our most intimidating location for an opening on-camera. But Gil was a gamer and despite his bad hip and a fear of heights, he made his way up. It took a while. And when we reached the platform we were greeted by a gust of strong tropical wind. The tower started to sway. Gil was now mainly concerned with two things—keeping his toupee from blowing away, and getting back down the ladder. He accomplished both, grumbling all the while.

When we made it safely back to ringside, it rained. And the rain went the distance, winning a soggy decision over Gil's toupee.

One of our more remarkable experiences together occurred during a fight telecast in Atlantic City at one of the hotel-casinos. For some technical-problem reason, we needed to "re-call" a couple of rounds of a fight that already concluded, and was to be played back to air on videotape. But it couldn't be done at ringside, since another match on the card was underway. Our technicians had hurriedly put an audio-setup together where wiring was already installed—in one of the boxers' dressing rooms, and the quietest space in there for us was in… a toilet stall. A video monitor could not be wired in time. A couple of blankets had been thrown over the walls of the stall to provide some soundproofing, and a sentry was posted to prevent anyone from using the nearby urinals.

Yes, Gil and I, standing up, flanking the bowl, actually called a fight on a national telecast from a toilet stall! Clancy was unbelievable—on cue, from memory, we re-created two or three rounds of what we had called earlier, and Gil's comments were virtually in sync with the action taking place on the video which we couldn't see.

That was a first—and a last, I am quite sure!

As one would expect, most of our boxing venues were indoor or outdoor arenas, and the occasional hotel ballroom or theater-stage. One would not expect to see a professional boxing match coming from a prison. But in fact, the infamous Rahway prison in Rahway, New Jersey became the site of several TV matches showcasing its most famous prisoner, light-heavyweight James Scott.

Scott was a guest of the State of New Jersey because he had been convicted of armed robbery. The state prison system had a boxing program and he became its 175-pound champion. Rahway allowed him to turn pro, but only if all of his fights were inside the prison confines. So there we were, going through security at the prison gates, in order to be in, well, more security! But it didn't feel that way. Prisoners were allowed in the small gym space where the fight against a former inmate, and a top contender himself, Dwight Braxton, took place.

Of course there were extra prison guards all over the place, but it was hard to get out of my mind that some of the most dangerous prisoners in the U.S. were incarcerated here, and just a few years before, Rahway featured a prison riot with hostages, stabbings, and all the stuff of bad prison movies. Only for real. Let's just say that while it was a memorable experience, I wasn't unhappy that Scott lost the fight and retired—from boxing that is—which meant we wouldn't be patted down by prison guards again.

CHAPTER 26

The Man With the Golden Gun

We were frequently in Las Vegas for boxing shows. Boxing draws customers who like to gamble. Las Vegas casinos are in the gambling business. And of course you can gamble on boxing in Vegas. Some people who gamble have checkered pasts, and sometimes checkered presents. The same can be said of some boxers. Vegas was created by Howard Hughes, and cultivated by mobsters who ran most of the casinos until recent times when major corporations got into the business, along with a few deep-pocketed individuals like Steve Wynn, Kirk Kerkorian, and Sheldon Adelson. Of course movies and TV shows have glamorized the Mafia portion of the history.

This brings me to Gianni Russo. He is a sometime actor, singer, nightclub owner, and by his own resume, "connected." He is also a likable, handsome guy who is a huge boxing fan. While Russo has played small parts in dozens of films and TV shows, his claim to fame is that he got the part of Carlo Rizzi in "The Godfather."

In the 1980s he owned a restaurant and night-club just off the Las Vegas strip called State Street. On one side of his establishment was a very good Italian eatery; on the other side was a bar, a dance floor and a small stage for live music. The entertainment most nights included a set or two featuring Russo singing and a trio to back him up. One night in 1988, Russo came over to our table and introduced himself to Gil and me, saying he was a big fan of ours. We became regulars there whenever we were in Vegas to cover a boxing match.

On arrival to Las Vegas one morning, the local newspapers' front pages were reporting that the previous night at State Street, Gianni Russo had shot and killed a man who attacked a woman with a broken beer bottle on the dance floor of Russo's night club. As the report went, Russo was on the restaurant side when he heard a commotion from his nightclub—screams above the disco music. He ran through the connecting door, saw a man on the dance floor, wielding a broken beer bottle as a weapon, and slashing at a woman. Russo approached them and the man took a swing at him with the bottle, whereupon Russo reached into his coat pocket, pulled out a small gun and shot the guy. Dead.

Big story of course. We couldn't resist going to State Street for dinner that night. Gianni comes by our table.

"Gianni, you have to tell us about what we read in the papers! It sounds like you had a gun in your pocket?"

Russo reached into his pocket, and gently took out a gold-plated Beretta pistol and placed it on the table.

"That's the gun?" I asked stupidly, stunned at his totally calm demeanor. And Gianni went on to describe how close the guy with the broken beer bottle had come to cutting Gianni's throat wide open.

"He was a maniac. He was going to kill that girl, and he damn near killed me." There were no charges, Gianni didn't even have to surrender his weapon. The woman had survived with minor cuts and major trauma. Gianni and his gold-plated Beretta remained together.

Gil and I had our spaghetti vongole.

State Street closed a year later. Russo resumed his acting career, and now has his own labeled wine and an Italian spaghetti sauce company.

CHAPTER 27

Fan-Man Takes a Dive

Las Vegas seems the setting for bizarre occurrences of all kinds—prompted no doubt by the "Disney for Adults" image and "What Happens in Vegas Stays in Vegas" slogan. Not to mention Hunter S. Thompson's book and movie, *Fear and Loathing in Las Vegas*.

So when a heavyweight championship fight is interrupted by a nut-case named James "Fan-Man" Miller who flies into the outdoor ring in a paraglider, we should neither be shocked nor surprised. Fearful maybe—if you are sitting in the audience—realizing that he could kill people with a miscalculation.

It was November 6, 1993, Riddick Bowe against Evander Holyfield, a rematch of a heavyweight title fight won earlier by Bowe. Gil and I were calling the pay-per-view telecast from Caesar's Palace. With a little less than two minutes left in round 7, the guy who became known as "Fan-Man," appeared out of the sky and hit the top of the ring ropes where he got tangled up as media and other ringsiders scrambled over each other. Obviously, both boxers stopped throwing punches and stared in amazement along with everyone else.

Miller had a small motorized fan strapped to his back. His paraglide fabric got caught on the light standards above the outdoor ring. That's what got my attention as I was describing to viewers this bizarre event on Pay-TV. Had he not been hung up on the ropes, his body weight could well have brought down the lights and his stunt could have been a deadly one. Or worse, he could have crashed directly into the lights.

He was pulled off the ropes by members of Bowe's entourage and took quite a beating—at least one of the Bowe "security" guys kept bashing him with a walkie-talkie until Caesar's security pulled him away. Miller was knocked cold and taken to the hospital. The fight continued, Holyfield won by decision.

With John and Bo Derek, avid boxing fans.

Later at the usual post-fight party hosted by Top Rank, I was still shaken—thinking of what might have been. The comedian Billy Crystal and the actor Gene Hackman were cracking wise about the incident, and when I offered my more somber take of the wild occurrence, Billy's response was "Calm down, Tim, calm down, you're making too much of it." My assumption was that Billy (whom I love) must have been in the men's room when Miller risked the lives of hundreds of people with his wacky grab for attention.

In another Las Vegas fistic fiasco, Holyfield found himself as the foil for a nut-case yet again. Holyfield had beaten Mike Tyson to win the WBA title seven months earlier. "Iron Mike" had lost much of his luster—mainly as a result of his more than colorful life outside the ring. This was the rematch, June 28, 1997. Clancy and I were calling it for a delayed playback on CBS. Gratefully, I think that has kept our call off of YouTube! Another announcing team was calling the fight live for pay-per-view.

The less said about the fight—or lack thereof—the better. Suffice to remind you that Tyson bit a chunk of Holyfield's left ear, and for good measure nibbled on his right ear after referee Mills Lane—who backed off disqualifying Tyson after his first taste of ear ligament (he spit it out), allowed the fight to continue. But bite number two was enough for referee Lane who called the fight over, and awarded the match to Holyfield.

It was not boxing's finest hour, or ours, for having not just to witness it, but to describe it on TV.

CHAPTER 28

Witness to Ring Tragedy

Gil and I never talked much about the night his great boxing champion Emile Griffith knocked out Benny "the Kid" Paret at Madison Square Garden in March of 1962. Paret did not survive the onslaught of Griffith's punches early in the 12th round, and died ten days later without awakening from the knockout.

Over the years of Griffith's career, Gil, who guided Emile to the welterweight and middleweight titles, had treated him like one of his own sons. He knew how badly Griffith felt about Paret's death, and he knew that death was more than an occasional visitor to the sport he loved. Like most people in the sport, Gil accepted the risk. But I knew the outcome of that night in the Garden had weighed heavily on him.

When I started my career as a boxing commentator, I knew the chance existed that I would be covering a fight in which someone might die—as I knew that could occur in downhill ski racing, or in the contact sports of hockey and football which I also announced. In fact, as the announcer for the Oakland Seals in 1968—in the hockey era before helmets were mandatory—I was doing the Seals radio broadcast in Minnesota when North Stars defenseman Bill Masterton, was knocked backwards with a body-check—his head striking the ice with what turned out to be a deadly thud. It remains the only fatality to an NHL player as a result of an injury during a game.

Still, one hopes to never see an athlete die while participating in a sport he loves and makes a living at. But I was not to be exempt from that in boxing.

On September 19, 1980, we were covering the WBC Bantamweight championship fight in Los Angeles' Olympic Auditorium. A frail-looking 24-year-old named Johnny Owen from a tiny town in Wales was challenging the champion, Lupe Pintor of Mexico. Skinny as he was, Owen was all muscle and European champion with a record of 24 and 1. He had scored eleven knockouts and his only loss was on points. After eight rounds, he was leading the fight against Pintor on all three cards of the judges.

Pintor, supported by a largely Mexican crowd at the Olympic, scored a knockdown in the 9th round and turned the fight in his favor. In the 12th he dropped Owen again, and then landed a knockout blow. The Welshman was completely unconscious as the ring doctor worked on him, and it was apparent it was a serious situation.

I described it as dispassionately as possible—lauding Owen's boxing skills that had given him the lead, praising Pintor's sharp punching ability and the combination which sent Owen to the canvas. But from my view at ringside, only a foot or two away from the prone Owen, something told me he would not be getting up. I kept that to myself, and tried to reassure the audience that excellent medical care was right there, and offered the hope that Owen would be alright.

He never came out of his coma and died several weeks later.

I learned recently that a sculpture of Johnny Owen was erected in his hometown of Merthyr Tydfil, Wales, in 2002. His family invited the long-retired Lupe Pintor to do the unveiling. Pintor made the long trip from Mexico and was warmly welcomed by the Owens family.

There is no greater mutual respect than boxers have for each other. You see it after virtually every fight. No matter the outcome, the two warriors embrace. Luckily, in most cases, both are able to stand to do so.

My only other experience with a fight ending in a fatality was on a much bigger stage and with a much bigger backstory. It has been recounted in numerous newspaper columns, a biography of the survivor, and a TV documentary about the young man who died after a grueling lightweight championship fight that took place under the broiling afternoon sun of Las Vegas, Nevada.

The date was Saturday, November 13, 1982. A virtually unknown boxer from South Korea, Duk Koo Kim was to fight for the WBA Lightweight title, scheduled for 15 rounds, held by American Ray "Boom-Boom" Mancini, who was making his second title defense at the age of twenty-one.

All of Kim's fights on his 17–1 record had taken place in Seoul. Mancini was 24 and 1 with 18 knockouts. The fight was scheduled to start at noon Nevada time, 3 p.m., Eastern Time.

The night before, Gil and Sugar Ray Leonard (a commentator on some of our telecasts) and I had been in Miami Beach, Florida covering the Alexis Arguello-Aaron Pryor fight at the famed Orange Bowl stadium. It had been a very dramatic fight. The unbeaten Pryor had stopped the favored Arguello in the 14th round. The popular Nicaraguan was slow to get up off the canvas after the TKO and there was some concern he had been badly hurt.

Arguello had scored a TKO win over Mancini a year earlier, retaining his WBC lightweight title and ending the rising young American's unbeaten run.

Promoter Bob Arum's plan was to have Arguello meet Mancini again in a title match for Arguello's WBA title. But now the exciting Pryor was in the picture. Mancini figured to win easily over the lightly tested South Korean Kim.

Arum, Gil, Ray and Mort Sharnick, CBS's boxing overseer and I left Miami after midnight on a chartered private jet in order to get to Las Vegas for a short night's sleep and a 10 a.m. production rehearsal at Caesar's Palace. A couple of hours into what should have been about a five-hour flight, the captain told us that because of strong headwinds, we are going to have to land in Albuquerque, New Mexico to refuel. By the time we got to Vegas it was about eight in the morning.

On about an hour's sleep we were at the makeshift outdoor arena at Caesar's Palace—bleary-eyed and hoping for a short fight. The Vegas bookmakers had Mancini a heavy favorite to win. Frank Sinatra, headlining in Caesar's showroom had already invited Ray to see his show Saturday night after the bout.

The morning sun was already searing as we rehearsed our opening on-camera. Bill Cosby was one of the early-arriving celebrities and came by ringside to say hello to us. Spectators filled the seats, unaware of the high drama and tragic outcome that would follow. Ray and Gil signed autographs as I went over my notes on the two fighters.

There had been no video available to us on Kim, and we had been in

Miami for the previous few days and so had not seen the South Korean in his final workouts in Vegas. He was a tabula-rasa—a blank sheet—to us, but we quickly saw what Mancini had learned about Kim. Not a big puncher, but with a big heart. A fighter who is busy, brave, and will not back up. In effect, a mirror of Mancini.

The early rounds were fought at a terrific pace. Both fighters were landing a ton of punches. Into the 12th round, Gil, Ray and I all had it close. In the 12th, it appeared to me that Kim was tiring, although he still fought in determined flurries. I said so in my commentary. But he wasn't going away. His fatigue looked more apparent in the 13th round.

In round 14, Mancini charged from his stool to the center of the ring. Nineteen seconds later he landed a straight right hand that decked Kim, his head striking the canvas as he fell backwards. Kim gamely grabbed the ropes, trying to pull himself up but referee Richard Green, who had done an excellent job through the fight, called it over.

There was the usual chaos in the ring. The fight doctors, commission officials, the Mancini camp, Kim's corner people all milling around as I climbed into the ring to do the interview with Mancini. Mort Sharnick was having a hard time corralling Mancini to get him to our camera.

Neither Mancini nor the rest of us knew that the young Korean boxer had suffered a brain hemorrhage, and would be rushed to a local hospital for surgery in an attempt to save his life.

That evening, reports from the hospital were not optimistic for Kim. CBS asked me to stay in Las Vegas to do an on-camera piece into our programming on Sunday afternoon.

Mancini went to Sinatra's show, and was introduced by Frank as our champion. But by then Ray knew it was unlikely Kim would survive. Sunday afternoon I reported on CBS from the hospital that Kim was still in a coma following surgery to remove the pressure on his brain. The prognosis was not good.

It was the most difficult report I had to deliver in my career—before or since. Three days later Kim was dead. Ray successfully defended his title twice more with knockout wins, before losing it to Livingstone Bramble. Losing the last four fights of his outstanding career was painful, but nothing like the pain he says is still in his heart from that bittersweet victory one sunny November day in Las Vegas.

CHAPTER 29

"And Now For Something Completely Different..."

Well back in this memoir I referred to a life-changing experience that Lee and I had involving our travels to Africa, which came about because boxing had taken me there in 1979 for the first of three bouts CBS televised in South Africa over the next two years.

My first attempt at a Hemingway experience had ended with a roll of film filled with animals' asses. That "safari" followed that first fight in Mmabotho, and since I didn't know if I would ever return to Africa, I wanted to at least take a look into the Kruger Park, a national wildlife reserve.

I had booked into a small lodge near the park, thinking I could hire a guide for a morning drive. I had only one day to see as much as I could. The desk clerk informed me that guides had to be booked in advance, but that I was allowed to drive myself into the park and follow the rules. Stay in your car, keep your windows up and do not leave the paved roads. At the park gate, I paid a small fee and was given a small map of the roads. It was about 7:30 a.m. I was told early morning and early evenings were the best times to find game.

Off I went, with more than a little apprehension. Kruger, I had learned, has the Big Five: elephant, lion, leopard, Cape Buffalo, and rhino. I drove slowly, my inadequate snapshot-type camera on my lap. The rental car was a right-hand drive with a manual transmission. For the first half-hour I saw absolutely nothing. Suddenly several antelope bolted across the road a few yards in front of me. I braked sharply, failing to get the car into neutral. The car lurched forward and stalled. The camera fell off my lap onto the floor. The antelope, impala it turned out, were gone—swallowed up by the bush.

The rest of the morning went pretty much the same. I broke the "keep your window up" rule several times, but by the time I got the left-handed gear shift into neutral, the hand brake on, the window open, the camera focused, the best I could capture were a lot of hind-ends of assorted game.

I saw no lions, leopards, rhino or buffalo. I did see an elephant or two, but stayed so far away from them while planning a hasty exit, they became specks seen through the windshield when the photos were printed a few weeks later.

Needless to say this morning in darkest Africa was not what I had hoped for, and was definitely not a safari. I determined to come back with Lee and do it properly.

Lee and I were still getting over the trauma of a horrible health problem with our son Jay, who two years earlier at the age of twelve, had suffered a brain aneurysm that caused him to fall while running laps during a phys-ed class at school. He underwent brain surgery at Columbia-Presbyterian in New York, and things were touch-and-go for several days. Thankfully, we had a great surgeon and Jay made a full recovery, although with rest and recuperation he missed most of his school year. Lee's nursing experience was invaluable and while I was off covering events for CBS, she was largely at home caring for Jay until he was able to go back to school. Kim was on her way to Georgetown University, Kevin was in high school in Mamaroneck, and Brendan was still in elementary school.

While still in South Africa for the first fight there, my father Joe who had been diagnosed with pancreatic cancer only three months earlier, died in Victoria, B.C. where he and my mother had lived since his retirement from pro football. He was seventy-seven.

The following year—with another CBS fight scheduled near Johannesburg, the chance for Lee and I go on a proper safari seemed to be a great idea for both of us to regroup from the recent sad events. By good fortune, my friend Paul Levesque was hosting a cocktail party in New York for a Kenyan safari guide who was drumming up business in the U.S. At the party we met two women, Ingrid Schroeder, a business executive and Babette Alfieri, who worked for South African Airlines. They had formed a fund-raising organization called Save African Endangered Wildlife Foundation, based in New York, and primarily aiding the beleaguered Zimbabwe Parks and Wildlife Department.

Ingrid recommended to us a safari camp she had been to in South Africa, in the Timbavati Nature Reserve adjacent to Kruger Park.

Neither Lee nor I knew whether or not we could fall in love with the bush. We had no idea what to expect, except that there would be some roughing it, along with mosquitoes, snakes, and proximity to dangerous wild animals. But we were certainly excited to go and find out what a proper African wildlife experience was all about.

We went and we were hooked. For the next ten years, Lee and I spent the month of May in southern Africa—primarily in Zimbabwe, with forays into Zambia, South Africa and Namibia. In the eighties, CBS still had the NBA television rights, and I was no longer working pro basketball, so it was the optimum time of year to take most or all of my five weeks of vacation. And May happened to be a great time of year in southern Africa—temperatures were not too hot and it was off-season for most tourists. So while there was still a lot of foliage on trees and bushes (which made game-viewing a little harder) it was a very comfortable time of year for us to have the animals to ourselves—except for poachers, who were to become a big part of our experience.

Lee and I became Trustees of SAVE and became close friends of Ingrid and Babette. And our love affair with Africa brought us even closer to each other. We had the same heartfelt—almost spiritual—relationship to the wild and its creatures. Walking in the African bush, quietly observing the flora and fauna with a tingle of fear despite being accompanied by an armed guide, is the most humbling human experience imaginable. One realizes you are on the animal's turf—an angry elephant matriarch protecting a baby, a near-sighted black rhino with a bad temper, a lion enjoying its hard-won meal of antelope, a leopard startled from its nap on a tree limb, a Cape Buffalo bull whose peaceful grazing is disturbed. Here, humans, armed or not, are unwelcome intruders. Respect and good sense must be shown.

For Lee and I the rewards were many and equally appreciated. Thanks to our involvement with SAVE, we met and safaried with many of the top commercial guides in Southern Africa. There is an expression that says, "Once you have the red dirt of Africa under your fingernails, you can never get it out." For most who have been there that is very true. It certainly was for us.

CHAPTER 30

Into Africa

Recounting all of our incredible experiences in Africa would fill another book. Many were simply sublime—nights in thatched-roof huts on the banks of the Zambezi River, listening to the roar of a hunting lion nearby, or the rustle of bushes as hippos foraged in the dark before retreating to their watery homes on the riverbanks. Or lying in sleeping bags on the sands of the desert floor of Namibia, gazing at the galaxy of the Southern Cross.

One of our earlier trips to southern Africa provided the most romantic backdrop possible. We had both read Isak Dineson's evocative book *Out of Africa*, and we were aware it was going to be filmed on location in Kenya. By sheer coincidence, our flight that time took us through Nairobi to Harare, with an overnight stop at Nairobi's historic hotel, the Norfolk.

As we went into the dining room for dinner, I could hear American voices around a corner of the room. We were seated within earshot, and I easily figured out it was the film crew shooting *Out of Africa*. I walked over, recognized the director and occasional actor Sydney Pollack and introduced myself. It turned out he was a sports fan and knew who I was. After being introduced to Lee, Sydney invited us to come out to the movie set the next day, where Robert Redford and Meryl Streep would be acting in a scene together.

Our flight south was late afternoon. Sydney sent a car for us and we were driven to the outskirts of Nairobi where Isak Dineson had lived. The house being used in the film had actually been lived in by Dineson at one time.

Sydney introduced us to his stars—Redford and I chatted about his film *Downhill Racer*, since his character was remarkably like the then-current American star skier, Bill Johnson. Streep was very polite to us but was clearly getting her game face on for the shoot.

LEFT: 1985: Lee on the set of *Out of Africa*.
RIGHT: Streep and Redford shooting a scene.

We watched Pollack work his charms with the scene, down to the details of a guttering candle that had not burned low enough to match the picture from the previous scene shot the day before. Lee was fascinated. While waiting for the candle to burn to the right height, Redford—asked about his experience filming in Kenya—said he couldn't wait to leave! They had been there for several months.

He and Streep did the scene in just a couple of takes. We thanked Sydney for his hospitality and headed to the airport, en route to Harare, Zimbabwe with quite a story to tell our friends waiting for us there.

Another year, we had more adrenalin-inducing adventures that could have been a feature film-perhaps called, *The Namib Affair*. Like *Out of Africa* it was a real-life story that saw Lee and I with Ingrid, Babette, and another woman, Chloe Rolfe, flying from Johannesburg, with our destination a tiny camp in the desert. Name of the nearest village: Wereldsend. Afrikaans translation to English: World's End.

Well it nearly was—at least for us.

We were to join up with the two rhino researchers who were working on a project to study rare desert-rhinos, which along with a small number of elephants and lions were subsisting in the arid climes of the desert— far from their more food-friendly environments of forest and bush. SAVE would provide some funding to them in their efforts.

Our pilot, Peter Joffe, flew us from Jo'burg in a six-passenger, single-engine Cessna, with a stop in Windhoek, the Namibian capital, for fuel.

That's where our troubles began. Namibia had become Namibia just days before—independent of South Africa. It had been known as Southwest Africa, so named when colonists from Holland, Germany and England had finished fighting over its mineral riches, particularly the diamond fields of the Skeleton Coast.

When we landed to gas up, we expected to be able to just fly off again. But we had to go through Immigration and Customs, manned by soldiers who knew nothing about their new jobs. By the time we waved a bunch of papers of no legal consequence at them along with an assortment of passports, we had lost nearly an hour on the ground. Our goal had been to arrive in the desert camp before dark. That now appeared unlikely, although our pilot thought we had a chance.

"If we don't make it there by dark, we can land in the desert and overnight," he said, "and then carry on at first light. Or, we can stay here in Windhoek and leave in the morning."

Since we had camping gear and sleeping bags, we voted unanimously to keep going, but not before asking him if he had landed in the Namib terrain before. "Oh yes, of course," he replied. "Shouldn't be a problem—but I think we can get there tonight."

I am not sure why we took him at his word, since during the flight over from Johannesburg, with me sitting in the co-pilot seat, it had become apparent that only one of the two radios was functioning. That didn't seem to concern him, even though he acknowledged the other one seemed to be working only intermittently.

Once off the ground and flying over the moonscape that it is much of Namibia, the pilot reduced his altitude to about 1,000 feet, telling us this would save us some time and enhance our chances of making it to Wereldsend. But after swooping over the only glimpse of civilization we had seen—the tin-mining village of Uis—Africa's curtain of darkness was dropping rapidly.

"Well, we're not going to make it there," the pilot announced. "We can either set down on the desert floor, or turn around and land back at Uis—they have a good landing strip there." Once again the vote was to land where we were, trusting his word that he had done so many times before.

Peering below in the fading light, I could see a vehicle track, which I assumed he was aiming at. But apparently he was looking at another landing spot—off to the left of the track. As the ground came rushing up at us, I could see that the terrain wasn't really as smooth as it had appeared from farther up in the air. In fact, it was littered with rocks and scrub bushes.

We were all silent as he picked his spot and lowered the nose of the plane. Within seconds of touching the ground, the nose wheel struck a rock, the propeller plowed into the sand. As we burrowed forward, the landing gear on the left side collapsed. Fortunately, we stayed upright, even as the left wing-tip began scraping through the sand.

We jolted to a stop. Peter's hands were in a death-grip on the stick. He appeared catatonic. Over his shoulder I could see fuel running down the broken wing. I pushed open the door on my side. Peter still hadn't moved. The four women and I pulled bags and other gear out of the open door.

The pilot finally clambered out and we moved away from the stricken Cessna and assessed the landscape around us. It was virtually barren with little that could be used as firewood, but the women gathered what they could find in the fading light, while the pilot gave me the coordinates of where we were from his aerial map, and instructions on how to use the radio.

We spread out a white plastic SOS marker from the plane. Peter muttered: "I'll walk back to Uis to get help."

That seemed crazy to us—it was a half-hour flying time back to that mining village. We tried to dissuade him, but he was insistent.

"I have a torch, I'm going." And off he went.

Of course we were all nervous and concerned, but everyone remained calm and industrious. We set up a makeshift camp: sleeping bags, a small fire, some of the food and water we were taking to Wereldsend.

The black drapery of the sky was now filling with tiny dots of gold.

About an hour and a half later, the pilot's flashlight became visible, bobbing up and down. He was back, exhausted and penitent.

"It was too far…"

Right.

Babette told us there should be a South African airlines flight coming in from Europe to Johannesburg that evening, maybe we would see its lights overhead. We all lay there, staring at the star-filled sky, ready to bolt to the radio. No planes were seen.

The night passed without much sleep, enlivened by the calls of Barking

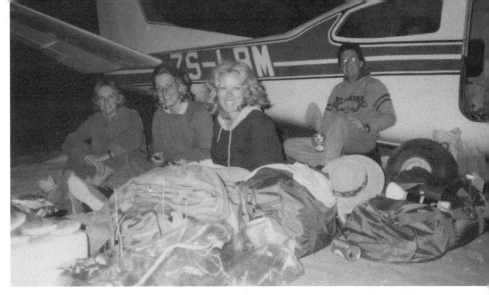

Namibia, after crash-landing in desert. Lee, Ingrid Schroeder, and Babette Alfieri.

Gekkos—nocturnal lizards that were presumably curious as to who we were and how we had dropped out of the sky onto their desert terrain.

At dawn, I roused Peter and off we went without a word to each other, walking east, hoping to find one road marked on the aerial map which led from Uis to a military base.

About an hour and a half into our hike we found the road, but an hour standing by it did not produce a vehicle of any kind. Back we went, following our own tracks to the Cessna. The women had had no luck with the radio calls.

Finally, at about 11 a.m., we heard a crackling response from a South African Airways flight. The captain took our coordinates, asked if there were any injuries, and said he would send help.

If you are old enough to remember a TV series called *The Rat Patrol* set in the Sahara during World War II, you may recall the opening scene each week of a cloud of dust materializing into a jeep churning across the desert with the soldiers manning a mounted machine-gun.

Well, minus the machine-gun, that's what we saw several hours after our rescue call. A jeep-like vehicle rolled up, with a cage-like flatbed behind the front seat, out of which leaped two armed policemen with no smiles and no English. They were Afrikaners from the mining town, Uis.

It turned out the mine manager had received the call from the SAA flight, but had been concerned as to our identity. You see there was still an armed conflict going between Namibia and Angola, the country to the north. No doubt, we were suspected of aiding and abetting somebody other than our rhino researchers.

After more than an hour of bumpy riding in the "paddy wagon", all of our gear stuffed in with the five of us while the pilot was telling his story to the cops in the front seat, we arrived in Uis. A less-than-friendly mine manager—who had not been amused at a low-flying plane waking him up the night before—grilled Peter and put him on a mining truck back to Windhoek to face the authorities. After a quick lunch, he said he would fly us on to Wereldsend.

Flying in daylight over the barren terrain of the Namib showed us just how lucky we were to have been found. The mine manager flew us past an isolated mountain peak, the Brandtberg, where the wreckage of another small plane lay rusting. Then, using the coordinates he had been given by our pilot, he descended a thousand feet or so to show us our crippled Cessna—a mere speck in a vast wasteland. But for our lucky contact with the jet which had flown over us, our bones may still be there in that desolate stretch of sand.

A short time later we spotted the makeshift landing strip of our researchers, who waved us in, smiles and obvious relief on their faces.

That evening, around an open fire, we shared a bottle of 1970 Chateau Margaux that I had been sure to salvage from the Cessna. It was meant to celebrate Lee's and my wedding anniversary a few nights later—but our survival and rescue seemed a good reason to have it early.

We spent the next three days searching for desert rhino, and on our final day were rewarded with a good long look at a mother and calf—which were somehow finding forage and water in an unfriendly clime.

CHAPTER 31

They Are Called "Wild Beasts" For a Reason

What's gnu about wildebeests? Well the spelling is from the Afrikaans language, and yes it means wild beast, and you can call them gnus if you prefer. There are black and blue wildebeests, although actually they are kind of brown-gray. They are related to cattle, but are far more unpredictable.

Which brings me to one of our bizarre African experiences in Zimbabwe.

Our friends in the Zimbabwe National Parks Department—a rapidly diminishing group since independence was won from the U.K. in 1980 by Robert Mugabe's Shona tribal insurgents—were gamely (pardon the pun) doing their best to protect and preserve the animals in the national parks so that tourism and legal hunting would continue to contribute to the livelihoods of the tribal villages adjacent to the reserves.

Poachers organized by foreign countries were depleting the rhino and elephant population for the valuable horn and ivory of those animals. But all of the game was suffering from lack of management as the Parks department continued to lose their top people who were being replaced by Mugabe cronies and inexperienced new hires.

One of the myriad projects being attempted was to relocate several species, including the plentiful wildebeest.

Ingrid, Lee, and I were there one May when a young ranger suggested a novel approach to herding and driving some wildebeest into corrals where they would be loaded onto trucks and transported to other areas. Well, novel by Zimbabwe standards. Americans would recognize the method instantly—

Tim and Lee spotting game in the bush in Zimbabwe.

cowboys on horseback rounding up cattle. Despite his skepticism, and total refusal to participate, the commanding officer, Clem Coetzee, gave the okay.

The ranger gathered as many of his colleagues who could ride horses as he could. That was less than a handful. We were asked if we rode. We did. We all assembled at a horse-safari camp near Lake Kariba. We borrowed their horses and saddles and headed into the bush where trackers had spotted a herd of "Wildies."

Clem rolled his old Land Rover to where the corrals were located with the trucks. He thought the whole idea was ridiculous and he hated horses. He stretched out in his Landy, propped his feet up over the knockdown-windshield, lit a cigarette and waited for the mayhem.

Lee, Ingrid, and I mounted our rented horses and joined the three or four rangers who were also crazy enough to give it a go. The trackers led us quickly to where the wildebeest were grazing. When they caught our scent, all hell broke loose. We crashed through bush, over ditches, under tree branches in what proved to be a hopeless pursuit of the ungainly animals who split up, turned in circles, hid behind bushes and confused the hell out of the horses. Staying on the horses proved to be a challenge. There were more than a few falls, remounts and near disasters.

The end result was maybe three wildebeest finally herded into the corrals. Clem was right, it was a crazy idea. But a memorable day!

There were many more years of incredible times in Zimbabwe, Zambia, South Africa and Namibia. Under Ingrid's leadership, SAVE's efforts to protect the black rhino from the increasing onslaught of poachers gave us the opportunity to provide an airplane, a truck for translocation, tents, uniforms, and other equipment. The National Parks department was being badly neglected by the Mugabe government. Brilliant scholars in the Department—Russell Taylor, Rowan Martin, Dave Cummings and many others were being pushed out, or left because of salary cuts. All of which meant saving the rhino was becoming a desperate cause.

While we managed to get a very generous donation to SAVE from the Coca-Cola Company, it was clear that getting the message out was critical so that other donors might decide to help the cause. I had been able to get a few stories onto CBS News programs, and of course my scary episode on the CBS wildlife show

Dan Rather and I had met several times at CBS events and in the studios. He was and is, an affable and generous guy. On one occasion I told him of my involvement with SAVE and he was aware that the rhino poaching in southern Africa was becoming an international story. I suggested that his weekly special on CBS *48 Hours* might be a great vehicle on which to follow the efforts in Zimbabwe to combat the perpetrators who were decimating this once-plentiful icon of the African bush.

Dan bought into the story idea, a CBS film crew was sent to Zimbabwe to spend forty-eight hours with Game Warden Glen Tatham and his rangers as they tracked and encountered poachers, and SAVE was duly credited for its contributions to the effort. Dan was also generous enough to attend a SAVE fundraiser in New York where we showed a preview of his program.

Lee and I continued our annual May travels with Ingrid and Babette to Zimbabwe, and also Zambia and South Africa in the latter part of the decade, doing what we could in our limited way to help wildlife conservation result in a better life for the villagers living in the rural areas where animals and humans need to co-exist.

The month of May for Lee and me was always a special one since our anniversary was on the 27th. Spending Mays in Zimbabwe and its neighboring countries made the month even more so. Every year brought lasting friendships with people of "good value," as they say in that part of the world—devoted stewards of their beautiful environment. We treasured nights around the campfires, under the stars, the sounds of night birds and nocturnal wildlife bringing an unmatched peace to us. That peace for us was soon to be lost forever.

CHAPTER 32

"The Heart of Darkness"

With apologies to Joseph Conrad, there is no darkness darker than Alzheimer's disease.

Our family discovered that horrible fact when Lee was diagnosed with the cruelest disease in January of 1991. We were at the peak of our joy together during the decade earlier—our time in Africa with dear friends old and new had drawn us even closer to each other. My career was providing us with the means and the opportunity to see more of the world together. Our children were off finding their own paths—Kimberley, was beginning a television career as a news reporter in Twin Falls, Idaho, Kevin was just back from running a restaurant in Val-d'Isere, France and about to start a career in television production, Jay was a recording engineer at a studio in New York and Brendan was finishing his senior year at Bowdoin College in Maine, where he would meet his future wife Caitlin and go on to law school at Fordham.

The previous May on our annual trip to Zimbabwe, Ingrid and I had noticed some uncommon behavior from Lee. Normally fearless and eager to get into the bush or onto Lake Kariba to get as close to animals as possible, she now seemed somewhat nervous and often disoriented. Lee had always been the first to jump out of the vehicle to follow our guides for chances to see lions or elephants. She had been first to crawl up the Zimbabwe riverbank to get a photo of the Cape Buffalo sentry guarding a herd of dangerous buffalo close by. From our boat on the river, he seemed a hundred yards distant. But when Lee crawled up the grade, he was staring at her from just a few yards away. She stared back though her viewfinder and fearlessly got the shot.

But on that May trip in 1990, something had changed. We turned back from a walk through tall elephant grass when she seemed to be overly bothered by mosquitoes. She fell into the lake when boarding a canoe we were paddling back from the dining area to our floating hut nearby. I was able to help her back into the canoe, but I felt something was wrong. This wasn't the Lee who had been so comfortable in the bush, who had become a talented poet describing her innermost feelings for the beauty and majesty of wild Africa.

Back home in Larchmont it was several months later that I became seriously concerned. As the treasurer of her tennis league, she paid the bills. I found her in tears one evening after dinner, seated at the dining room table struggling to deal with the invoices and her checkbook. A few weeks later, a tennis friend told me she was having trouble keeping the score during the matches.

Alzheimer's? I knew nothing about it. Not many people did in 1990. But after several visits to various doctors, a top neurologist at Columbia Presbyterian Hospital said, "Mr. Ryan, there is no true diagnosis of this disease until autopsy, but I feel sure Lee has Alzheimer's disease."

My response to that horrible news, the research I did with many experts in the field, the decisions made in consultation with our children have all been recounted on television news programs, on Larry King's CNN, in *People* magazine and during testimony before a Congressional committee—a public journey I took after being invited to serve on the National Board of the Alzheimer's Association. The devoted doctors and researchers working on the disease were desperately seeking to create more awareness and funding to help their cause—our cause.

Realizing I was managing a disease that could not be cured, I sold our home in Larchmont and bought one in Sun Valley where we had owned a vacation condominium for several years.

With all of the children already off on their own from the house in Larchmont, we moved to Sun Valley in October of 1991, a quieter environment in a small town with caring friends we had made vacationing there over the years, and where I felt Lee would be safer.

And so began a new life. With hired caregivers to look after Lee when I was traveling for CBS, I carried on with my career. Gratefully my income— if I kept working—would cover the enormous costs of care for Lee. An otherwise good health plan did not provide coverage for Alzheimer's care. Even reimbursement for Lee's medications were severely limited. As the disease rapidly progressed—common in early-onset Alzheimer's, (Lee was only fifty-one)—her symptoms become more unmanageable. She was soon living in a state of terror, as her brain deteriorated and her ability to speak diminished.

I was worried sick every time I had to leave her, but over time I realized that the weekend covering football, or ski-racing, basketball or boxing, tennis, or Olympic sports were a needed break for me from my caregiver role. Still, as her condition worsened and capable nurses became harder to hire, it became obvious that we would have to find an Alzheimer's care facility for Lee. I was lucky to do so—a small assisted-living home in Santa Barbara, California.

After nearly four years at our home in Ketchum, Lee spent the remaining years of her long goodbye, first at the excellent facility in Santa Barbara where I would visit every couple of weeks, and then closer to Sun Valley at the Good Samaritan nursing home in Boise, Idaho, where Kevin was living in the mid-nineties. Kevin had married, and knowing he and his wife Sylvie were nearby to Lee gave me some comfort.

The children were of course devastated by their mother's illness. But they were very supportive of my thinking as to her care. We had regular telephone conference calls over the ensuing years, on which I would update them on their mom's medications and the inevitable changes in her abilities to listen and understand me when I came to visit. They were also glad that I was continuing to work, and to have the experiences of the various locations around the world that covering sports on television afforded—even though they knew it could not be the same without having their mom to share things with me.

So we all carried on, secure in the knowledge that would be what Lee wanted for each of us. More than two decades in the business lay ahead for me, with a million air miles taking me to almost every corner of the world. I felt that somehow Lee was still sharing the journey with me, at least in spirit. She loved adventure.

CHAPTER 33

Ice Follies and the Fall of the Wall

Just as boxing had taken me around the world, so did other international sports. I was designated as the winter sports guy at CBS—mainly because I had my identity with hockey, and also because no one else on our staff was familiar with the cold-weather sports. So I found myself in Switzerland and Austria with alpine ski racing, Norway for speed-skating and cross-country skiing, France, Hungary, and Yugoslavia for figure-skating, Japan for ski-jumping and alpine skiing, and of course the U.S. for most of those same sports as well as bobsledding and freestyle skiing.

Alpine skiing became a passion for me. Having grown up in Toronto, I was a hockey player as a youngster, and didn't learn to ski until I was in my mid-thirties and we had bought our condo in Sun Valley, Idaho. Seven years later, in 1980 I found myself in Wengen, Switzerland, a picture-postcard village that sits in a valley surrounded by the Jungfrau region of the Alps known as the Roof of Europe. There I was, on skis, staring down the steep slalom racecourse with famed American skier Billy Kidd, exhorting me to "make nice round turns" down the icy patch.

CBS Sports Executive Producer Terry O'Neil had assigned Kidd and me to cover the World Cup Downhill race in Wengen. Billy had won the silver medal in the slalom event at the 1964 Olympics. He was now a rookie announcer for skiing on CBS.

Billy wanted me to experience how icy the slalom course was at Wengen, since we would be covering that race as well. Right. The gates weren't set up when we stood—alone, at the top of the course. A good thing, it turned out, since I would have taken several of them out. Having managed to make only one turn on the near-vertical pitch I careened down on my butt to the midway part of the track before sliding off to the side of the course into the snow. I certainly learned how icy a World Cup slalom course could be. Billy laughed.

As for the Lauberhorn downhill course, the scariest part for me to navigate during the media inspection on the morning of the race was a narrow path adjacent to the dramatic Hundschopf jump near the top of the course. The jump itself was closed to the press to preserve the snow for the race, so we media types had to follow one another, ski-tips to ski-tails down a three-foot wide, roped off, very steep slope. Luckily I didn't ski into any of my fellow journalists, and managed to make it down standing up. Billy applauded.

The rest of our inspection down the two-mile-long course was fascinating to see from the skier's perspective, but at a much lower rate of speed. When the track is fast, racers reach as high as 100 miles per hour on the straightaway, known as the Hanneg-Schuss. I came to know it intimately a few years later.

I see Billy Kidd once or twice a year. He is a valued friend, and a very warm human being. Inevitably he will recall that first trip we made to Wengen, most particularly the opening stand-up we did for our CBS show. At the top of the Lauberhorn course, there is a flat meadow where the race begins. Behind that meadow the terrain rises gently, then dramatically into a sharply chiseled, enormous rock face known as the Eiger. We chose to do our on-camera with the Eiger in the background.

I couldn't resist.

"Hello everyone, I'm Tim Ryan joined by Olympic silver medalist Billy Kidd, to bring you the Lauberhorn Downhill World Cup race, and we are also joined by the greatest rock star in the world... the Eiger." (Pull back the camera shot to expose the North Face of the world famous Eiger.)

The star on the course that year was a taciturn Swiss, Peter Müller, whose victory sent the beer taps flowing and a serious run on bratwurst as the home-country fans celebrated a homeboy win.

Billy and I had a couple of great adventures together during that time. Once, after covering a women's alpine race in Laax, Switzerland, he and I were flying from there to Zurich by helicopter, carrying the videotapes on to

LEFT: Aspen: With Patrick Lang, Billy Kidd, and Franz Klammer.
RIGHT: Schladming, Austria, with Billy Kidd.

London where we would do a voiceover with the edited show. We were in a small Bell Ranger, with a bench backseat behind the pilot. Up we went from the ski village, into a bright blue sky. As we gained altitude and cleared the peaks surrounding Laax, the view over the Alps was breathtaking. Suddenly our breath was literally taken away, as the copter plummeted straight down. A minute seemed like seconds as the ground rushed up at us. I found myself gripping the bench-seat in an effort to lift the copter back up—at the same time a thought raced through my mind as we kept dropping, "No one will ever find us down there." As if that would matter.

The pilot, who hadn't said a word into our headsets, tipped the nose of the copter forward, tilting the rotors into the new wind, and he calmly brought the copter back to horizontal and began climbing again.

Billy hadn't said a word either—out loud—but back on the ground in Zurich we agreed that we used up prayers and expletives combined in silent speech to ourselves, certain we were done for.

"What was that all about," I asked our Swiss pilot when we were out of the copter.

"The foehn," he replied. "It's the warm wind we get at this time of the year in the Alps. When we came over the top of the Jungfrau we had a following wind. But when we were clear of the mountaintops, we were met by the foehn blowing in the opposite and downward direction. That's why I had to turn the rotors into the wind to re-stabilize us. It's nothing to worry about; I'm very experienced with it."

Billy and I were glad he was, and even more glad to be in a taxi on terra firma on our way into Zurich. Our next adventure together—a few years later—was a little less dramatic, but also somewhat tense.

Thursday December 21, 1989, Billy and I were in a rented Mercedes driving from Schladming, Austria to Munich, Germany. We had been in Schladming for CBS to cover a men's World Cup downhill race scheduled for Saturday. However, there was a distinct lack of snow in Schladming, and the race was cancelled two days in advance. Our flights back to the U.S. were scheduled for Sunday the 24th, Christmas Eve.

What to do. "Let's go to Munich for a couple of nights," I suggested. Then Billy realized something better was also in Germany. The Brandenburg Gate was to be opened on Friday, symbolically ending the nightmare of the Berlin Wall separating East and West Germany. We quickly checked flights and found we could get one from Munich to Berlin Thursday afternoon, and one back on Saturday to Munich.

"Great idea Billy, let's go for it!"

We packed our gear hurriedly and left for Munich. All went well for several hours until we were about thirty minutes from the Munich airport. We ran out of gas, which was pretty stupid since the gas gauge had been indicating we were in reserve for about the last hour. We had to pull off the autobahn onto the shoulder and I was out trying to wave speeding cars down, hoping one would stop. One did. I hoped he would agree to drive us to the next gas station and we would fill up a gas can and call a taxi to drive us to our stranded car.

The chances of making our flight to Berlin were now dim and slim.

Billy is never without his cowboy hat and neck bandana. That's his look. That's Billy. Never mind that he had been very thin on top for many years. When the man, who was driving alone, walked back to our car from his, he looking in astonishment at the cowboy with a big smile.

"Billy Kidd!!" he exclaimed, and then in German-accented English, "What are you doing here? Can I help?" He was so excited, he offered to drive us to the nearest gas station and BACK with the gas can! The clincher was when Billy opened the trunk and asked the man if he would like to have an autographed picture for his son—both were apparently avid skiers. And the father was obviously old enough to remember "Billy the Kid" from his racing days.

What would the odds be that this kind man would stop to help a driver in distress and discover it was a ski-racing idol of his from America? The guy was overcome when Billy, black marker in hand, carefully wrote the boy's name on the photo and signed his.

We made the flight.

But the best was yet to come. We found a room at a hotel near the Berlin airport and hopped a taxi into town. Neither of us had ever been to Berlin. Our woman cabdriver was ecstatic about the opening of the wall at the Gate. She babbled on in German, and Billy understood enough to know that this was one of the happiest times of her life, and all of Germany's. I asked her to take us to the Gate, and said to Billy we could try to bullshit our way into the media compound with our credentials from Schladming and then find our way to the CBS News trailer.

The area near the Brandenburg Gate was ablaze with lights—most of them erected by news trucks from around the world. Traffic was thick. We paid our driver and walked through a maze of barriers waving our credentials and spotted the CBS News site. We were welcomed by technical and production people who were busy preparing for the next morning. None of the correspondents were there as yet, but the vibe was definitely in the air. News people from all around the world would be reporting an historic moment when that wall would be broken open—in the heart of Berlin—ending the twenty-eight-year nightmare of the division of East and West Germany.

Billy and I knew we could not be there at the Gate the next morning—our flight back to Munich was early. Almost casually, Billy said, "Let's go over to Checkpoint Charlie and see if we can get into East Berlin."

The checkpoint was the most famous crossing point through the wall, manned by Western Allied forces on the western side and East German soldiers on the eastern side controlled by the Soviets.

"Okay, let's give it a try," I replied, "but what happens if the good guys let us go over, and then we can't get back?" But Billy was confident we could pull it off—why I am still not sure! The West German soldiers saw the American-looking cowboy, Stetson hat with stampede string hanging loosely, red bandana neatly knotted around his neck, denim jacket and jeans, cowboy boots.

"Americanisch cowboy!" one said with a smile to the other and a quick glance at our passports, "Why do you go there?"

"We just want a look at East Berlin, and maybe have a beer," the cowboy replied.

A few feet away, the Eastern Guards could see us being checked through by their Western counterparts. They could hardly say no. Didn't even bother to look at our passports. We were in.

It was after 10 p.m. there were few lights on in the dull, gray buildings in view from where we entered East Berlin. The streets were deserted, unlike in West Berlin where parties were already underway. After walking a few blocks, carefully keeping track of our return route to Checkpoint Charlie, we saw some lights and heard voices, music, singing. We picked up our pace and came to a beer hall packed with young people—obviously celebrating the end of a dismal era. Once again, Billy's cowboy hat brought smiles and calls in German—and English, "Americanisch cowboy." We were swarmed over by young people, brandishing beers. "Come join us. This is a big night, how did you get here? Where are you from?"

It was one of the most spine-tingling, emotional moments imaginable.

About an hour later, we made our way back to the checkpoint, me still a little nervous about the border guards. Fortunately, the same ones were there, and on the Eastern side, there were now smiles on the faces of the soldiers, who waved us through. Tomorrow, they were free.

Early the next morning, Billy and I watched on television from our hotel rooms near the Berlin airport. The cameras were focused on the section of the wall at the Brandenburg Gate. The sound of sledgehammers could be heard as thousands watched from the streets of West Berlin. You could see the wall shake, and suddenly a long crack brought dust and broken concrete. A hole appeared and then grew larger. An East German officer stepped through the gap, smiled, saluted and then shook hands with his Western counterpart. The crowd roared with joy, music played, and Germany was unified.

I sat alone with a cup of coffee in one hand, and rubbed a small piece of concrete in the other—scratched from the Wall at Checkpoint Charlie the night before.

CHAPTER 34

More Snow, and Sake the Hard Way

CBS Executive Producer Terry O'Neil had made a commitment to ski-racing—and other winter sports in the eighties—hoping that we could break the hold on ABC's grip of the Olympic Games, and feeling that the Winter Games were the most vulnerable of ABC's Olympic portfolio. CBS brass had its eyes on the 1992 Winter Games in Albertville, France.

After dipping his toe into the snow with the World Cup ski races, in Europe, O'Neil acquired the rights to the Aspen, Colorado men's downhill in 1981 and promptly gave the race a television title of "America's Downhill." Neil Diamond had a hit song out called "We're Coming to America." That became our theme music over the opening graphics. 1976 Olympic champion Franz Klammer was the star attraction. He had literally launched ski racing into American sports culture with his electrifying run for gold at the Innsbruck Games in his home country of Austria—nicely packaged in the U.S. by ABC Sports. The ratings for our our race in Aspen were decent. An Austrian won, but it wasn't Klammer. It was Harti Weirather, another accomplished racer from that bastion of alpine skiing success.

Billy Kidd and I continued to work together through the eighties covering World Cup events—men's and women's races—although ABC Sports had the rights to the 1984 Sarajevo Olympics and the World Championships. In 1982 I was sent to Verbier, Switzerland to cover the Women's World Cup races there. The U.S. women's team figured to be medal contenders in Sarajevo having shown strong results on the tour. Tamara McKinney led a strong squad that included Christin Cooper, Cindy Nelson, and Debbie Armstrong.

McKinney had a tragic family story. She was in a fragile state of mind, and the U.S. coach, Michel Rudigoz, whom I was meeting for the first time, at first refused to allow me to interview her. I realized he was trying to protect her, and keep all of his team focused on the racing. But I needed the interview. He wound up allowing me to do it, Tamara was willing, and I kept it short. The next day, she won her race. Rudigoz and I became great friends and remain so to this day. (We both had homes in Sun Valley, Idaho; Michel still does, and owns a popular French restaurant, Michel's Christiania.)

Billy and I went to Furano, Japan during this era to cover a women's race. Furano is on the island of Hokkaido, better known for the city and ski area of Sapporo, which hosted the Winter Olympics in 1972. We stopped overnight in Sapporo and Billy insisted we go night-skiing on the Olympic run. It was spectacular. There are two or three runs lighted for night skiing, and the views from the top are mountain peaks under moon and stars and the neon-lit city of Sapporo below. Hard to concentrate on your skiing, and the nighttime temperatures guarantee icy conditions. But it was worth the effort and made for a unique way to spend an evening!

Furano provided more classic Billy Kidd. It is a small fishing village that in recent years had developed as a modest ski resort. Both men's and women's World Cup races have been held there, and we were there for one of the first women's events. We had been booked into the Prince—a western-style hotel with all the modern amenities.

But Billy being Billy, suggested he and I and the CBS producer and director stay instead in a *ryokan*, a traditional Japanese inn. Naturally he had already done this before and thought we should have an authentic experience. We acquiesced. The deal is you sleep on an unpadded futon—effectively a mat on the floor, in one big co-ed room screened off into bamboo cubicles. Privacy is obviously quite limited. The toilets are communal, although separated by sex. You receive your own wash-basin and a towel, and settle for a sponge bath.

In the morning, breakfast is brought to your "room." It's your choice of fish and seaweed, or seaweed and fish, and of course, green tea.

As I recall we moved into the Prince Hotel for the remainder of our stay.

The first night there Billy and I ventured into the village looking for a restaurant open late. We found a *robata*, which is a Japanese grill—where we had a delicious dinner of grilled fish. Your choice from a number of whole fish, fresh from the waters of the Sea of Japan, is selected by pointing to the one you want. The ice chest has a counter the same length and chairs in front. Behind the fish chest, a team of four or five kitchen staff command an enormous grill. When you have pointed to the fish that appeals to you, one of the team scoops it up with a long handled wooden paddle, and deposits it onto the grill. You choose your veggies to be grilled as well. All of this occurs in a general din. The waiters bark at the grill chef, he barks back. Another is offering sake or beer to the customers at the counter.

When your food is ready, it is paddled back to you unceremoniously. It is good to be watching so that the paddle doesn't knock over your drink.

The barman appeared with the bottle of sake, two small square wooden boxes and a stack of saucers. When he saw Billy—cowboy hat with stampede string, red bandana, denim and boots—a broad grin crossed his broad face.

"Ichiban skier, ichiban skier," he exclaimed to no one in particular. Could it be? Yes, it could be that this man recognized Billy Kidd the "Number One" skier. That Colorado brand reached across the seas all the way to the Far East!

Sake was on the house, and soon on our laps. I had never seen the wooden box trick. The waiter filled the box with sake, and placed several saucers under it. Drinking out of a square box takes a certain technique. We tried several techniques, only to quickly understand why they give you saucers. When you have drunk and spilled enough from your box, what you missed is on your saucer (if not on your lap). You then dump that into your box, get a refill, then see how many saucers you can go through.

The next night, we—well, CBS—hosted the women and coaching staff of the U.S. ski team at another restaurant, sitting on tatami mats and sharing sake (in glasses) with those old enough to drink. It was a great chance to get to know them and better present them to our audience. Several, including Christin Cooper—my TV-partner-to-be several years later—wrote charming thank-you notes saying it was the first time U.S. TV had ever done such a thing. Credit to our producer Ted Shaker, who eventually went on to be the head of CBS Sports for a time.

Here's to Billy Kidd, a great friend and a great American. There is no more respected and loved U.S. ski racer in the history of the sport.

CHAPTER 35

Other Icy Endeavors

While ski-racing kept me busy in beautiful alpine locations through the eighties, it was only part of the winter sports agenda. When CBS obtained the rights to the World Figure Skating Championships, the first of those was on home soil in Cincinnati. I became the CBS voice of Figure Skating, and leading up to those championships we covered the European Championships in Lyon, France. My expert commentator for that was a former World Champion from Great Britain, John Curry. Having never done a compulsory figure on hockey skates, I relied on John. In return, fancying myself a patron of the culinary arts, I felt obligated to take him to lunch (on CBS of course) at Michelin-starred Le Restaurant Alain Chapel in nearby Mionnay to establish some rapport. We talked about the Russian men's favorite Alexandre Fadeev, and rising East German teenager, Katarina Witt. And about the food. And the wine. We were in France after all.

More preparation followed with the entire CBS production crew at the Le Restaurant Paul Bocuse in Lyon. I had made contact by mail with Monsieur Bocuse, suggesting that I could bring a CBS TV crew to do a little feature on him and his restaurant while we were in Lyon for the skating. Of course I was as much hoping to land a free lunch at his famous Michelin establishment. I had seen that M. Bocuse was marketing-savvy, and already had plans for a restaurant in the U.S. His answer to me was yes, with one proviso, he would like me to show off his collection of antique musical toys.

It turned out the toys were displayed adjacent to the restaurant, in a building larger than the restaurant itself! He was a very gracious host and very proud of his fascinating collection, some of which dated back to the

18th century. Lunch of course was spectacular. There were about six or eight CBS folks, including our director, a long-time good friend and colleague.

There was no menu. Chef Bocuse came to our table before each course to explain, in French accented English, what he had prepared. Each time after he left, our director would ask, "What did he say?" and go on to complain that he didn't like it, or wouldn't eat "that!" Our gourmet also declined the fine wines being served with each course, opting to stick with his Chivas-on-the-rocks throughout the meal.

When the cheese course arrived, (with M. Bocuse himself pushing the wheeled tray to us!) I was petrified that our now well-oiled outlier would make some embarrassing comment as he surveyed the selection of chèvre, several wearing traditional ash coatings. Fortunately, M. Bocuse pre-empted him by explaining to our table the reasons for, and tastes of, ash-covered goat cheese!

Our director opined that he would have preferred McDonald's, but that was out of earshot of Monsieur Bocuse. For the rest of us, it was an epic dining experience—one which none of us could have afforded on our own.

And there was no bill.

The Bocuse feature made a nice set-up for our figure skating coverage, since Lyon is known as the gastronomic capital of France. And M. Bocuse's antique musical toys made the show.

In ensuing years, I traveled to Sarajevo, and Birmingham, England for European Championships, and covered the World Championships in Cincinnati 1987, which was special. It marked the emergence of Katarina Witt as a glamorous superstar of the sport, in a heated battle with U.S. champion, Debbie Thomas, a Stanford medical school student.

Witt had already won two World Championships and Olympic gold in the 1984 Sarajevo Olympics. She was at the top of her game. Thomas had won her first U.S. Championship the year before. Both had their eyes on the 1988 Calgary Olympic Games. Thomas had strong U.S. competition from Jill Trenary, Caryn Kadavy and Tiffany Chin. But Debbie had a big following, and was skating on home ice.

My expert was now Scott Hamilton, newly retired from a brilliant career on the ice. We had the pleasure of covering a thrilling Ladies Long Program to decide the World Championship. In the final group of six skaters, Witt skated second to last, and set the leading mark. Thomas, skated brilliantly,

Sun Valley, Idaho, with Katarina Witt.

but fell short in the eyes of the international judges. The East German star had won the hearts of American figure-skating fans, and her third World title.

My biggest contribution to our otherwise scintillating coverage of the event, was to identify the music being played for Debbie Thomas was being performed by "the musical group Yanni." My musically inclined producer David Michaels, came quickly into my headset to inform me that "Yanni" was not a musical group, but a musical guy. Embarrassing moment!

I had met Katarina briefly at the Lyon European Championships. She was just seventeen at the time and spoke no English, but at twenty-two, she was very self-assured. Scott and I had gone to watch her practice in Cincinnati (which Katarina charmingly pronounced "Chinch-inatti"). I had asked him to be sure to tell her that a great ice-show takes place in Sun Valley every summer, outdoors under the lights. All of the top skaters—including Scott—perform there and I had promised the ice-show director that I would try to get Witt to come.

She was quite intrigued, and was a big fan of Scott's. So after winning the Calgary Olympic gold, Katarina became a regular in Sun Valley, and eventually bought a piece of land to build a house on. She was a guest in our home frequently, and in the nineties brought her parents over from Berlin and spent the summer there in our house while we were in Europe.

My speed-skating commentary was limited to just one event—as a last-minute choice to cover a last-minute CBS purchase of the 1990 World Men's Sprint Championships in Tromso, Norway. As I said, I was the winter-sports guy, although all I knew about speed-skating I read in the kid's story of *Hans Brinker, or the Silver Skates*.

All I remember about Tromso was that it was north of the Arctic Circle, damn cold and totally dark for most of the twenty-four hours I was there.

It also has a nifty statue of Roald Amundsen, the Norwegian arctic explorer who was a rival of Admiral Byrd in their race to the South Pole. I don't remember who won either race, but I think I got a call saying the speed-skating event wasn't going to make the show anyway, come on home.

"Twenty-Four Hours in Tromso," would not be a likely travel feature in *The New York Times*.

I had been to Norway once before, to do a piece in Oslo at the Holmenkollen Ski Festival, and to cover the jumping portion of that event with former U.S. coach John Bower. It was an extraordinary show—more than 10,000 people gathered on the grounds watching a mass start for a fifty kilometer cross-country race, galvanized by the cheers of the passionate Norwegian fans. Almost fifteen years later I would be back in Norway for the 1994 Olympic Games.

Bobsledding was also a "one-off" for me, when CBS acquired the rights to the 1981 World Championships in Lake Placid, New York. To call it a breathtaking experience is putting it mildly. Lake Placid was the site of the Winter Olympics the year before, and had registered a temperature the day before the competition of 36 below zero.

I had driven north from our home in Larchmont with a suitcase full of ski clothing that I had expected would be adequate. When I arrived and felt my skin stinging from the cold, I went directly to a ski-shop and bought heavier long underwear, a down-filled jacket, and knee-high sheepskin-lined snow-boots. I have never been so cold in my life and I have been in a lot of cold places. (Minneapolis, Minnesota gets second place, where I was covering the NHL All Star Game in 1972. When I stepped out of the hotel lobby to go to the Met Center arena, the 30-below temperature sucked the breath out of my throat so I couldn't speak for several minutes.)

Since it was a World Championship at Lake Placid, there were several days of racing on the Olympic bob-run. It did not warm up. On the day of the men's four-man event, my expert analyst, Paul Lamey—who had raced on the U.S. Naval Academy bobsled team that competed in the Olympics—suggested we take a run on the track and he would analyze the course on the way down. Our director, Bob Fishman loved the idea and said we could videotape it and make it part of our opening.

We would get two experienced sledders; Lamey would drive, and I would be in the number two seat. Paul would have a wireless microphone and describe each turn. I would simply hang on and enjoy the ride, then at the finish line, I would jump out, be handed a mic and do the, "Hi everyone, we are here in Lake Placid for the World Bobsled Championships etc.," thing.

The concession to my welfare was that we would start halfway down the track, so that the risk of dying in a high-speed crash was lessened.

It was still more than 30 below zero.

I hunched behind Lamey in seat two, my crash-helmet pressed against the back of his. I had no idea what to expect as the brakeman in seat four pushed us off. The sled quickly gained frightening speed, and the G-forces in the high turns tied my stomach in knots. I closed my eyes. I could barely hear Paul's commentary over the whooshing sound of the sled as we barreled down the course. When we scraped to a stop at the finish area, I felt like I had been in a washing machine on the spin cycle. I extricated myself from the sled and clumsily removed my helmet, slapped on the head-set the CBS audio man handed me and with a shaking hand, took the microphone.

"Hhhh… eeee… lll… oooo… e… ve… ry… one…"

My voice was barely a squeak as I tried to get air up from my chest into my throat. I could hear laughter from the production truck in my earphones.

"III'm… Ttt… iii… m… R… y… an…, what a ride down…(deep breath) the bu… bu… bob… rr… un here at the World (deep breath) Champion… ships in Lake Placid."

Fishman was hysterically laughing into my head-set. "This is great, this is great!"

When I finally got my voice back I said into the microphone, "Sorry Bob, I guess that didn't work the way we wanted. I guess my voice literally froze up! We can't use that."

"Are you crazy?" came his reply, "It's great, and we are absolutely using it!"

And so we did.

Obviously I survived that questionable decision to rocket down an ice tube in 30-below temperatures, but lady luck can smile on us in less dramatic ways.

CHAPTER 36

Lucking Into America's Cup History

Two years later, in early fall and lovely weather, Lee and I were in Newport, Rhode Island having just dropped off son Kevin for his freshman year at Boston College. We hadn't ever been to Newport and decided to stop there for lunch and have a look. There was a lot of activity in the harbor, which turned out to be the challenger competition to determine which yacht would challenge the United States for the America's Cup.

The 12-meter yachts (remember those?) were moored dockside. Britain, France, Italy, and Australia had entries in the competition. I saw a press tent and told Lee I would go in and see if we could get closer to the yachts. Xerox was the main sponsor, and I was introduced to an executive, Michael Kirby, who promptly invited us to join him for lunch on the Xerox yacht and then to watch the afternoon races. Conversation led to his inquiry as to CBS interest in airing a filmed version of the upcoming Cup series. I said I had no idea, but could introduce him to the right folks at CBS. Kirby also asked if I thought our famous news anchor Walter Cronkite would consider being the narrator of the film covering the final series. I said I would be happy to make the inquiry for him.

Cronkite, an avid and accomplished sailor, was not interested. I arranged a meeting for Kirby with Neal Pilson, then head of CBS Sports. Pilson was not interested in airing a filmed documentary more than a month after the races took place. Kirby stopped by my office to say thanks anyway, and by the way would I like to do the film narration? I told him I knew very little about sailing, and absolutely nothing about the America's Cup. Not to worry he

The America's Cup Summer

OFFICIAL GUIDE
America's Cup
International Exposition

$2.95

The Hottest Cup Chase Ever: A Six-Nation Battle
The Insider's Newport — Maps, Guides, Listings

1983: First ever U.S. loss
in sailing's America's Cup.

had replied, it will all be scripted. "Okay, why not," was my answer.

So it came to be that I was the official voice, and only U.S. broadcaster of the historic 1983 America's Cup. The U.S. had never lost the Cup since its inception in 1851—twenty-four successful defenses. But outside of the sailing community, it was not a big audience-grabber. Xerox was going to have a tough time getting it on the air. There certainly was no interest in the U.S. for a live telecast from Newport that would be cost-prohibitive anyway.

The final series saw Dennis Conner skippering the American 12-meter, *Liberty*, and John Bertrand at the helm for *Australia II*, the boat financed by the crusty Aussie Alan Bond. It was football season; I was working NFL games for CBS and so was only able to get to Newport to see three of the races in the best of seven regatta. But I was in Newport for the decider with the series tied 3-3. I had talked the film producer into having me do a "live" call of portions of the seventh race from the Xerox boat on the course. As Conner made his last desperate tack trying to catch the leading Australian boat, I was able to call the finish: *Australia II* becoming the first challenger to beat the United States for the oldest trophy in sports.

Because of the history involved, it was a big story that September, but not seen on television until six weeks later, and only in syndication, not on a network.

In 2013, as I watched on television from Switzerland the U.S. boat *Oracle* stage an incredible comeback—winning eight races in a row to overcome New Zealand in San Francisco bay—I thought back thirty years to my good fortune of being the sole announcer of still the most historic of America's Cup races—the first time the U.S. had lost the Cup in 132 years.

CHAPTER 37

A Family Copes as Olympics Approach

For my career, the 1990s brought great promise of more adventure, interesting travel, and the prospect of covering an Olympic Games. That promise was tempered by the continuing reality of Lee's descent into the darkness of Alzheimer's. While continuing to cover NFL football and college basketball at CBS, I was able to visit her regularly in Santa Barbara, and later at the facility in Boise.

Our children were coping, each suffering in their own way and trying to move on with their own lives. Kim and Kevin were both in TV news in the West. Jay, in the music recording business, and Brendan, after graduating from Fordham University Law School, were living and working in the New York area. I had become very active as a National Board Member of the Alzheimer's Association and spoke at their annual Public Policy Forum, served on a policy committee, and did numerous TV appearances, telling Lee's story, including an emotionally wrenching one in 1995 with Connie Chung of CBS news that I agreed to do at my home in Ketchum. Richard Sandomir, *The New York Times* sports-TV columnist, generously wrote a lovely piece that brought attention to the cause, as did a long feature in *People* magazine.

The big news at CBS was the acquisition of the TV rights of the Albertville, France Winter Olympic Games. In the late eighties I had turned down a contract offer from ABC and re-signed with CBS. At the time it was a tough call, but I chose to stay because I enjoyed the people so much—particularly Ed Goren, a producer I worked with quite frequently, and who in 1994 went on to become president of sports at FOX, along with many others. I knew nobody at ABC, but was tempted because they were known as the Olympics network. But as it turned out, I was getting my first Olympics shot at CBS.

Executive producer Mike Pearl invited me, (the winter sports guy!), to lunch. "We'd like you to be our hockey announcer in Albertville," he began. "You are the only guy we have with that experience, and you were well known in that sport, so I figure you want to do hockey."

"Well, Mike," I replied. "Actually no. I haven't done a hockey game in ten years, and although it's been a big part of my life and career, I want to be outside at the Winter Olympics, not in an arena every night."

Somewhat taken aback, Pearl went to his second choice for me—figure skating, since I had done three World Championships and three Europeans.

"Well if it's okay, Mike, I would prefer to do alpine skiing. Figure-skating is indoors every night also."

"Then I guess you'd like to do the men's events at Val-d'Isère. Open the Games with the men's downhill…"

"No Mike, I would like to do the Women's events at Meribel. The U.S. men do not have any medal contenders, the women have two, Diann Roffe and Hilary Lindh."

I thought I might be pissing him off at this point, but to my pleasant surprise Mike said fine, do the women's skiing.

I had fallen in love with ski-racing, and when we moved from Larchmont to Sun Valley in 1991, I was skiing every day I was home during the snow season. Sun Valley's history with skiing—as the first resort built in the U.S. in 1936—included many accomplished racers such as Olympic medalists Gretchen Fraser, and Christin Cooper, and several other U.S. ski team racers. To have a chance to call the Olympic races was a thrill, not knowing if I would have another opportunity after Albertville, since CBS's deal was for only the '92 Games.

CBS hired Christin Cooper, who had won a silver medal at the 1984 Games in Sarajevo, to join on the commentary along with Mary Carillo as a reporter. There were two venues for Alpine. Billy Kidd worked with Dick Stockton on the men's events at Val d'Isère, Christin with me and Mary at Meribel, the site of the women's events. (I was able to get son Kevin a job as a runner at a couple of the venues. He had also had a job with me in 1983 at the Pan-American Games in Caracas, Venezuela—nice duty!)

I was also able to convince CBS we should hire two people for our crew who could be very helpful to us in our first Winter Olympics, especially since our producer Bob Dekas was new to ski-racing. One was Patrick Lang, from Basel, Switzerland, a ski journalist whose father Serge had started ski racing's World Cup series. He had grown up with the sport, spoke several languages, and had worked as a researcher with ABC Sports on their ski racing coverage. The other was my previously mentioned friend Michel Rudigoz, a former French ski racer and coach of the U.S. Women's Team that had won medals at the '84 Games, including Christin Cooper's silver in the giant slalom.

Rudigoz knew all of the French organizers working the alpine events, and many of the team coaches from various nations. His connections would prove valuable when we wanted to mount the first ever "come-and-go" lipstick-sized camera on the course. It provided a unique look on a fast part of the track, but had to be approved by the ski federation and the French TV guys. Michel made it happen, earning himself an Emmy for his part in our production.

The Emmy sits handsomely in the entrance hall of his restaurant in Sun Valley.

The first Olympic Games for me is marked in memory by two faux pas of my very own. The first occurred in the Women's Downhill. We were calling the races in "voiceover" following the event. I was down in the finish area during the race. We had spent some time with the U.S. team during our research for the events, and I had been most impressed with Hilary Lindh, one of the favorites for a medal in the downhill. She was from Juneau, Alaska, a shy, thoughtful young woman with a quiet confidence.

When she skied dynamically over the very demanding course designed by the famous Bernhard Russi and clinched the silver medal, I couldn't help myself. I completely forgot I was working the event and wearing a jacket with the CBS logo on it. I dashed from the media area onto the out-run of the course and gave her a big hug! Of course TV cameras were all over the place.

It might be the most unprofessional thing I have ever done in my career. But I don't regret it. Hilary and I have laughed about it when we have seen each other at ski events over the years.

My other faux pas was an avoidable accident. Christin and I had finished doing a voiceover that ran until after midnight. It was a starless night in Meribel, and while walking to our car in the parking area I slipped on black ice, fell, and turned my ankle badly. The pain was excruciating. Christin and

Michel (who was Coop's coach all over again in the voiceover booth) came to my aid and got me into the car and back to the hotel. I was actually in shock from the pain—something I had never experienced before. Michel recognized it, and roused the French ski team doctor, who was in our hotel. He sent some medication for me with the advice to see a doctor in the morning for an X-ray. Michel, God bless him, stayed with me the whole night, something he reminds me about constantly all these years later!

It turned out the ankle was not broken, but the ligaments were badly sprained. The Giant Slalom was that day. Christin and I had planned an opening on the ski slope, where she would point out the trouble spots for the racers. I was determined to stay with the plan. Meanwhile, someone had asked U.S. team doctor, the noted orthopedic surgeon Richard Steadman, to come and check me out.

"Yes it hurts, Doc, but if I have my ski boot on, I'm sure I can manage to ski down the course," I said boldly. In his calm fashion, Richard said okay, try putting the ski boot on. I could tell he knew the result in advance. Even with the painkillers, I couldn't even put my foot all the way into my boot.

"It would actually be better if it was broken," Richard smiled, "that's going to take a long time to heal. I'm afraid your skiing is done for the year."

I was totally angry and disgruntled. We had planned an on-camera for each of the remaining races—Giant Slalom and Slalom—with Coop and me on the mountain. Instead, I put on one ski on my good foot and pushed over to the finish area from the TV trucks, and we did the usual two-shot stand-up. Boring.

We did have another American medal win to bring to our audience, when Diann Roffe raced to silver in the giant slalom. At least I had the satisfaction of knowing I had selected the right sport and the right venue at those games—thanks to Hilary and Diann. Christin did a great job as our expert analyst despite having to put up with her former coach Michel Rudigoz offering his expertise to her voiceover work for the two weeks we were in Meribel! Coop would continue to do great work for the next twenty years of ski coverage as my partner, and she and her husband Mark Tache continue to be dear friends of mine.

CBS contracted for the next two Winter Games, Lillehammer, Norway, and Nagano, Japan. Former American downhiller Andy Mill was added to our crew for men's events at Lillehammer, where two Americans won gold medals—Tommy Moe in downhill and Diann Roffe in super giant slalom.

Andy and I got to work a few World Cup races together after Albertville, which led to one of my more thrilling days on skis. We were covering the men's downhill on the Lauberhorn at Wengen, Switzerland. I had been there before with Billy Kidd, and we had skied down the course during media inspection, going slowly to check out the camera positions, slowly also because I had already had that harrowing trip down a narrow trail alongside the famous Hundschop jump!

Lillehammer, Norway, with Andy Mill.

With Andy, we were going TOO slowly for the likes of the race organizers since we were the last ones on the run just thirty minutes before race time.

At the top of the long steep known as the Hanneg Schuss (where racer speeds can reach ninety miles per hour) race officials alongside the course yelled at us, "You must go straight, go straight," meaning get the hell down the hill and out of the way. Andy, ahead of me, pointed his skis down the hill and dropped into a downhiller's tuck. I had planned to make long, sweeping turns to control my speed, but the officials' rant ringing in my ears, I flattened my skis and let them go. I had never gone this fast in my ski life. I could see Andy ahead, standing in the compression at the bottom of the steep—laughing as he saw me speeding toward him. I knew if I hit the flat at the bottom, I would probably die, or at least break every bone in my body. Deciding discretion was definitely the better part of valor, I steered over to the side of the course, and tipped my skis into a hip slide. With Andy grinning and clapping, I slid to a stop on the flat and got back upright—not glamorous, but still in one piece. When I regained my breath and lowered my pulse rate, we carried on to the finish line without further incident.

Ever since, my nickname from Andy remains "Hanneg."

CHAPTER 38

Loveable Lillehammer

Having done ten Olympic Games in all, I am frequently asked which was the best—the most rewarding. My answer is always quick, Lillehammer 1994.

Norway is a small country, but its love for sports and the culture of winter runs deep. Winters are long, cold, and beautiful. Its citizens embrace the climate, the snow-covered mountains and villages with a nationalistic passion. Every sport is valued, with the favorites being cross-country skiing, biathlon, ski-jumping, and speed-skating where Norway has had consistently good Olympic and World Championship results. And the country's Alpine skiers were already making their mark. But hockey, figure-skating, and curling are also popular. Getting the Olympics for Lillehammer was the first time in this snow-mad country since the 1952 Games in Oslo.

The excitement in the country was palpable and the spirit was infectious. You could feel it in the frigid morning air and hear it in the packed pubs in the evenings. Two scenes stand out in my mind as though they occurred yesterday. The speed events, downhill and super-G took place in a tiny village called Kvitfjell. It wasn't actually even a village. The organizers had purchased a mountain property from a sheep farmer in order to have an Olympic-standard downhill length and pitch. The course started high in the tree-line and ended near the farmer's barn, which he rented to the ski federation to act as the ski-tuning facility for all of the teams. His wintering sheep were allowed to keep their pens nearby.

Kvitfjell was a half-hour's drive from our hotel in Hafjell. We would leave at 6:30 each morning with temperatures of 20–30 below zero. By 7 a.m. hardy Norwegian ski-racing fans were already filling the parking lots, some a half-mile away from the race hill. Under still-gray skies, they would step into cross-country skis, backpacks stuffed with food, drinks, and often—babies—and ski to the finish area to get the best standing room viewing spots. Once there, with folk music blaring from loudspeakers, they would jump and dance to keep warm, join in singing the vocals, and paint one another's faces with Norwegian flags.

It was the most joyful expression of national pride and exuberant celebration at any of the Olympic Games I have worked and watched. Of course we did an on-camera opening with Andy getting his face painted!

The second scene would have made a good bit on a TV comedy show. We had seen the farmer's sheep in a corral next to the barn he had rented out to be a ski-tuning house. It was simply too good to pass up for an on-camera as a feature or a race-open for the Women's Combined event. My pitch to our producer Michael Burks was that Coop and I would get into the pen with the sheep, and briefly tell the story of why they happened to be at the finish area of an Olympic ski event, and then set up our race.

"Okay... let's give it a try," was his hesitant reply.

We arrived around 7 a.m. The race was scheduled for 9:30. Spectators would be arriving around 7:30 to get good vantage points in the standing area. Our camera crew of three men were city guys. A sheep pen was not a familiar workplace for them. They weren't comfortable with the sheep, but in we went. The sheep, about fifteen or so, immediately went to the farthest corner of the pen. We followed them, hoping they would stay put and be in our camera shot. That was the point after all. Once we moved toward them—five of us human-types, one carrying a big thing on his shoulder (the camera) another waving a pole (the microphone), they bolted. In several directions.

We had limited time to get this done. My suggestion was that everyone stand still, let's set up our shot, and I would talk—or in this case sing—the sheep over to us. I launched into the Whiffenpoof Song, a Yale University Glee club song that my late father had loved and from whom I had learned it. "We are poor little lambs, Baa, Baa," etc. Sure enough, some of the sheep wandered over. Amid laughter all around, Coop and I rushed through our opening comments. Suddenly, all hell broke loose. Several of the sheep, who apparently didn't like my rendition of their anthem, squirmed through the fencing and dashed up the road—the only road where the skiers, officials and public could get to the finish area and ski-room.

A couple of our CBS group tried to keep the sheep from getting out, but with no success. One admitted he was actually afraid of them. Coop and I and one other brave soul rushed up the road to try and turn the strays back to the pen before the traffic started arriving. The caper would be a hard one to explain to the race officials.

Oh for a good border collie.

But after a few minutes and much yelling and waving of arms we got the mavericks back in the pen and all of us breathed sighs of relief.

I was not asked for an encore of the Whiffenpoof Song.

To make it completely an unhappy ending, the video never made air. No reason was given to us. Maybe I sang it in the wrong key?

Meanwhile the U.S. ski team turned in great results, Alaskan Tommy Moe—with Norwegian heritage—won gold in the downhill and silver in the super-G. Diann Roffe won the gold in the women's super-G, and Sun Valley's Picabo Street made her Olympic debut with a silver in the downhill.

CHAPTER 39

Picabo and "The Herminator" Do Nagano

The 1998 Nagano Olympics were exotic, wet, and filled with drama. The alpine events were held in two locations: the speed events were near the small village of Hakuba, and the slalom-gate events were in Shiga Kogen, closer to Nagano itself. The Sea of Japan influenced the snow conditions, and while there was plenty of the white stuff it was wet and sticky. In fact, there was so much snow the first days of the Games, the men's downhill was postponed for five days! Christin Cooper and I would dutifully ski to our broadcast position each morning all pumped up to call the opening alpine event of the Games, only to be giving weather reports every half hour or so, until the race was officially called off each day.

Half of the fun of going from our tiny hotel in Hakuba each day was trying to outwit the security guard on the ski runs. With the language barrier, there was no talking them into give us access to the training courses. We would be greeted at the ropes by neatly uniformed, unsmiling soldiers who would cross their arms and shake their heads—a "no go" sign. But Coop would not be denied. We would slide down the mountain until we were out of view, duck under the ropes, and hope our credentials wouldn't be confiscated if we were caught.

On one of the downhill delay days, our producer Steve Milton had me do a live stand-up report in the finish area and by the time we got to do it, I had about four inches of snow on the top of my hatless head. This scene would wind up playing a more-than-minor role in my ongoing career.

But the annoying weather delay was worth the wait—for two reasons.

This would be the first time in U.S. television Olympic history that the men's downhill would be broadcast live. Secondly, the then-young Austrian Hermann Maier provided the most spectacular crash since the Polish guy flew off the ski jump on ABC's Wide World of Sports.

Japan's humid weather produced some foggy conditions at the top of the race course. About five gates down it was clear and bright, but the seventh gate, which led into a steep drop, had been shifted a few feet sideways since the training runs. Several racers had problems there. But nothing like what Maier encountered as he blasted between the panels and then got airborne completely out of control. The Austrian's head smacked the packed hard snow on the course then his back and hip took the brunt of the fall before he cartwheeled into the first safety net, took out the second one and careened down a steep incline into deep, soft snow. He should have been dead. But within seconds, he was getting himself upright, rubbing his left knee, and climbing back up to the race course.

His downhill day was over, and most of us thought his Games were over as well.

To this day, I'm not sure how well I called the Maier run. It was a thrill to call it live—and in this case, be part of U.S. TV and ski-racing history—I just hope I captured the moments and did justice to what was a memorable scene for all who watched it. Of course most big event ski-racing is described in "post-production," the advantage being you can correct a mistake or add something you didn't see watching it live. There are other good reasons for taped calls—it offers the chance to include short bios or features and family reaction shots that there isn't time for before each racer leaves the start house. But you have to develop some acting skill too—to keep that live sound, when you already know the result.

My guy Patrick Lang got to the Austrian team officials and learned that not only was Maier not seriously hurt (although plenty sore), but was planning on racing the super-G just three days later. Better yet, Maier's quote borrowed from his film idol, fellow Austrian Arnold Schwarzenegger, was, "I'll be baaack!" That gave me a good idea—but with little time to explore it.

I had met Arnold a few times in Sun Valley. His then-wife Maria Shriver and I had worked together briefly before at WNBC-TV in New York. His ski-instructor, an Austrian named Adi Erber—was an old friend of mine. What if we could get Arnold to go to the ski hill in Sun Valley with a camera crew, and just do his famous line from *The Terminator* films? We could open the Olympic ski segment with a clip of the downhill crash, and see and hear Arnold, in ski gear, deliver, "I'll be baaack!" We had a thirteen-hour time difference to the U.S. in our favor, but could I get to Arnold, find a local cameraman in Sun Valley, get it shot, and have CBS organize satellite transmission of the piece to Nagano.

Yes, yes, yes, and yes.

I decided first to make sure Arnold was in Sun Valley, I had Erber's number, woke him up and he told me Arnold was there and they had watched the crash on our coverage together earlier that day.

"Ask Arnold if he would do this for me—will he be skiing tomorrow morning?" He would and all he asked for was a phone number for Maier in Hakuba. Patrick Lang was able to get that for me.

I found another local Sun Valley friend, John Plummer, a good cameraman who said he could do the job.

He staged Arnold at the bottom of Sun Valley's Warm Springs run, and the actor did his thing: "The Herminator—I'll be baack!" Our producer Steve Milton—who had loved the idea—made one crucial mistake. He told the big bosses at CBS Olympics what we were pulling off, and when they saw the clip, it suddenly was being taken away from our super-G opening and instead going into the primetime studio show!

Of course that was great for our Olympic coverage and no doubt boosted the audience for the super-G race segment, but our crew was a little upset that it was not in our opening since it was our idea.

Unbelievably—Maier won the super-G gold, got a congratulatory phone call from Arnold who invited the "Herminator" to visit the "Terminator" in Hollywood, which Hermann did in the spring.

Meanwhile, Picabo Street was the focus of attention on the U.S. ski team. After dominating the World Cup tour and World Championships downhill races and wearing a silver from Lillehammer, her quest for gold at Nagano had suffered a severe setback when she had crashed in a World Cup race in Vail, Colorado in 1996, just fourteen months before Nagano. A lengthy rehab from severe injuries to her knee and leg had reduced her chances of being in top shape for the Japan Olympics, but she had willed her way to a gold in the super-G. With the constantly changing weather conditions affecting the Nagano downhill course, she finished outside the medals. When I spoke to her at the bottom of the course afterward, she admitted that it was too dangerous to risk yet another serious injury. She would settle for one gold in Japan, and set her sights on Salt Lake City in 2002.

Ironically, a couple of weeks later in Crans-Montana Switzerland, she crashed in a World Cup race, injuring her knee again, forcing another long, brave recovery in order to compete in the Salt Lake Games.

With the Maier crash-and-comeback, and Picabo's gold on an icy super-G course, the Nagano Games had already provided U.S. ski fans with plenty of excitement. When the venue switched to another mountain at Shiga Kogen for the technical event, Christin and I thought things might be a little calmer.

We had enjoyed our quaint little hotel in Hakuba, and our introduction to soba noodles in the nearby restaurants. Shiga Kogen lacked the same charm—we were lodged in a tourist high-rise hotel—but it did increase my knowledge of sake. After all, as a knowledgeable oenophile it was my duty to bone up on rice wine. At an excellent sushi and sake bar I quickly learned the pleasures of chilled sake as compared to the traditional warmed stuff, and was pressed to sample the variety of sakes—sweet to very dry.

Our broadcast position at Shiga Kogen was similar to that at Hakuba—temporary construction of prefab cabins mounted on scaffolding. We were five levels up with spectator seating below us. Producer Mike Burks, in the interest of time, suggested we call the races live-to-tape, with the caveat that we could repair any mistakes in post-production. This decision came in handy on the day of the men's Giant Slalom event.

It was also the day that the Japanese Emperor Akihito was in attendance. He had been escorted around to the various sports events at the Games, and this day was his ski-day. Of course his appearance brought added excitement to the races—spectators were busily snapping away with their cameras in the Japanese tradition. But their photography of the emperor and our call of the race was interrupted rather rudely while a red-haired Norwegian GS racer, Hans Peter Burras, was on course. With a clean run through the upper set of gates, he suddenly missed a gate for no apparent reason.

Well actually there could have been a reason. An earthquake in fact, that may have thrown him off course and violently shook our already shaky scaffolding—sending TV monitors, and other equipment off of our desktops.

Christin's usually studied commentary on how the Norwegian had missed the gate deteriorated into "Holy fuck, what was that!!" The tremor lasted only a few seconds, but long enough to scare everyone there as the broadcast compound shook violently and the sounds of equipment being thrown around was more than distracting.

Mike Burks came into our headsets with a calm rejoinder, "Guess we'll have to fix that in post, I know you guys can re-create that as though you are doing it live."

"Do want the 'fuck' left in?" I inquired.

The emperor was unhurt, Burras said he hadn't noticed the tremor, but his team asked for a re-run anyway—which was declined by the officials.

As I recall, we retired to the sake bar after the race was over, and I think I sampled more of the offerings than usual.

Arigato and *sayonara* Nagano.

Back in the States after the Nagano Games, the traditional visit by U.S. Olympic teams to Washington D.C to be welcomed by the president was scheduled for April.

I guess most people in America would like to have a chance to visit the White House. Millions have made the effort and have made it happen. More millions have not.

It was not on my to-do list, but when I had the opportunity I didn't say no. I was hosting a series called *Olympic Gold* for the U.S. Olympic Committee and a feature was planned on the Winter Olympics team being honored by the president—in this case, Bill Clinton.

All of the necessary credentials had been provided. The team arrived on time. President Clinton did not. Which gave us the chance to tour the Press Room (nicely captured on the TV series *The West Wing*) and see the space where the world press and broadcast media scramble for the best positions at White House press conferences.

When President Clinton arrived, the U.S. athletes were all assembled in neat rows outside in the Rose Garden. Mr. Clinton, accompanied by wife Hillary, seemed somewhat distracted, and didn't stay too long. Still, the team members have the photographs to mark the recognition of their achievements by the president himself, and to remember all their lives.

After the ceremony—on the lawn with the White House in the background where all of the network news correspondents do their reports—I did an on-camera stand-up to lead in to the feature we shot for *Olympic Gold*.

Bill didn't stop by for a sound-bite.

CHAPTER 40

A Very Busy Decade

More Olympic adventure lay ahead after the turn of the century, but the last of the gay nineties proved very eventful.

Settled in the West, my business travel was generally longer, involving commuter flights from Sun Valley to Salt Lake City and connections from there to NFL cities, college towns for football, and European venues for ski-racing, tennis, and the Olympic Games in Europe and Japan. My plate was even more full than it had been in the eighties.

Earlier I talked about our NFL weekly routine, and how difficult some head coaches could be with the TV announcers. Others I named were helpful and fun to be around. Two more of my favorites were hugely successful—Bill Walsh and Mike Holmgren. I was fortunate to work a number of '49ers games when Walsh had his Super Bowl runs with Joe Montana and Steve Young, and the brilliant receiver Jerry Rice. My partner for a time was former '49er Randy Cross which helped when we worked games in San Francisco on CBS.

Walsh, now deceased, was one of the classiest men in the NFL. He was always welcoming, informative and willing to give us material we could use on the air. He was also an excellent tennis player, and having seen me on telecasts of the U.S. Open, asked if I played. I made the mistake of accepting his offer to play with him the next time we were in San Fran. He beat me easily, but was fun to play with, and a very gracious winner!

His disciple Mike Holmgren became the coach of the Green Bay Packers in 1992 and with Brett Favre as his QB won two National Conference championships and the Super Bowl in 1996. In all the right ways, he was almost a clone of Walsh—patient and helpful with the TV guys, interested in our work, and in us as people. I got to know him well over the years, and during one off-season was delighted to host him and his daughter at a figure-skating event I was involved with in Green Bay.

In 1992 Matt Millen retired as a player after a distinguished career—eight years with the Oakland Raiders and finishing up with Washington. He became a game analyst with me and a couple of other CBS announcers and in his second year had become so good we moved up to the number three slot on the CBS NFL roster. When CBS lost the NFL rights to FOX, Matt joined a number of CBS announcers and production people in moving to FOX where he would be groomed as the successor there to John Madden.

I mentioned Matt earlier in the book as one of my favorite colleagues in the football booth. As tough and nasty as he was as a player, he was as nice and classy a guy as I ever worked with in football. I had hoped we could stay together as a team, but it was not to be. But that last year of CBS football for me, spent with Matt, producer Richie Zyontz, director Artie Kempner on what we called the "Z Team" was the most fun I had doing NFL football.

Matt would frequently bring one or both of his two sons along on road trips, and Matthew Jr.—then about nine or ten—made his mark in NFL television history by crawling under our table in the booth during a game and accidentally unplugging a cable, which took us off the air.

"Ladies and gentlemen, we apologize for our brief technical blackout...."

Along with Matt, Pat Summerall was among the CBS NFL announce staff to move to FOX after the 1993 NFL season, and finally I would become CBS's top tennis announcer in 1994 getting the important matches on Center Court, including the men's finals with Pat's longtime partner, Tony Trabert and the women's finals, with Mary Carillo.

In 1995, Executive Producer Rick Gentile had a bold idea for our Open coverage. When John McEnroe had retired from the circuit, he had joined the USA network, which had the cable coverage of the Open. In 1992 he was signed by NBC to work Wimbledon with Dick Enberg. Gentile was eager to get him onto CBS's U.S. Open coverage.

Gentile's idea was to team up McEnroe with Carillo, with me as the referee. McEnroe had been publicly hostile when Carillo had been used on some men's matches as well as on the women's. The irony was that McEnroe and Carillo had both grown up in the same part of New York, both became tennis pros and teamed up to win the French Open Mixed Doubles while

1995 U.S. Open with John McEnroe.

they were still teenagers. But they had grown apart, taken separate paths, and the idea of getting them to work together on TV seemed a highly unlikely prospect.

Meanwhile, NBC boss Dick Ebersol wanted to hire Carillo as an analyst on Wimbledon's women's matches. Gentile suggested an arrangement that would have NBC allow McEnroe to work the Open on CBS and Carillo to work Wimbledon on NBC. But it was Gentile's idea to pair them together at the Open.

"What do you think, Tim?" Gentile asked, "Would they do it? You're friendly with both of them—would you approach them and see what happens?"

Well I thought it was a great idea—as much as I was opposed to three-person booths covering any sports on TV (and remain so!). This was different. And a challenge. If I could get them to agree, it could be fun at the least—and maybe a hit with tennis fans.

Mary was easy—despite having been hammered in TV columns by McEnroe, she was more than open to the idea. She also saw it as a chance to reconcile with the volatile Irishman. "I've never had a problem with

John," she told me, "but I'm not surprised at his attitude about me working men's matches."

Rick and I sat with McEnroe who was watching a match on an outside court at the Open, a few days before CBS's weekend coverage in 1994. To our surprise, John agreed to try it with Mary and me. We knew that John's wife Patty Smyth had been on him to drop the chauvinistic attitude towards Mary's commentary on men's matches. Now it was up to me to create a platform for a civil, but entertaining dialogue in the TV booth.

We debuted on the Saturday of Labor Day weekend 1995. John arrived late for rehearsal, which became an "as usual." In that now familiar—almost bashful—style of his, he barely looked Mary in the eyes, asked what we wanted him to talk about in the opening, and then promptly left the booth. We were going on the air in about five minutes. Producer Bob Mansbach was yelling into my headset, "Where's McEnroe!"

"Don't worry," I replied, "He'll be here." Nerves were a little taut.

John reappeared (just in time) opening titles rolled, we were off and running. John and Mary re-unite. They were a hit—viewers and TV media loved the banter between them and the expert commentary provided. So for the next four years—including the move in 1997 into the new Arthur Ashe Stadium Court at Flushing Meadow—we had a great time covering many of the big matches on CBS's traditional weekend coverage.

That span saw the dominance of Pete Sampras and Steffi Graf each winning two in a row, and then Patrick Rafter of Australia and Martina Hingis winning in 1997. That final year for me in the CBS broadcast booth at the Open saw the emergence of Venus Williams, who at age seventeen, made it to the final against Hingis, marking the beginning of the historic tennis saga of the Williams sisters.

CHAPTER 41

People of Good Value

By the time I left CBS in 1998, I had covered tennis for them since 1978—twenty U.S. Opens and a handful of other tournaments they owned. Tennis people, like ski people, not only compete in individual sports, but enjoy a special culture that I was lucky enough to get next to and treasure to this day. Some of my best friends in life come from these two sports. The first to make an impact from the tennis world was Billie Jean King.

Before my CBS days, I covered the Open in reports for WPIX when the tournament was still played on grass courts at Forest Hills. I interviewed Billie before and after her wins there in 1971 and 1972. My wife Lee—an avid tennis player—had come with me to the '71 championship match. After her win in the final over her friend Rosie Casals, Billie Jean was clutching the engraved trophy and prize money check and the gold tennis-ball charm each champion received. When we finished the TV interview Billie asked Lee about her tennis, and then suddenly said, "Here Lee, I want you to have this," and handed her the gold charm.

"And remember, drink lots of water during your matches—even if you have to go to the bathroom on the changeovers! Hydrate, hydrate!"

The following year, when I was at NBC, Billie won again, beating Kerry Melville of Australia and insisted I take the gold tennis ball charm home to Lee—to add to her charm bracelet. Through the years I would see Billie at the tournaments, interviewing her several times and most often listening to her pitching her sport and her creation—"World Team Tennis"—to anyone who would listen. We worked together on CBS telecasts of the Open in 1978 and 1979.

She is a remarkable woman, a remarkable person—with a remarkable history.

Often I am asked who are the greatest athletes I have covered—from any sport. My response is always the same. There are many great athletes, but two in my lifetime have taken their sports and their athletic achievements outside of their field of plays and made an impact on a greater, world-wide society: Muhammad Ali and Billie Jean King. Ali became an unofficial ambassador for his country and race relations and Billie has become one of the most significant spokespersons for women's rights and equal pay for women tennis players.

Many years after her kind gestures to Lee, Billie Jean was among several of my tennis friends who, when learning about Lee's Alzheimer's made a point of offering her sympathies to me in person. On one of those occasions at the Open in the late nineties I asked Billie to lunch and told her I had something to give her. I returned the two tennis ball charms. She was surprised and grateful, telling me that her mother had the other two gold tennis balls from her wins at the Open and would now have all four on her charm bracelet—and would know that two had come from Lee Ryan.

During that horrific period when Lee was inexorably drifting away from us, my friends in tennis were among the most thoughtful and kind.

At one of the Opens, Martina Navratilova—another great lady—actually stopped her game-day practice session on Center Court when she spotted me nearby, and came over to me to offer her sympathy for our ordeal. Fellow commentators, Bud Collins, Mary Carillo, and Pam Shriver were especially sweet and caring during that time.

Best of them all was John Newcombe, the great Aussie champion. I had actually met him for the first time in the late seventies when we worked together on one of Billie Jean's World Team Tennis championship matches. We became instant friends, and worked together on World Championship tennis events and in my early years for CBS at the U.S. Open. I got to know his Aussie beer-drinking buddies, Fred Stolle and Tony Roche and with other of his American friends, Bill Dorman, a cheese company owner, and Gene Barakat an executive with Eileen Ford's modeling agency, we spent many late nights during the Opens at Jim McMullen's saloon on the Upper East Side.

"Newk" holds a special place in my heart as one of the best people I know, period. I think of him as a brother, not just a friend. We have visited in each other's homes—and have helped each other through difficult times. His wife Angela ("Angie") is indeed an angel, and I miss seeing them more often since our homes are now so far apart.

Ah, yes… the McEnroes.

John and I had met professionally—when I was the studio announcer and courtside interviewer on CBS coverage in the early eighties—during his greatest years as a player. He was the biggest thing in tennis, winning four U.S. Opens between 1979 and 1984. My most memorable interview with him was at courtside after a win in the late eighties when he brought his young son Kevin (his first-born by first wife Tatum O'Neil) onto the court beside him. It had been another tumultuous winning performance for him with obscenities heard over the TV microphones. I bravely (since we were already friends) asked him if he wasn't embarrassed about swearing on national TV with his young son within earshot in the family box seats.

Somewhat taken aback, he dropped his chin, and said ruefully, "I'm not proud of that and I've got to get over that stuff now that I am a father."

Over the next few years John—and in fact his father John Sr. and mother Kay—and I became casual friends, and when Lee's Alzheimers became public news nationally, they were graciously sympathetic. The true colors of the "brat" John McEnroe and his pugnacious father, and his quiet, talented brother Patrick came to the fore in a request I made of John in 1997. But telling that story will have to wait because part of it is linked to other events in the nineties.

CHAPTER 42

A Diamond Investment

When Lee and I moved to Ketchum, Idaho in October of '91, one of the first people to welcome us was a man named Pete Smith. I hadn't known him during our previous "second home" life in Sun Valley in the eighties. Pete had heard about why we had chosen to settle there full-time. His father was also an Alzheimer's victim and he was offering his understanding and experience. It was a generous and helpful gesture on his part. Knowing of my life in sports, he told me I should meet Bill Pereira, a local friend of his with whom Pete had invested in the Boise Hawks minor-league baseball team. (Boise was a two-and-half hour drive from Ketchum/Sun Valley.) Bill and his investors were forming a company called Diamond Sports with which he planned to buy another minor-league team—in Sioux City, Iowa—and Pete thought I might be interested in joining their group.

Pereira is a die-hard baseball fan. A Stanford graduate, he had been in advertising, journalism (with *Newsweek* magazine) and a founding partner in Air California—a commuter airline. His family, wife Susan and five children had come to Sun Valley from California so that daughter Susan could pursue her interest in figure-skating at the famed Sun Valley Lodge ice facilities. When the Boise Hawks baseball team came up for sale, he had jumped into his passion. Now he wanted to grow the company and involve his three sons in it along with invited investors.

What intrigued me was that Diamond Sports would have a chance to partner with investors in Boise to build an arena and acquire a hockey franchise in the expanding West Coast Hockey League. I would be buying into a chance to return to my roots in hockey—but in Boise, Idaho, not Canada.

I signed on with Bill, Pete Smith, and a handful of other investors just as the group was buying its second baseball team, the Sioux City Explorers (Iowa) of the independent Northern League. By 1995, we had joined up with the business and real estate people who had built the arena in Boise, modeled after Toronto's baseball stadium by featuring a hotel with luxury suites overlooking the ice surface, and topped with penthouse apartments. We obtained the hockey franchise in the West Coast League, and named our team the Steelheads after a salmon-trout popular with Idaho anglers. In the fall of 1997 pro hockey arrived in Idaho and I was back in the puck business.

Being the only hockey maven in our ownership group, I was elected to hire the general manager and coach. Matt Loughran had worked in the New York Rangers organization, and a friend of mine recommended him to me. While normally the GM would hire the coach, I felt Matt was too inexperienced to have that responsibility. I was still friends with many NHL execs who could recommend a coach. My old friend Bill Torrey of the Islander days, and who was now GM of the NHL Florida Panthers, suggested one of his former Islanders stars, Dave Langevin, who was just starting a coaching career. I hired Matt and Dave.

It turned out I was wrong on both counts—after our inaugural season with a poor record, and infighting between Loughran and Langevin, I fired them both. Then I fired myself!

The Steelheads are still in business and have won two championships in the expanded East Coast Hockey League.

Our group also bought a World Team Tennis franchise, which we named the Idaho Sneakers, and my friend Billie Jean King—founder of the league—was delighted to have me involved. Two then-unknown twins from California, Mike and Bob Bryan were our doubles stars, and have since gone on to become the best doubles team in the history of the sport. We also bought a local radio station in Boise, KTIK, to carry the games of the Hawks and the Steelheads.

Diamond Sports formed an entertainment company when Bill Pereira's son Cord hooked up with another entrepreneur who had created an innovative scoring system that enabled spectators to electronically vote from their seats at contests taking place in arenas. Another Pereira son, Kirk, was well connected in the figure-skating world, and together they came up with an idea called *The Great Skate Debate*, featuring top professional skating stars in competition for prize money, with the fans in the arena, and later those at home watching on TV, determining the winners instead of professional judges.

We sold the idea to CBS Sports, and in May of 1996 *The Great Skate Debate* made its debut with stars including Scott Hamilton, Kurt Browning, Katarina Witt, and Nancy Kerrigan. A second show in 1998 added internet scoring from fans watching in their homes. Our success led us to open a Diamond Sports office in New York, and we hired former CBS Sports executive Rick Gentile to run the operation. Our plans were to create other competitions in other sports to include fan-voting, but an internal dispute over the rights to the voting technology led to a lawsuit, and ultimately to the dissolution of the company.

Meanwhile we bought another minor league baseball team—the Double A Texas League El Paso Diablos. But by 2005, the fun was over, and we sold all our properties, took our profits (somewhat diminished by my ill-fated idea of opening the New York operation) and closed the doors of Diamond Sports.

A highlight of that era for me came in 1997 when with the help of Cord Pereira, who was managing the arena in Boise, and our Sneakers tennis team, I was able to stage a fundraiser for the Alzheimer's Association. I was still then a member of the national Board of Directors, and there was not a moment in the day that my thoughts were not about Lee and the devastation of the disease. She was now being cared for at the Good Samaritan Village in Boise, and would have loved to be able to enjoy watching our tennis team. That, unfortunately, was impossible due to the rapid advance of the disease that had already stolen her mind and disabled her body. But when I came to visit with her, I told her of my plans anyway, holding her hands and pretending to myself that she could comprehend what I was saying to her.

Still, her eyes seemed to light up when I told her that Pete Sampras and John McEnroe would be playing at our arena in Boise—playing for the "Lee Ryan Trophy."

CHAPTER 43

Promises Kept and Class Prevails

It was called the Rally against Alzheimer's which I and my Diamond Sports partners had organized at our Bank of America Center in Boise—a fundraiser for Alzheimer's research in honor of my wife Lee. My idea was that maybe I could prevail on a couple of U.S. tennis stars to play a fun exhibition match in Boise at our arena, and have our Sneakers team play an opening match featuring our star doubles pair, the Bryan brothers.

It could only happen if I didn't have to pay fees, just expenses, to the players. While covering the 1997 U.S. Open for CBS, I learned that four pros—all Nike endorsers and clients of IMG, the same talent agency that represents me—were playing an exhibition for Nike in Oregon in November. That is in the down season on the tennis tour—after the U.S. Open and prior to the year-opening Australian Open.

The players who had agreed to Nike's request to play the event in Portland, a short flight by private jet from Boise, were John McEnroe, Jim Courier, Marcelo Rios and…Pete Sampras.

Sampras had won the two previous U.S. Opens in '95 and '96. I covered those matches for CBS. In 1997 he was upset in the fourth round by Peter Korda. After his loss, I made my way to the men's locker room to speak with Pete; he was unhappy with his loss of course, but polite. I had known him since his first U.S. Open appearance and had interviewed him in our CBS studios and on-court.

I told him Lee's story—that she was dying from Alzheimer's, losing more quality of life day-by-day, unable to speak or walk on her own. I told him I was a member of the Board of Directors of the Alzheimer's Association and was doing whatever I could to help them raise money for more research.

I told him my idea for the tennis event in Boise and that I knew he would be playing the Nike show in Portland. I told him that John McEnroe had already agreed to play him if it was just a two-of-three sets match or a pro-set (one ten-game set, first player to win eight games). I told him that we would arrange for a private jet to fly him from Portland to Boise and return the same evening and that Nike had agreed to fly him home to California from there. I told him that it had been suggested by IMG that maybe I could get all four players to come to Boise and make it a "fun-doubles" match. (McEnroe and Courier were fine with that, but the surly Rios declined.)

Pete said yes, he would play. I said I would work out the details with his agent from IMG, whom I knew, Jeff Schwartz. That was early September. Our date in Boise was set for November, the night after the four would play in Portland. One of our partners in the arena operation offered to provide a private jet free of charge.

Then things started to unravel. Just as we were beginning ticket sales and preparing the souvenir program. Rios had IMG tell me he was not available, period. Jim Courier suggested Jim Grabb, an experienced doubles player, to replace Rios. While I was mulling that, Sampras' agent called me about two weeks before the scheduled date in Boise.

"Tim, I'm sorry but Pete can't play in your event. He's very sorry."

"Why not, Jeff? He had committed to me. He knows the whole story about my wife and my involvement in Alzheimer's fundraising. Why is he not playing?"

"He's tired," said Schwartz, "It's been a long season, he's just too tired and he's going to take the rest of the season off."

"Jeff, I already knew that. But he's playing the Nike event in Portland right?"

"Well… yes, of course but…"

"And he didn't have the nerve or class to call me himself. The program is going to press in a few days—we have already promoted that he will be there—this is devastating to me! You tell him I want him to call me himself, not to use you."

Sampras did call the next day, but was unmoved by my plea to play or my obvious anger and frustration.

So there we were, no Sampras, no Rios, and so I decided to go with a singles match between McEnroe and Courier. We get to the Boise media, tell them about the change (covering for Sampras with some excuse) and print the program just a few days before the event. On the cover:

"Tim Ryan and his Tennis Friends Present *Rally Against Alzheimer's* Featuring John McEnroe vs. Jim Courier"

What else could go wrong now? Well I was in Denver, Colorado in a recording studio doing a voiceover for a ski show when I was interrupted by an urgent phone call. Two days before our event. It's Jim Courier.

"Tim. You won't believe this, and I am so sorry, I know what you've been through with Pete, but I have a torn bicep muscle. I just did it a few days ago, and I have been trying to hit with it, but it's impossible."

I believed Jim because he is a high-quality guy I had known since he turned pro.

Now what? Program printed. Two days to go.

I take a break from the voiceover session and try to find John McEnroe to tell him about Courier and ask if maybe he can get his brother Patrick on very short notice to fill in. I had no luck locating him. I call his father John Sr. at his law office in New York.

I reach "Big John," explain where I am, and explain my problem. Does he have Patrick's number?

"Don't worry," says John Sr. "Patrick will be there. Go back to your work. I'll have him call you. I'll tell John what's happening. Good luck with the fundraiser."

Within the hour, I hear from both John and Patrick. They will play each other, will put on a great show, not to worry anymore about anything.

I still don't know who paid to get Patrick from New York to Boise. I had rooms booked in our hotel. We flew John from Portland after the Nike event. The next morning, he appeared on the arena tennis court unasked, unannounced, where the Sneakers were holding a juniors clinic as part of our event. He hit with some of the kids, joked around with the Bryan brothers (who would later be his doubles team when he was Captain of the U.S. Davis Cup squad).

The abrasive, combative, occasionally even rude John McEnroe showed the side that I had known for years—a sensitive, caring man (yes, with an Irish temper!), a man of his word, a great husband and father, generous to a fault, loyal to friends, entertaining, and always willing to help a good cause.

His brother Patrick—a little less excitable—has all of John's good

LEFT: Lee Ryan Trophy.
RIGHT: With John and Patrick McEnroe and Harlan Estate wine.

qualities in kind. I still can't thank him enough for jumping in literally at the last minute to help us out. And of course I owe eternal gratitude to John Sr., who no doubt gave Patrick no choice when he tracked him down and got him to Boise!

The show was terrific. We had 5,000 spectators who helped us raise $75,000 for the Alzheimer's Association. The McEnroes put on a competitive and very entertaining best-of-three set match, complete with John faking a temper tantrum with the chair umpire before winning the match in three sets.

Then John borrowed Cord Pereira's guitar and took the stage joining the Bryan brothers and their father Wayne in an impromptu rock session that the audience loved.

His victory over Patrick earned John the Lee Ryan Trophy, a unique prize consisting of a double-magnum of the world-famous Harlan Estate red wine, donated by my friends Bill and Deborah Harlan of Napa Valley. An engraved sterling silver necklace on the bottle identified the event.

Friends at CBS Sports, HBO Sports and Rolex bought ads in the program along with local Boise companies, adding to our fundraising effort. All told, the event was a great success, thanks to the classy commitment of John McEnroe and his family.

177

CHAPTER 44

Dinner with "the Chairman of the Board"

Two years earlier in 1995, I was visiting friends in the Palm Springs area, when a serendipitous event turned into a very entertaining evening, featuring a champion of a different kind.

Bill and Phyllis Dorman, whom I mentioned in a previous chapter as friends of John Newcombe, invited me to their winter home in La Quinta for drinks. They had invited a woman friend of Phyllis's to join us. Joyce Bosworth was a real-estate agent, single and very nice. After cocktails, she went on her way, whereupon Bill told me that the following evening she was going to a dinner party, and didn't have an escort. The party was at the home of her friend Barbara Knox, better known as Barbara Sinatra—the fourth wife of Frank.

In his wonderful bombastic fashion, Bill said I should go with her. Phyllis agreed and said she would call her friend right away and that Joyce would be delighted if I agreed. I said that sounded just great but that I had a flight home in the morning.

"Change it!" thundered Bill, "It's at Sinatra's for goddsake... are you crazy, who would turn that down? You gotta go!"

"Okay, okay you two, I'll go!"

So I went. Their friend was nice enough to pick me up with her car. This was my first "date" and that made me a little nervous, but the Dormans had explained my circumstances to Joyce and she was very kind and respectful.

The Sinatra home was actually a compound of buildings in Rancho Mirage, a suburb of Palm Springs. A valet took our car. Joyce explained that it was movie night—on Sundays, Frank and Barbara invited ten to twenty people, served cocktails, and then showed a movie following dinner.

There was a kind of reception line as we entered the house. Frank was first to greet the arriving guests, Barbara next to him. Joyce preceded me and introduced me to Frank. I reminded him that we had met once before, several years ago at Bill Fugazy's Collegiate Golf awards dinner in New York (which I had emceed that year), but that I didn't expect him to remember that occasion. He looked at me blankly, and there was something in his eyes that I recognized. It was that lifeless glaze that I knew so well in my beloved Lee. I surmised to myself that perhaps Frank was in the early stages of Alzheimer's. Of course it was an unprofessional, if somewhat informed diagnosis on my part. But it stayed with me. Sinatra was about to be eighty. Barbara and friends had planned a big birthday celebration a few weeks later in Palm Springs.

After cocktails in a lounge room with a bar area, a waiter serving drinks with paper cocktail napkins embossed with "Old Blue Eyes," we were then directed to the dining room. Dinner was a hoot. There were two large tables each seating eight to ten people. Barbara sat at our table to be near her friend Joyce. Our table partners included the actress/dancer Ginger Rogers, the former Vice President of the United States—he of Moral Majority fame—Spiro Agnew, and the widow of the great musical lyricist Jimmy van Heusen (a Sinatra favorite) who was confined to a wheelchair but whose spunk was displayed when asked if she would like to check her purse and replied, "Hell, no," and opened it to display a small jeweled handgun!

Sinatra sat at an adjacent table with what can best be described as the supporting cast from the film *Goodfellas*. I don't mean to suggest they were not good, law-abiding citizens—they were possibly just friends of the chef who turned out a terrific spaghetti dinner.

Following dinner, we were all directed to another building in the compound, a two-or three-minute stroll in the desert moonlight to what was Frank's cinema—a full-on large-screen theater with plush, comfy chairs and settees, and of course a bar and wait-staff at the ready. Joyce and I parked ourselves in adjacent cushioned chairs and Barbara sat nearby. Frank hovered near the door behind us.

Lights were dimmed and the film began: *Priscilla, Queen of the Desert.*

Yikes! A film about a cross-dressing, gay-lesbian band touring small villages in the Australian outback!

Frank's audience was in his age-group. Gradually and silently, within the first fifteen minutes of the film, most of them slipped quietly out of the screening room. Joyce and I were actually enjoying the amusing send-up, but were taking our cue from Barbara Sinatra.

She was obviously embarrassed by the film's racy content and said to us she had no idea what the movie was about when she asked one of the staff to order the weekly film for her.

"What does Frank think of it?" I bravely asked.

"Oh he's already gone to bed," replied Barbara. "I don't think he would have liked it—but he doesn't usually make it all the way through the movies anyway."

I didn't return to Palm Springs for Frank's eightieth. Two years later he died of heart failure—according to information offered by the family.

Old Blue Eyes—still the most important singer of the American Songbook. My Sirius satellite radio is always tuned to "Siriusly Sinatra."

CHAPTER 45

Changes

When I moved from NBC to CBS in 1977, I was in control of my destiny. That was not true when I returned to NBC in 1998.

After my spat with CBS Sports President Sean McManus over my role at the U.S. Open tennis tournament, his course of action was to reduce my roles across the board, and my contract dollars as well. My agent, Barry Frank, now a vice president at IMG had hired me away from NBC back in 1977 when he was the sports boss at CBS. McManus—son of famed announcer Jim McKay—had been Barry's protégé as an agent at IMG and eventually got the CBS job. When I consulted with Barry on the reduced deal offered by Sean, he said there was nothing out there for me at the moment and recommended I take it.

The 1998 Nagano Olympics still lay ahead in February, as well as the NCAA basketball tournament a month later. My contract would expire after the tournament. I had a bad taste in my mouth after McManus had reneged on my arrangement with former CBS president Neal Pilson to take over the top role on tennis when Pat Summerall left for FOX. I had the big-match spot from 1994 to 1997, when Jim Nantz was assigned to it, and I was dropped to number two. Jim had just signed a big contract with the network and was annointed, "the face of CBS Sports." I knew then my days at CBS were numbered.

Barry said he would shop me around during the Olympics when I would have good exposure covering the alpine skiing. He and I were on the phone regularly. ESPN showed some interest, although Barry warned me it was a "factory"—working its announcers heavily and not paying very much since it was cable, with a smaller audience than broadcast TV.

My thoughts were that we should wait until the Japan Olympics were over—the rights for the next six Games had been acquired by NBC, and I thought they might give me a look. But Barry called me in Japan with an offer from ESPN. When I said let's wait, he said he had committed me. I was not happy with that, but I hadn't signed anything. I would wait until I got home from Nagano and make a decision.

This circumstance was unlike in December of 1986 when my CBS contract was up. I was in the driver's seat. CBS wanted me to stay and offered more money in a new deal. I held the leverage, since ABC boss Dennis Swanson was campaigning mightily to get me to move to his sports division. He was offering me a number of different sports, including boxing, college football, some tennis and the role of hockey announcer at the '88 Olympics in Calgary. Ultimately I chose to stay at CBS, with a new and better contract and more money—matching the offer from ABC.

Sure enough, the morning after arriving back in Ketchum from the Nagano Olympics, the phone rang. It was Dick Ebersol, the president of NBC Sports who had pulled off the bidding coup of grabbing the next six Olympics starting with Sydney, Australia in 2000 through 2012.

"I've been watching you from Nagano," he said, "I especially liked your weather reports when you were outside with the snow piling up on your head!"

He wanted me for the alpine ski events at the Winter Games, and to cover boxing at the Summer Games.

A couple of hours later, Ed Goren, president of FOX Sports called. One of my best friends during our years together at CBS, he had a need for an NFL announcer, and offered a two-year deal.

I called Barry and told him of the day's windfall of offers from two networks.

"That's great Tim but I have you committed to ESPN—I can't tell them you are not coming."

"But Barry, I haven't signed anything—you have to admit this is a much better offer, you just have to tell ESPN I'm not signing."

"Okay Tim, but I guess this means we are 'divorcing,'" meaning he would no longer represent me after twenty years together.

Well, when things cooled down, Barry negotiated my deals with both

NBC and FOX, making me the first sports announcer to have contracts with two broadcast networks at the same time.

Said Barry, "I guess we're married again!"

Well, not exactly. But the decade was ending on a high note in my business life and in my personal life as well.

I finished my CBS contract with my 17th NCAA basketball tournament, working the last one with my much-loved Al McGuire. It was bittersweet. Knowing it was my last event for CBS after twenty-two years, I made a point of speaking to our entire sports department at the production seminar before the tournament began in March of '98. I wasn't invited to speak—I just walked to the microphone after the new executive producer Terry Ewart had finished his remarks, and took the podium.

I said goodbye to all of my friends and colleagues, thanked them for the great times and great events we had worked together over two decades, and assured them that I would not be out of work.

Sean McManus, who entered the room later to speak to the troops, made no comment about me then, or after I finished my March Madness tournament schedule with Al McGuire on the weekend of the "Elite Eight."

Show biz is not all tinsel and glamor!

That fall of 1998, I returned to NFL coverage after twenty years of doing it on CBS. Ed Goren asked me to try a three-man booth with two rookies—the great defensive back of the '49ers Ronnie Lott and an all-pro tackle with the Kansas City Chiefs, Bill Maas. I appreciated Ed's trust in me to help the rookies succeed, but despite effort on everyone's part, including our game producer Mike Burks, (another former CBS colleague) it just didn't work.

My return to NFL football ended at the end of that season.

CHAPTER 46

Can't We Do More?

As for my family life, my children and I were still struggling with the harsh reality of Lee's illness. Now that my schedule was lighter, I would visit her more frequently in Boise at the Good Samaritan Village skilled nursing facility—each time seeing her disappear from us a little more. She would smile and nod vigorously when I came into her room but couldn't speak a word, or walk under her own power. Her days were spent in a wheelchair, her nights in the darkness of Alzheimer's. I remain grateful for the wonderful caregiving provided by the loving staff at the Village.

When I was asked to become a member of the National Board of the Alzheimer's Association, I served on various committees—including the Public Policy Committee, chaired by the late Maureen Reagan who had watched her father succumb to the terrible disease. We would advocate for more research funds by visiting congressmen during our annual Forum in Washington, D.C., and testify at Senate hearings. I was among those who spoke at a hearing, telling my story of Lee's agonizing disease and excoriating health insurance companies for not providing coverage to Alzheimer's victims with "pre-existing conditions."

I remember several senators wandering in to make saccharine comments in our support (just to have their remarks be included in the Congressional Record) and then departing apologetically for "other Senate business."

One of the most moving experiences during my eight-year tenure on the board occurred one year at the Forum when we had a candlelight ceremony at the Lincoln Memorial, honoring victims and their families.

I had done several emotionally difficult interviews in print with *People* Magazine and in *The New York Times* and on television, with *CBS Morning*

News, twice with CNN's Larry King and a wrenching one at home with Connie Chung, then host of CBS's *48 Hours*. I had offered to come to the CBS studio in New York, but Connie and her producer wanted her to come to our Sun Valley home where I could provide photographs of Lee and our family in better times.

It was not an easy day. But I realized these interviews and speeches were worth the pain if we could increase awareness of a still little-known disease and help to eradicate it.

That night in Washington, I was introduced by the accomplished actor David Hyde-Pierce whose mother had died of Alzheimer's. David gave a kind introduction and I felt ready to read my stump speech about the loss of Lee to that horrific disease. But looking out at hundreds of flickering candles under the night sky held by fellow family victims in front of me, with the lights beamed on the statue of Lincoln casting a glow from behind, I found myself choking up as I recounted Lee's dark journey of terror over twelve years—a wife, a mother, an athlete, a poet taken before her time.

With the help of a reassuring hand of David's on my shoulder, I was able to complete my remarks to gentle applause from the folks with their candles, whose own stories were much the same as mine.

CHAPTER 47

New Beginnings

The nineties had been packed with life and career events, experiences and changes. Some had been easier to deal with than others. The things I had hoped for in my TV sports life had been achieved. My bet that my versatility would pay off in the chance to see the world on someone else's nickel was a win. Boxing, ski racing, and tennis had delivered the opportunity to soak up the cultures of Europe, Africa, Asia, and South America, to learn bits of language, sample foreign cuisines, see historic places and meet interesting people—many of whom remain lifelong friends.

Yes, I sacrificed the big money paid to the "face-time" people like my contemporaries Brent Musburger, Bryant Gumbel, and later, Bob Costas. But I had enough time hosting studio shows to know that the real fun and life-enhancement was on the road—covering the sports dramas in stadiums and arenas around the world. And I was paid well enough to pay the rent, college tuitions, live comfortably and as it turned out, to cover the enormous expense of Lee's care.

Even the otherwise excellent health coverage provided by AFTRA—the performers union of which I was a longtime member—paid little of the caregiving and medical costs of Alzheimer's disease—a travesty that will be ameliorated somewhat under the new Affordable Healthcare Act. Thanks to my TV earnings, from the time Lee was identified with the disease in early 1991 until her death twelve years later, I was able to pay for all the costs of her care "off the hip." But of course it meant continuing to travel to work, and limited time to be with Lee as the disease took its inevitable toll.

Also inevitably during that time—after Lee had been moved to the care facility in Santa Barbara following four years with nursing care at home in

Sun Valley, well-meaning friends encouraged me to consider dating. I was not ready to even consider that idea—my focus was on doing all I could do to care for my loved one in the best ways possible. It took a couple of more years before I put my toe in the water, seeing a recently divorced local woman friend in Sun Valley. That tentative attempt at a social life was followed soon after by a relationship with another divorced lady who lived nearby. That brief romance ended badly when she realized that my heart was still with Lee, and would be until she died—and even longer.

Meanwhile my great friend Jack Hemingway (yes, that Jack Hemingway—first-born son of Ernest) and his wife Angela had been plotting to introduce me to a new friend of theirs in New York. It was late August, 1996—I would be in New York for the U.S. Open tennis, Jack (my neighbor in Ketchum) was speaking at a salmon-fishing organization dinner in the city and hoping that I could get him tickets to the Open. When we assembled in New York, I suggested to Angela we have drinks at their hotel.

Her name was Patricia Benedict. She was tall, green-eyed and beautiful. Divorced, with two adult children. Vivacious and bright. Angela cleverly suggested that since my off-night from calling the tennis was the same night Jack was speaking at the salmon dinner, why didn't she, Patricia, and I have dinner together?

At a small neighborhood Italian near my hotel, we learned over pasta that Patricia and I have the same Taurean birthday, May 16, and that Angela—another Taurus—was a May 13 baby. This coincidence seemed to hold great weight with the ladies.

I didn't see Patricia again until the following year, although I had called her a couple of times from Sun Valley suggesting we get together when I was in New York. That would again be for the U.S. Open. We dined together again. Romance blossomed, and love soon bloomed. She came to visit in Sun Valley, and a long-distance relationship began.

Patricia was extremely respectful of Lee and our circumstances. She understood my commitment and accepted that my first priority would be Lee until the inevitable end came, and that the long goodbye would bring a painful period of mourning.

CHAPTER 48

The Gift of Lee

September 13, 1939–December 17, 2002

The phone call had come from Boise's Samaritan Village—a call telling me I better come as soon as possible.

A week before, I had received a similar call at home—at about nine in the evening. It was December, but luckily driving conditions were dry through the flats of ranchland below Sun Valley and through the high mountain pass and twisting two-lane highway to the freeway leading to Boise. Wildlife crossing the roads were a bigger concern than slippery roads at night. A range of emotions and tearful fears that I may not make it to the nursing facility in time had me tightly gripping the steering wheel.

When I arrived near midnight, visibly shaken by the circumstances, the nurses told me that Lee was actually doing a little better—her vital signs had improved. When I entered her room, she was sleeping comfortably. I kissed her forehead and held her hand.

I overnighted at my son Kevin's house and drove back to Sun Valley the next morning—knowing I would be making the drive to Boise again very soon. In fact, it was just a few days later, on the 17th, that I was again at Lee's bedside. When the doctor told me she was failing, I called Kevin, and my daughter Kim, who were both living in Boise at the time. Brendan had flown in from the East. All three had been with their Mom earlier that day. But before they could get back to Samaritan Village, their Mom slipped away—finally free of the prison that is Alzheimer's disease. I telephoned son Jay back East with the sad news.

I can't be sure that Lee knew it was me beside her bed when she breathed her last, that I was there holding her hand, kissing her cheek, whispering a loving goodbye. I hope so.

If there was a consolation, it was that Lee had finally escaped the terror of her killer, Alzheimer's disease.

Arrangements were made. A small funeral in Ketchum at Our Lady of the Snows, her ashes

The beauty that was Lee.

buried in the cemetery where Ernest Hemingway is an honored guest, a memorial service planned in New York so our Westchester County friends and old friends and family from Toronto days could more easily attend. Nearly a hundred of them came.

I gathered the collection of Lee's inspired and lyrical poetry, along with some of my favorite photographs of her and privately published an anthology titled, *The Gift of Lee*. It has brought both tears and smiles to great friends around the world who loved her so.

She was 61, but the thief of Alzheimer's had stolen the last eleven years of what should have been the prime of her life. The inscription on her gravestone in the Ketchum cemetery is the same as the book title. Lee was truly a gift to us all.

CHAPTER 49

Horses, Courses, and Courts

2000 had been an Olympic year with the Summer Games in Sydney, Australia scheduled for August. In May, Patricia and I had traveled to Paris for the French Open, and were guests of NBC at Roland Garros. In June, I was hosting the Wimbledon coverage for my old network and when I arrived at the NBC hotel in London, Ken Schanzer—the Number Two to Dick Ebersol—took me aside to tell me that my role for Sydney had changed.

When I signed the Olympics deal with NBC, Ebersol had said since I was the long-time, award-winning boxing announcer at CBS, he would assign me to boxing in Sydney. But NBC had just re-hired Marv Albert, who had been their boxing announcer until a well-publicized legal issue involving a woman other than his wife had briefly sidelined him from his announcing career. Schanzer had been assigned to tell me that Marv would be doing the boxing and they would like me to handle the Equestrian events.

Of course I agreed, although my knowledge of the horse sport was confined to a one-off coverage of the Royal Winter Fair—Canada's top equestrian event—nearly forty years earlier in Toronto. The upside of having to learn about dressage and cross-country and update myself on jumping was that those events in Sydney would take place outdoors in the afternoons, while boxing was indoors and at night. Having never been to Australia, I was grateful to have the evenings free. Patricia was going to make the trip with me, and we would have a chance to visit with my great friend John Newcombe and Patricia could meet his wife Angie.

The one event that had me spooked was dressage, but by the strangest of luck I learned that I would be able to get expert advice right at home in Sun Valley!

ON SOMEONE ELSE'S NICKEL

A prominent family headed by Parry Thomas, a former Las Vegas banker, had a lovely horse farm down the road from Ketchum in Hailey. I knew Parry's daughter Jane and her husband Peter Sturdevant, but didn't know the family had an interest in dressage and the Hanoverian horses that are among the best breeds in the sport. Most of the ranches south of Sun Valley raise beef-cattle and sheep. Hailey has an annual rodeo featuring quarter horses and bucking broncos. Dressage doesn't fit the history of horses in the West.

But not only did the Thomas' own a world-class Hanoverian—bought at auction in Germany—they had a top rider in Debbie McDonald, who with her husband/trainer Bob ran the Thomas farm. Jane Thomas invited me to come and watch Debbie work with Brentina—their goal was to make the U.S. equestrian team and compete four years later at the Athens Olympic Games.

The time I spent at the Thomas farm was an enormous help for my work at Sydney Games, and led to much more in the preparation for Athens.

Sydney was everything as advertised—one of the most beautiful cities in the world, set on a grand harbor with beautiful beaches, the elegant Harbor Bridge and the stunning Sydney Opera House. Patricia and I stayed at the NBC hotel very near the harbor, but it was a forty-minute drive each day to the equestrian venue. Melanie Smith-Taylor, a former U.S. Team gold medalist in jumping was my expert commentator, and we had a great moment of excitement during the individual jumping competition when America's top rider David O'Connor won the gold medal, despite nearly losing his way and having to course-correct quickly with the allowed time ticking down. It provided a dramatic finish to the event, which naturally made NBC's primetime show.

We managed to fake our way through the dressage competition, but were just spectators for the eventing, which was relegated by the NBC brass to a videotaped feature with narration by newsman Harry Smith.

The highlight for Patricia was a water-taxi ride to the famous Doyle's fish restaurant across the harbor, with great views of the bridge with its lighted Olympic Rings, under a clear sky showing off the Galaxy of the Southern Cross. It was a highlight for me too! We also got to see the Newcombe's beach house north of Sydney, meet their daughters Gigi and Tanya and son Clint, and journey up to their farm where Angie—a former tennis pro herself—has become quite the farmer!

LEFT: 2000 Olympics, Sydney, Australia: Patricia with Angie and John Newcombe.
RIGHT: Vail with Picabo Street.

My highlight—apart from covering my first Summer Olympics, was a tennis match Newk arranged at White City, the famous old tennis club in Sydney where pro matches and Davis Cups had been played for years. But because the Australian Open in Melbourne was switching from grass to hard courts, White City—which still staged an ATP tournament, was tearing out its grass courts and replacing them with hard. One of the grass show courts was still there—for about another week! Newk got former Aussie stars, Ashley Cooper and a good club member at White City, to come and play doubles with us on one of the days before the Olympics began.

To say it was a thrill for a mediocre club player (me) to team with John Newcombe and play another Aussie great is putting it mildly. We split sets and then went to a tie-break to settle it. Fortunately for me, it was Newk's serve at match point. Ace.

Of course Newk carried me through the match, and the other guys gave me some balls to hit, but nevertheless, it was great fun and to find out we had just played the very last match on that historic court. It was gone the next day.

Meanwhile another star athlete from the Sun Valley area was prepping for the 2002 Olympic Winter Games in Salt Lake City—Picabo Street. Picabo had dominated women's downhill racing since the 1994 Lillehammer Games and winning gold in super-G in 1998 at Nagano, after missing all of 1997 with a knee injury. A month after the Olympics she crashed in a World Cup race and was off skis for nearly two years, missing the 1999 World's in Vail where she worked with me as our expert commentator on NBC's coverage. But she was set on making a comeback for the only Olympic Games where she could compete in her own country, the 2002 Salt Lake Games.

I have often said to folks who ask about her that she is one of the most remarkable and interesting athletes I have known. Tough as nails, honest and forthright, funny, talkative, and determined. Dr. Richard Steadman, the renowned orthopedic knee surgeon who operated on her (and many other famous athletes) several times was astounded that she wanted to know everything about the surgeries, learned all of the medical terms, watched the operations on a video screen, and was able to describe her symptoms to him as though she was a medical student!

Unfortunately, her dream of another Olympic medal at Salt Lake City was not to be. She simply didn't have enough training time after the surgeries, and finished 16th in the downhill. Now retired, she is part-time TV commentator and mother of three boys.

Canadian Olympic downhiller Todd Brooker and I debuted as a team at the World Championships in St. Anton in 2001, and went on to do several more World's and the Olympics in Salt Lake, Torino, and Vancouver, joined along the way by reporter Steve Porino. Our team also called the World Cup races in Aspen and Beaver Creek each World Cup season.

The St. Anton, Austria World Alpine Championships were animated by the unexpected appearance during the racing of Russia's President Vladimir Putin. We were staying at a small family hotel in St. Christophe, a tiny village next to St. Anton. It was across the street from an historic, luxurious hotel, the Arlberg Hospiz. We could see the entrance from our hotel room. We knew something was up when the hotel staff was lining up outside to greet someone obviously important—the women in dirndls, the men in lederhosen, a band in military attire. A caravan arrived with lights flashing, Russian flags on the limousines.

That night, Todd and I were doing a voiceover in the broadcast booth at the bottom of the race hill. It was about 9:30, and we were the only TV people at the venue. To our left was the slalom course, where the next night the men's race would take place under the lights. Right now, it was pitch dark. Just as we were about to finish our work, the lights on the course suddenly switched on, and the ski lift started moving. It was now 11 p.m.

What could the course workers be doing at this hour?

Four men got onto the chairlift. A few minutes later we could see two of them skiing down the hill. You guessed it—Putin! He was skiing with what we presumed was a bodyguard, and two more were waiting for him at the bottom. In a few minutes he was gone as quickly and silently as he had appeared.

It's good to be czar....

The lights went off, and would be off until the race the next night, which was won by the way, by hometown Austrian Mario Matt. He had no bodyguards, and didn't need them!

CHAPTER 50

Carwashes, Bode-Bites, and the Dancing Horse

Salt Lake City was my fourth Winter Olympics and first for NBC. It was great to have Christin back on the women's events and Todd Brooker and I readily connected as broadcast partners and friends—not to mention fellow Canadians! The Games were the first Winter Olympics in the U.S. since 1980 when they were staged in Lake Placid, and the U.S. team had high hopes for the success of rising star Bode Miller, good wishes for the comeback try of Picabo Street, and eyes watched on two young American women, Lindsey Kildow and Julia Mancuso.

We were billeted in a dumpy condo complex on the edge of Salt Lake City, nearly an hour's drive from the Snowbasin ski race area in Ogden. Security was the tightest it had been at any Olympics site ever—it was, after all, less than a year after the events of September 11. At the entrance to the ski area, credentials were checked and then vehicles had to go through a tent where a security crew poked under the hood, screened the chassis, and checked the interior before waving cars through. The line was inevitably long, even at seven in the morning.

Once in, then we had to go through an airport-type security check at the entrance to the TV compound. Necessary or not, this all proved to be a bore, knowing we had nearly three weeks of this routine.

So naturally, being teenagers at heart, we turned it into a game—seeing if we could beat the system—especially through what we came to call the "carwash," the tented area with the long lines, where they made you get out of your vehicle and ran a metal detector under the car. We noticed a few days

LEFT: 2002: Salt Lake City with Todd Brooker.
RIGHT: Brentina video cover.

in that some vehicles were waved through into the venue without having to go through the carwash. One of the credentials we had to place on the windshield, if altered slightly, might get us into the line that bypassed the car wash. I did the altering. An Ogden County sheriff was the man checking those credentials. On our first try, he waved us through! And it worked several more times. I think we won at least a bronze in beating the carwash!

On the slopes, the charismatic Bode Miller was doing even better. He won silver in the giant slalom, and silver in the combined. But the men's events were dominated by Austrian Stefan Eberharter, who won three medals, and the Norwegian Kjetil Andre Aamodt won two golds. The star of the alpine races was Janica Kostelic of Croatia, who won three golds and a silver skiing every discipline. To my mind she remains the greatest woman overall racer ever.

The quirky Miller—he of the hippie parents in the backwoods of New Hampshire—had served notice his unorthodox and daredevil style would remain in the spotlight of alpine ski-racing.

With the Salt Lake Games behind me, I was now looking ahead to Athens 2004, although in between I would have busy winters with the World Cup ski events in Colorado, and the 2003 World Alpine Championships in St. Moritz. The Athens Summer Olympics were the target of Debbie McDonald and Brentina. Since the Thomas farm was only twenty minutes away from my house, I was spending as much time there as possible to soak up the subtle moves of dressage—and the possibility that the U.S. would for the first time have a serious chance at an Olympic medal.

Brentina came from the finest breeding heritage in Germany. Parry Thomas had paid more than $400,000 for her, hoping that maybe she could bring Olympic glory to tiny Hailey, Idaho, and knowing that when her competitive career was over, she would be a very valuable broodmare. Jane Thomas, Parry's daughter approached me with an idea. The family wanted to have a video made about Brentina to have as a memento for friends and relatives, it would focus on a performance they were planning—a fundraiser for the Sun Valley Summer symphony, and the idea was to have the orchestra perform at the Thomas farm, with Brentina as the star soloist—doing her Grand Prix musical routine to live accompaniment. Could I help with the video?

My answer was quick—of course I could. And then I suggested making a longer video, following Brentina—from Idaho to Athens. I told Jane that there was a chance that it could be a TV program—I couldn't promise it would get on—but if Parry wanted to give it a try, I would put a budget together.

The story had a chance to become a salable TV program: A beautiful horse, and appealing rider training to take on the best in the world at the Athens Olympics and the first-ever live performance of dressage with a symphony orchestra. At the very least, we could make a home video and try to recover the production costs with its sales online and at horse shows.

The Thomases said go for it. Suddenly I was a producer—and as it turned out, a director, a screenwriter, and a program salesperson. My plan was to follow Debbie and Brentina as they trained in Hailey and competed at important annual events in the U.S. and Europe between 2002 and the Games in Athens in August of 2004.

This was uncharted territory for me. I built a budget, including hiring a full-on TV production truck with cameras, crew and lighting for the symphony performance at the Thomas farm. Parry had built a brand-new outdoor ring on his property, surrounded by trees with a mountain range in the background. The setting was beautiful, a tented roof would cover the orchestra, and seating would be on the opposite side.

I contracted an old CBS friend, producer George Veras, to handle the concert portion of the show. But the most fun for me was to utilize two of my children, both in the TV business at the time—to help make the video. Son Kevin had a small production company in Boise. He and a partner of his would shoot and edit all of the footage. My daughter Kimberley, who had been a TV news reporter and anchor in three Western markets, would be my host/narrator. I would write and direct.

At the Thomas farm, we did interviews with Debbie and Jane, and a dressage instruction piece with Debbie mic'd aboard Brentina explaining some of the fundamentals and subtleties of Grand Prix level skills. Then we joined the Brentina team in Del Mar for an event against other top U.S. horses and riders that would give the Thomases a sense of how good an Olympic contender they had.

Brentina won that event and we followed her to the World Championships in Jerez, Spain, (home of the world's great sherry wines!) where in a controversial judging decision, she just missed a bronze medal. Another European trip, this time to the famous Equestrian Festival in Aachen, Germany saw her score well again, sending her into the U.S. team Olympic trials in New Jersey as the number one dressage horse in America. Our story ended with the spectacular night at the Thomas Farm, where Brentina turned in a flawless performance of the freestyle routine that she would use at the Olympics—dancing under the stars to the live rendition of her music played by the Sun Valley Summer Symphony Orchestra. She seemed to love every second, her ears perked as she went through her intricate movements in perfect time to the music. Debby was ecstatic and it provided a great sendoff to the Olympic test in Athens.

We sold a good number of video cassettes and DVDs, and after a long sales struggle—with the help of Rolex, and CBS-TV executive Dennis Swanson (the man who years before had tried to hire me away from CBS to ABC)—I was able to get it on a group of CBS-owned stations, all in major markets. The next time I would see Brentina and Debbie would be in Athens, Greece where I would be covering her medal-quest for NBC, as well as the other equestrian events.

CHAPTER 51

Athens: Hot Winds, Hot Horses, and Death-Defying Waiters

Athens was my second Summer Olympics, and since I had done so well identifying head-from-tail in Sydney, NBC implored me to do it again in Greece! Of course equestrian is not a headline sport in the U.S., or in many other places for that matter.

But the U.S. team has always done well at Olympic Games and it brought several contenders to Athens in jumping, eventing, and in dressage—Brentina and Debbie McDonald.

So while the notion of sitting for eight to twelve hours a day identifying horses and riders from dozens of countries, frankly held little appeal—but, well, it WAS the Olympics, and Brentina was here, with a chance for a medal, and I would get to make the call as she tried.

Since much of our coverage would be on NBC's cable channels, we would be calling every horse in every event live-to-air.

Melanie Smith-Taylor's husband was very ill with cancer, and she bowed out of her assignment as our expert. Another former U.S. rider, Robert Ridland, had taken her place. Like Melanie, Robert had been a jump rider, and while nervous about being a commentator for the first time, he had done his homework well.

We hit it off immediately, which meant we could bitch about the usual things together—security as a pain in the ass—we even needed to show our credential each time we entered and left our hotel, it was a 45-minute drive to get to the venue (twice a day) we had a different driver each day some of whom didn't know the way, or drove slowly, or both. As for the hotel, named for some Greek sea-god naturally (Pegasus—well at least it was a horse of sorts), while it overlooked the Aegean, it also overlooked a busy two-lane road and a trolley line before sand and sea were in view.

My third-floor balcony was about three feet by five feet, with two plastic chairs and fumes from the traffic below. The shower (there was no tub) was about two feet by two feet and featured a light plastic shower curtain that as soon as one turned on the shower and stepped in, the flimsy curtain immediately enveloped your body and didn't let go until you peeled it off to get out.

But I digress. (Again!) More from the balcony later.

Robert and I quickly found a little fish restaurant a few blocks walk from the hotel, which became our "local." When you entered you were greeted warmly in Greek, and taken to a chest of drawers a few feet away—an ICE chest of drawers, wherein was the nightly selection of fresh fish. You pointed, asked the name of the fish, and having made its acquaintance, proceed to your table to await its arrival on a plate. Simply grilled, olive oil, lemon. Spectacular. Salad with feta cheese, maybe some spanakopita while you waited for the fish, a white wine from Santorini—all made a long day of horsemanship worthwhile.

The Greeks were great—proud, friendly, embarrassed by the drama over whether their country was actually ready for the Games (they were, but it was close) and eager to please. I spent my first night, alone, at a special concert in the spectacular ancient arena near the Acropolis—the London Symphony Orchestra played under the stars.

For the full two weeks of competition, the weather was unbearably hot—steady strong winds blew scorching heat all of the sunlight hours, so sitting outside at the equestrian venue was totally uncomfortable. The horses couldn't have been happy either.

Our coverage went well, considering we had no communication with our producer onsite, so we didn't know what replays were coming from the world video feed and Robert had to quickly react to the replays as they came up. And the U.S. team had a great Games—Chris Kappler won a silver in jumping, as did Kim Severson in eventing, the jumpers won team gold, and the dressage team won bronze.

Brentina was part of the bronze team of course, and she and Debbie had another close miss individually—finishing fourth—by one point—out of the medals. Still they would bring their share of the U.S. team bronze medal back to the Thomas farm. *Brentina: From Idaho to Athens* had a very happy ending.

Back at the hotel, an unofficial Olympic sport had caught my attention. During my rare moments spent on my balcony, I had become fascinated with the lunch-hour food service. The hotel operated a small restaurant on the beach across the speedway that separated the hotel from the sand. Olympic officials had put a concrete barrier down the center of the road and created Olympic lanes for credentialed athletes, officials, and media to get from downtown Athens to venues in the suburbs. The nearest pedestrian crosswalk to the beach was about 200 yards beyond the hotel. The beach restaurant was directly across the street. But the kitchen was in the hotel.

This created a new Olympic sport for the waitstaff. A waiter would have his tray loaded in the kitchen—plates of food, cutlery, glasses etc.— leave the hotel through the front door, approach the curb, view the speeding traffic, and then, without benefit of a starter's pistol, take off running—tray held high as a means of identification to the spectators. There were two options, turn left through the pedestrian traffic, try to catch a green light at the crossing and then loop back on the beach-side, down the stairs to the restaurant, *or*, looking both ways, opting to bolt across the near lane, hurdle the concrete barrier, dart between speeding cars on the far lane, then sprint to the stairs down to the beach.

All without losing anything from your tray or your life or limb.

Gold medals go to those who arrive safely with trays intact, silver to no food lost, and bronze to those who were only slightly injured by passing vehicles.

Fortunately, I was able to award a gold to all those I happened to watch from my balcony, but I held my breath every time a waiter would give it a go.

CHAPTER 52

The ESPN Years: "Who Knew?"

During the year preceding the 2004 Athens Games, Sandy Montag, who had taken over my representation at IMG from his mentor Barry Frank, called one day with a seductive proposal: "How would you like to go to London next week to work Wimbledon for ESPN?"

It was to be a one-off gig, but was still very appealing. ESPN had learned from two weeks with expanded coverage of the French Open that they had too few announcers for all of the on-air hours.

I had worked a handful of Wimbledons for NBC as a studio host of weekend daytime matches, and the previous year had the same role with Turner when they took over HBO's long run as the cable broadcaster of the Championships. I got to do a couple of play-by-play matches for Turner, and that year I also doubled as a host of NBC's late-night highlight show with John McEnroe and Chris Evert. But now, with ESPN, I was getting a chance to call matches again, which I much preferred.

It was certainly quite ironic that I was going to work for ESPN, nearly ten years after our contract squabble that had led to my temporary divorce from IMG. I was greeted at Wimbledon by an executive producer, Jed Drake and given a warm welcome. ESPN President Mark Shapiro had arrived from New York to be a guest in the Royal Box. When Drake introduced me to him, Mark told me he had been a huge fan watching me do Bears and Blackhawks games when he was growing up in Chicago. By the end of the tournament Shapiro said he wanted to sign me to a long-term contract to cover more tennis and other sports. I told him I didn't want a full-on deal, but would be willing to do a dozen or so events in addition to tennis.

Sandy—God bless him!—put together a great package, including three years with good money to do tennis, ESPN's new Friday night national coverage of college football and possibly some boxing. This was manna from heaven. My NBC deal was only for the Olympics and other Olympic-related events—World Cup skiing, a few equestrian events and the occasional figure-skating competition, so the ESPN opportunity was a perfect fit.

At the age of sixty-two, I had a new TV life—doing only events I wanted to do, and in control of the number of them.

From 2003 through 2006 I worked the Australian Open, Roland Garros, and Wimbledon doing play-by-play with a variety of expert analysts, among them Martina Hingis (who was delightful but didn't last too long!), Brad Gilbert, Mary Joe Fernandez and my old pals Pam Shriver, Mary Carillo, and Patrick McEnroe. While I wasn't the top play-by-play guy on the slams (Cliff Drysdale, and later Dick Enberg had that role), I wound up being the lead-announcer on the U.S. Open series of women's tournaments in Palo Alto, Manhattan Beach, La Costa—all nice stops—and Toronto.

Patricia joined me for most of the tennis trips—she fell in love with Melbourne, always loved Paris, and took a new view of London, a city she previously hadn't cared for. The first year with ESPN, we stayed at their hotel in Melbourne—a modest Hilton near the tennis grounds—but we soon learned other tennis folk were staying in more appealing accommodations.

So in ensuing years, we stayed in hotels of our choice, paying the difference in the rates between them and the ESPN choices. In Melbourne we liked the venerable Windsor, across from the Parliament Buildings. I cajoled the manager into a suite—at a reduced rate for our two-week stay—which featured a full-on dining room with a gorgeous chandelier! In Paris we found a little boutique in the Golden Triangle called Chambiges Elysées, around the corner from major-glam hotels, the George V and the Plaza Athenée—but considerably less pricey! In London, we chose the Milestone, a small five-star on Kensington Court across from the palace and park of the same name. Each of the Grand Slam cities including New York of course, had much to offer visitors who had the time and inclination to take a good look around, engage with the locals, and try all the available cuisines.

When we stayed at the Windsor in Melbourne, we would walk through a lovely park to the tennis venue. On weekend afternoons it would be filled with families using the children's playground, picnicking, or listening to impromptu musicals. Often little girls would be dressed in butterfly dresses, each one prettier than the other. In the evenings one was advised by warning signs to not approach the possums, nocturnal animals, which nest in the trees.

The influx of Asians—resisted by older Australian nationalists for decades—had brought an exciting diversity to "Oz," not to mention a dazzling array of Chinese, Thai, Vietnamese, and Malaysian restaurants. One of the more established Chinese restaurants, the elegant Flower Drum featured top-level Cantonese food, and because Chinese New Year falls during the Open in January, it is a tough ticket. But Patricia and I were lucky enough to walk in and get a table on the big night when the brilliantly costumed dragon-dancers come through the restaurant to add to the atmosphere.

Melbourne being a port city, where the Yarra River flows into the Tasman Sea, is naturally home to outstanding fish restaurants, many of which are located along the river near downtown hotels and shops. Our favorite became Donovan's on the seafront in the St. Kilda neighborhood. It turned out the owners are a couple from Connecticut!

In 2006, my sister Cindy and her husband Terry Casey, joined us for a few days from their home in Victoria B.C. Cindy was dealing with high-grade melanoma that was moving to her brain. Calmly seeking all options for treatment, she had been to Adelaide, Australia to see a doctor recommended to me by John Newcombe. The doctor was running an experimental trial, and with Newk's help, had included Cindy.

The four of us had dinner with Newk, who gave Cindy an inspiring pep talk, and she was clearly moved by his obviously sincere interest. Meanwhile she and Terry were enjoying Melbourne, visiting some Canadian friends who had moved there, and going to the shops and museums with Patricia while I was working the tennis.

One evening we had dinner along the Yarra and Martina Navratilova was seated at the next table. When Martina saw me she came over, met Cindy and Terry and had her picture taken with them. They were thrilled. They were also thrilled to have great seats for the men's final, when the upstart from Cyprus, Marcos Baghdatis took a set from Roger Federer, before losing in four. It was a raucous affair, with a good portion of Melbourne's sizeable Greek population singing and chanting for Baghdatis throughout the match.

Cindy, a college professor, a wife and mother with two grown children, Ryan and Megan, a lively woman who took up competitive rowing at age fifty and attacked life with vigor and humor, died in her sleep at home a month after returning from Australia. She was just fifty-six.

Patricia, who had become great friends with Cindy, often talks about their time together in Melbourne. We both miss her greatly.

CHAPTER 53

I Love Paris…and London When It Doesn't Rain

Clearly, working the French Open for ESPN was one of my favorite gigs. Paris is one of the most beautiful cities in the world with unmatched charisma that only the most parochial cynic can ignore.

Even driving out to Roland Garros each day from our little hotel in the 7th arrondissement was pure pleasure. Fifteen minutes along the Seine with a view of the Eiffel Tower, then a turn through residential areas neighboring the Bois de Boulogne and down a shady street to the entrance of the tennis grounds named for a World War I French fighter pilot. The red clay courts seem just the right decor for the French, and it's amplified by the most fashionable tennis fans—even those in the "cheap seats" (which are not cheap!)

The soon-to-be-remodeled Court One is a total throwback, resembling a small Roman amphitheater. And the Place des Mousquetaires between Court One and the center court is the prettiest place to check the scores on the big screen while sipping a little champagne or vin rouge.

Of course the rest of town isn't bad either! Even though the Champs Elysées has been dumbed down to fast food joints and electronics stores, there is still Fouquet's on the corner at Avenue George Cinq, and L'Arc de Triomphe and L'Obélisque in the Place de la Concorde bookending the boulevard. On one of our ESPN trips to the French Open Patricia and I went to dinner in Montmartre at a bistro called La Pompanette. White asparagus was in season in late May, and that was followed by typical bistro fare. To add to the fun, the cheerful owner telling us her grandmother designed the ample red linen table napkins—and then happily selling four of them to us.

On another night we went to a late-night locals' haunt called Le Lapin Agile (The Agile Rabbit). In the cellar of the building patrons sit communal style at big wooden tables and are immediately served a cherry liqueur. A floor-show follows, with singers and instrumentalists providing a repertoire of traditional Parisian songs, many of which are designed sing-alongs for the audience. Very authentic and much fun.

We are always asked where we like to eat in Paris. Well, having dined at a few of the Michelin-starred famous restaurants over the years, we now avoid them for the neighborhood bistros and old reliables like Le Dome in Montparnasse, Chez Andre and Le Pichet in our hotel's neighborhood.

London is loveable (when it's not wet). And the food is much better than it was fifteen years ago. The world has come to London Town, and it's better for it. One of our favorites is a very authentic Spanish restaurant called Cambio de Tercio that has a bullfight motif and during Wimbledon reserves its back room for the Spanish tennis stars (including Rafa!)

Pretty hard to beat the historic city for walking, and so much to see in central London—no matter how many times one has been there. Great theater and good jazz.

Of course Wimbledon is still champion of the Grand Slams. From the glorious green grounds, to the queues of fans sleeping overnight to line up for grounds passes (no seating, except on your butt on Henman Hill), the cathedral-like feel of Center Court (even with its new roof) and of course, strawberries and cream.

For many years, John Newcombe and some Aussie buddies have rented the same house two blocks from the All-England Club. We have been lucky to have had many good times there, especially the night before the tournament begins when Newk invites all of the Australian players in the draw for an outdoor dinner picnic and a pep talk from the Great One.

They listen. After all, Newk won Wimbledon three times, was a Davis Cup star for Australia and captain of the Davis Cup team.

One night at the gathering, Lleyton Hewitt, and his Mom and Dad were there. Lleyton listened attentively, and went out and won the tournament—at twenty-one, he was one of the youngest male players ever to win at "Wimby."

Staying in London was an added treat for Patricia and me since we both

London, 2004: With Patricia at an ESPN party for Dick Enberg.

have long-standing friends there and were able to squeeze in some visits in the city, in Wimbledon Village and in Oxford, where our friends the Duguids were living at the time. But much of our travel together came later—on the Continent as the Brits like to call Europe.

Patricia was less interested in the small college towns back in the U.S. that I spent Friday nights in for ESPN while calling college football games with Rod Gilmore, an excellent and underrated analyst. Stops included glamour spots like Toledo, Ohio; Greenville, North Carolina; and Huntington, West Virginia—not exactly London, Paris and Melbourne! But it was fun for me to be back doing some football, and just enough games.

As it turned out, my final football telecast ever, came in my final ESPN season, Baylor at Army.

I had never been to West Point, even though it had been a short drive from my former home in Larchmont, N.Y. It was as special as I had been told—the setting on the Hudson River, the lovely grounds, the cadets in their grays, the traditional game-day breakfast in their dining hall, the march into the stadium.

Unfortunately, I didn't get to finish the last telecast of my twenty-six-year football broadcasting career. By a quirk of fate, ESPN's production trucks lost electrical power in the 4th quarter and we were off the air. By the time the power was regained, the game was over! Maybe ESPN was trying to tell me something—it was the last gig on my contract, which was not renewed.

CHAPTER 54

Why Switzerland?

During the three-year run at ESPN, the tiny country sandwiched between Germany, Italy, France, and Austria literally became the center of my universe. The emergence of Roger Federer as the best male player in the world put Switzerland at the center of the tennis map, and no doubt increased sales of Rolex watches, Lindt chocolates, and assorted other Swiss products he endorsed—not to mention Wilson racquets and his own line of "RF" tennis clothing.

The last Swiss player anyone had noticed was Martina Hingis, a Czech immigrant as a child to the land of milk and cheese. Marc Rosset, a largely forgotten player outside of his own country, was the top Swiss male player, but his best Grand Slam result was a semi-final at the French Open. He did win an Olympic gold medal in men's singles in 1992, but he was no Roger Federer.

While Federer couldn't beat the rising young Rafael Nadal on the clay at Roland Garros, he dominated the grass of Wimbledon winning five in a row, including the four years I was part of the ESPN coverage. When I have been asked to describe Federer's significance in tennis history, I usually reply that whether he is the best ever is irrelevant to the fact that fans have been so fortunate to live in his era—to see his tennis magic live in person or on TV, much like we have been lucky to be around during the time of Luciano Pavarotti, and Mikhail Baryshnikov and Leonard Bernstein—artists who come along only once in a generation.

In fact, Roger has elements of all three of those geniuses—the compelling presence of the great tenor, the agility and grace of the Russian dancer, and the ability to compose points and games with the thoughtful versatility of the brilliant conductor.

Being able to cover many of his matches over the stretch on ESPN was a privilege, and again when I returned to the U.S. Open to be the lead announcer on the USTA's world feed telecasts.

But the more significant story of Switzerland for me was that Patricia and I had decided to be married, and to have the wedding in Geneva!

Starting in 2004, during the two-week period between the French Open and Wimbledon, we had made trips into France and Switzerland with a view to maybe having a second home in Europe. Patricia is virtually fluent in French (not to mention strong in Italian with a smattering of Spanish and German). We looked first in France—a little wine village in Burgundy called Meursault—well known for its pristine Chardonnay wine. We stayed at a charming small hotel, and looked at a lovely old house being renovated for sale. Geneva is a two-hour drive from Burgundy, and I suggested we have a look at villages along the shore of Lake Geneva, or *Lac Léman* as it's known in Switzerland.

At first, Patricia wasn't all that interested in Switzerland even though she had gone to school in Lausanne one summer as a teenager. Because I had driven the autoroute between Geneva and Lausanne several times over the years while covering ski-racing, I thought we should look at that area— particularly since it is in the French part of the country.

By the time we got back to London for the Wimbledon tournament, we were both thinking more seriously about Switzerland—and in fact, getting married there. Since it would be a second marriage for both of us, we wanted a small wedding that would not impose on our children's finances to travel to attend. Not incidentally, my four children and Patricia's son John and daughter Celeste—both married with children—had embraced the idea of our marrying, which was a great comfort to us.

I had looked into having the wedding in Italy or France, but the paperwork involved was predictably onerous. Switzerland was less so, but still required some organization. First we had to travel to San Francisco—the nearest Swiss consulate to Sun Valley—to turn in documents in person. Next was to organize a venue—preferably a Catholic church, although we were also required to first have a civil ceremony at the Geneva City Hall.

The whole idea seemed very romantic—(the kids thought so too!) and we decided we would have no guests, except for the required two witnesses. We immediately thought of asking our long-time friends, Lorne and Margie Duguid, who still lived near Oxford, England and so would have a short flight.

On our first trip to Switzerland, we had stayed a couple of nights at the elegant Hotel d'Angleterre in Geneva which had a personable general manager by the name of Jacques Favre and a great concierge, Bruno. I called Mr. Favre (who later with his wife Margreth became new friends of ours) and asked if there was a Catholic church nearby we could be married in. Well, Bruno put that together in no time, giving us the name of the pastor at the Basilica of Notre Dame (minutes from the hotel), and booked the hotel limo for the short trip across town to the City Hall.

But there were a couple of glitches in this idyllic plan. We had hoped for the wedding to be May 16. We would fly to Geneva from New York, get married, and have a week to look at some of the villages along the lake to decide where we might like to rent a house, then travel to Paris for my work with ESPN at the French Open.

However, May 16—our obvious choice since Patricia and I share that date as our birthday—fell on a Monday in 2005, and was a " bank holiday" in Switzerland, meaning all public offices were closed.

The Monsignor at the cathedral—after being assured that we were Catholic and requiring us to get papers from the U.S. to that effect—said we could have the church on Monday the 16th and he would have an English-speaking priest available for the ceremony. But the civil ceremony would have to take place on Friday the 13th, before the City Hall closed for the long weekend. That meant the Duguids, (pronounced do-good) who were playing in a golf tournament Saturday in England, would have to make two trips! Which they did. The Duguids done well.

The wedding at the Basilica of Notre Dame was something special. Our priest was Father Peter Henry from Dublin, Ireland, the Monsignor provided an organist, ordered the church bells rung at the wedding time of 3 p.m., and we had the huge cathedral to ourselves! Well, except for a handful of sleeping pilgrims with backpacks who were startled to see the lights turned on, to hear the organ playing the Wedding March, and a priest in gold vestments leading us down the aisle. They scrambled to leave but I waved them back and said they were welcome to stay if they chose. It turned

Geneva, 2005: Our wedding day.

out they were on a religious hiking pilgrimage to France, and had come into the cathedral to rest.

So we had some guests after all!

By the time we left from Geneva to get to Paris, Patricia and I had had a brief honeymoon driving through a number of villages in the vineyards along the lake between Geneva and Montreux, including a spotless town called Cully just east of Lausanne, enveloped by the spectacular terraced vineyards of Lavaux. We had seen enough to decide this French part of Switzerland, centrally located in Europe with an airport in Geneva, was where we wanted to have a second home. And by the fall of 2006 we had found a charming little house in the vines of Fechy that we rented for the next five years, commuting back and forth to our home in Ketchum as my work schedule allowed.

CHAPTER 55

Boondoggles and Bangkok

One of my best boondoggles came in 2006 when my schedule had me going to Melbourne for the Australian Open in late January, to be followed less than two weeks later in early February by the Winter Olympics in Torino, Italy. It seemed pointless to travel all the way back from Down Under to my home in the Pacific Northwest and then a week later, fly across the U.S. and the Atlantic to Italy.

So I looked into an "Around the World" airline ticket (or tickets, since I would take Patricia with me) and suggested to ESPN and NBC that they split the cost of my ticket that would result in savings to both networks. Surprisingly, they agreed!

Now, where to go for the week in between? How about Bangkok, where we had never been, and which made a sensible route from Melbourne back to Europe for the Olympics.

Game on!

I shipped my ski-gear and winter clothing—(or rather NBC did!)—from Sun Valley to our hotel in Sestriere where the ski-racing would take place, booked flights to San Francisco to Melbourne to Bangkok to Frankfurt—where Patricia would carry on back home and I would connect to Torino.

Then I decided to try for a discounted rate at the world famous Oriental Hotel in Bangkok by meeting with the General Manager, Kurt Wachtveitl and hoping he was a sports fan. And if possible, could we stay in one of the famous Writer's Wing suites? Kurt (now retired after forty-two years at the Oriental), who is considered to be the greatest hotel manager ever, met us for coffee in the lobby, and no doubt thanks to Patricia's charm, immediately moved us into the Somerset Maugham Suite, one of three named for famous authors who were frequent visitors to the Oriental. (The other two were Noel Coward and James Michener). We stayed four nights, had a great tour of the city with a guide recommended by old friend Bob Arum. Being Bob, he had also organized a lunch for us at Lord Jim's seafood restaurant in the Oriental hosted by the General of Police! Because of our lack of fluency in the Thai language, conversation was limited—but the General was an enthusiastic boxing fan who had done business with Arum at fights in Bangkok and so he had brought along English-speaking colleagues to fill in the gaps.

Bob's tour guide, whose English nickname happened to be Tim, was a scholarly expert on Thai history and gave us an exceptional trip through Bangkok, his driver maneuvering through the city's teeming streets to drop us off at the many spectacular temples then magically reappearing at the appointed time to pick us up and deliver us to the next stop. We learned from Tim that all young men of the Buddhist sect in Thailand are expected to spend two years as a monk before then choosing their path in life—his choice was to share his immense knowledge with visitors from other parts of the world.

Another day was spent on the Chao Phraya River as passengers in a "long tail," a lengthy wooden skiff driven by old inboard automobile engines, and used by tour guides and merchants to travel through the dozens of communities on the shores of the river where markets thrive selling fish, vegetables, flowers and other commodities for the locals.

A visit to the Jim Thompson House was de rigeur and not disappointing. The American entrepreneur was a silk trader and former architect who designed and lived in an opulent wooden house in Bangkok for many years following his service in the O.S.S. in World War II. He disappeared after going for a walk in the woods while on vacation in Malaysia. His house is now a museum, and seeing it was one of the highlights of our Bangkok tour.

But nothing topped our ride to the airport from the Oriental. If only every airport experience could be like that one! Our bags were whisked from our Somerset Maugham Suite into a waiting limousine, the driver dressed in a white naval-style uniform. When we arrived at the airport, before we were even out of the car, the bags were on a trolley and three (three!) of the Oriental's own porters were guiding us into the airport, our boarding passes in hand, through expedited security, onto a golf-cart to the gate where we were given our boarding passes and baggage claim tags—all with much bowing, and *"Sawadee kas and kops,"* the Thai all-purpose greeting, *"ka"* for women and *"kop"* for men.

Unmatched before or since, Thanks Kurt Wachtveitl!

P.S. Kurt was a huge fan of Roger Federer (who had stayed at the Oriental of course) and Kurt had never been to Wimbledon. That June he was my guest at The Championships, and he, his delightful wife Penny, Patricia and I had dinner together in London.

Having changed from cotton to goose-down at the Frankfurt airport, I arrived in wintry Torino where the next morning an NBC driver would take me up to our accommodation in Sestriere. With Patricia en route home, I dined alone in a very formal, elegantly decorated restaurant with superb Piedmontese cuisine and wine from Barbaresco. It was near the central piazza, where the *Today Show* and our NBC Sports anchors would be located for the Games. Most of the buzz was about Bode Miller and how many medals he would win for the U.S. on the ski slopes. Miller was favored in all but the slalom, and even given a solid chance in that event.

But it would all go terribly wrong for Bode, in more ways than one.

CHAPTER 56

Bad Times For Bode

NBC had a lot riding on Miller. In 2006, alpine ski-racing was still the number-two event, behind figure skating, in terms of viewer interest at the winter Games and the U.S. figure skaters did not have a well-known contender for medals in either the women's or men's singles, although young Sasha Cohen would surprise with a silver medal.

But Bode was a known quantity on a young U.S. ski team, having added to his silver medals at Salt Lake with four World Championship Gold medals (in four different disciplines) since the 2002 Games, and the World Cup Overall title as the racer with the most points in all events in the year before the Torino Games. Not only that, but his flamboyant style on the slopes, good looks, quirky personality and unusual name had made him the most famous ski racer alive. People wanted to watch him.

Our NBC ski team, former racers Todd Brooker and Steve Porino, producer John McGuinness, director Andy Rosenberg, and expert researchers Patrick Lang and Hank McKee were all psyched up, knowing our sport would get lots of attention at the Torino Games.

Unfortunately, Bode wasn't as psyched up as we were. For reasons still largely unexplained, Miller chose to stick to his "winning isn't everything—it's how well I ski the course" mantra that fans don't understand and don't want to hear. He did apparently entertain other athletes and Olympic patrons off-piste, sharing beers at a selection of Sestriere bars and nightspots—an activity that was duly recorded by photographers.

As each event he raced in ended with him out of the medals, Bode became more surly with the media, skipping post-race interviews and after one of his most mediocre performances skied off the hill before the finish area, eluding the media entirely until Porino caught up with him walking down the road, skis on his shoulders, to his own private accommodation—a mobile home. He didn't have much to say, despite Steve's excellent efforts.

NBC was not amused. Even esteemed news anchor Tom Brokaw in an interview with Miller was stern with him about his carousing, but Bode remained unrepentant.

It must be said that some of us later learned that Bode came into the Torino Olympics still bothered by an ankle injury he acknowledged having, and by an aggravated knee injury he chose to hide. He had not been able to train normally and had gained weight as a result. Apparently he knew he wasn't really ready physically for Torino, and chose his "I'm here to enjoy the full Olympic experience" line rather than reveal his injuries.

In retrospect—while he annoyed the hell out of us at the time—his fifth and sixth place finishes in the speed events were actually quite remarkable. It was Bode being Bode.

CHAPTER 57

Baubles and Beads

While Bode was dominating the ski coverage at Torino by not skiing like Bode, the U.S. ski team still grabbed two golds. A young upstart from Park City, Ted Ligety, upset the field by winning the combined with a blistering slalom run to go with his more than decent downhill. And a spacey young woman from Squaw Valley, Julia Mancuso, motored to a gold in the giant slalom, but not without some controversy, partly fired by yours truly.

Mind you, it was Julia who wore the tiara, not me!

Mancuso and Resi Steigler, two young racers both appeared in the start gate for the slalom portion of the combined event sporting bright beaded necklaces over their Olympic number-bibs. On our NBC coverage from Torino I was critical of their fashion choice, feeling it was undignified and disrespectful to the U.S. team at an Olympic Games. My opinion was shared by former U.S. ski team star Picabo Street, who was doing studio commentary for NBC's *Today Show*, and said Julia "should lose the tiara," referring to the plastic headdress Mancuso wore on the podium after she won the gold in the giant slalom.

Julia's rebuttal to our point of view was to later start a fashion lingerie line branded "Kiss My Tiara!" And while she abandoned the beads and has won four Olympic and four World Championships medals, she did not give up her tiara on the podiums.

I did notice a certain coolness toward me when we would meet at team interviews in subsequent years. But her success on the ski hill is undeniable. Since she made the U.S. team as a teenager with Lindsey Kildow (now Lindsey Vonn), the pair of friendly (and often unfriendly) rivals have been the best one-two punch for the American women since the eighties when Tamara McKinney and Christin Cooper were terrorizing the World Cup.

Lindsey was ready to make her move in the speed events at the Torino Games, but a horrific crash in a downhill training run sent her to the hospital in Torino. Her idol, Picabo Street—until Kildow the toughest female athlete I have ever seen—came to the hospital to see her. While Lindsey was bruised, battered and depressed—she still wanted to race the next day. With nothing broken or torn, and with Street's encouragement, Kildow checked herself out of the hospital and raced the next day—in pain from a severe hip contusion. She finished with a respectable eighth place result.

For Lindsey Kildow, marriage, medals and much more lay ahead. Her misfortune in Torino disappeared in her rear-view mirror.

CHAPTER 58

Home Sweet Homes

Our new half-life in Switzerland brought a whole new dimension to my work life. After the 2006 Wimbledon we flew to Geneva, rented a car and drove to nearby Fechy where we set up shop in the little house in the vines that had been the family home of a *vigneron*, or winemaker, whose sons we were renting from.

We had shipped Patricia's furniture from her former New York apartment and some she had in storage from her house in Connecticut. I bought a couple of beds for the two guest rooms and some furniture for the kitchen and we were set. From our second floor balcony we had a view of the lake over the lower part of the village of Fechy, and on each side of the house we looked out on the vineyards. On warm nights we ate outside under a canopy of grapevines and looked up a slope filled with more vines to the upper part of Fechy, which featured a tiny church with a conical steeple lit up each evening at dusk. It was a Swiss postcard.

Under our tourist status we were allowed a total of six months a year of residence, but only three months at a time. That first year we stayed until September, then went back to the U.S. for what turned out to be my final season of broadcasting football. For the next five years in the Fechy house, we scheduled our time around my schedule of ski-racing, equestrian events, U.S. Open tennis and Olympic Games—along with visits to our respective families in the East and West.

People back home would ask "What do you *do* there in Switzerland?" and our reply would be, "The same things we do back in the States—except in French!"

Patricia's command of the language was indispensable since in the villages around where we were, very little English was spoken. I had schoolbook French, and bought the Rosetta Stone, but must confess I didn't study it enough. I was able to hack through in Français and handle most daily discourse, and found that I was learning—slowly—by immersion.

Still, I never felt intimidated by a language barrier, and I was soon able to converse somewhat with our neighbors and shopkeepers, and over time became comfortable going to local events where there were few English speakers. And we felt very welcomed in the community—especially by the *vignerons*, at whose wineries—a dozen or more in Fechy alone—I became a frequent visitor.

Over the five (half) years in the Fechy house we ventured into other parts of the country. One can drive from nearby Geneva, in the southwest corner of the country, diagonally to the north-east part—where St. Gallen (home of great sausage!) sits on the German border—in less than four hours.

We made day trips to the nation's capital, Bern, to Lucerne and Basel where our good friend Patrick Lang lives, Gstaad, Gruyere—to see the cows and the castle—the ski resorts at Crans Montana and Verbier.

Going back to the eighties when I had the condominium in Ketchum, if I wasn't working over Christmas, Lee and I and the kids were in Sun Valley where we joined up with friends, the Capozzi family, for a lavish Christmas dinner. When Patricia and her family came into my life, our table became even bigger—especially when grandchildren arrived! I believe our record high was twenty-six, which included some relatives of Patti's daughter-in-law who were visiting from Holland.

But with the two families growing in number, it had become more difficult to organize everyone from New York City, Rye, N.Y., Grimsby (Canada), Las Vegas, and Boise, so when we began to divide our time between the U.S. and Switzerland, we decided to alternate years of Christmas gatherings.

The first year, 2006, Patricia and I had a quiet Yuletide in Fechy, going through the grapevines "up the hill" to the little Calvinist church. For the Noël service Christmas trees were decorated with real candles on the boughs, and the congregation of our neighbors joined a small choir in singing carols. While we did feel like outsiders, even the stern lady who ran the tiny post office greeted us with a smile and "Joyeux Noel" when she saw us entering the church.

Over the next several years when not in Sun Valley for Christmas, we spent the holiday in neighboring countries—France, Austria, or in another part of Switzerland. We drove to Megeve, France, took the train to Vienna and Salzburg, and on another occasion to the famous Swiss resort of Zermatt. Each of those trips was very special—and eventful. More on them later in our narrative.

CHAPTER 59

"The Second Time Around..."

It had been ten years since I called a match at the "toughest tournament in tennis," the U.S. Open.

Thanks to my agent Sandy Montag at IMG, I had a chance to return to one of my favorite assignments—not with my most recent tennis employer ESPN, and not with my old network CBS where I had worked twenty-two years of the Open in several capacities and where, in 1997 I had called my last matches at Arthur Ashe Stadium.

This time, I would be working for the United States Tennis Association, as their lead play-by-play announcer on the English language world feed— the live telecasts that Grand Slam tournaments are obliged to provide to networks in countries around the world that pay rights-money to carry the Open.

The best thing about it—along with a more than decent fee for world-feed rates—was that I would do all of the primetime featured matches, and the semis and finals for both the men's and women's tournaments.

The deal also included an American Express radio report during the daytime matches and a live evening preview show with Nick Bollettieri, the tennis coach and an old friend of mine.

The fact that I would be mainly in English-speaking outposts outside the United States really didn't matter to me—it harkened me back all those years to the 1971 Ali-Frazier fight when my call was only heard outside of the U.S. market. What mattered to me was that I would be calling all of the big matches over the entire two weeks of the tournament, in an era when the new "Big Four" in the men's game—Federer, Nadal, Djokovic and Murray—would be contesting a Grand Slam and the Williams sisters, Maria

Sharapova and Justine Henin were the favorites in the women's draws at the USTA-Billie Jean King National Tennis Center in New York. It was a great era to be part of the U.S. Open telecasts again.

My hours were a little nuts, but the fact is I loved being out there at Flushing Meadows all day and all night (some matches would go beyond midnight under the lights with the encouragement of cocktail-infused patrons). It took me back to my CBS days at the Open, only this time I was with a different crew: producer Brian Williams, whom I knew only slightly, old friend Virginia Wade, Aussie Rennae Stubbs, and Kathy Rinaldi on the women's matches, Taylor Dent and Luke Jensen on the men's. We worked the primetime matches that started at 7:30 on the Arthur Ashe Stadium court.

At 6:30 I would be on the plaza outside the stadium doing a live show with Nick that could be heard on speakers near our small stage where tennis fans would gather on their way into the Stadium for the night matches. It could also be heard by folks who had picked up small transmitters with earbuds by showing their American Express cards at nearby booths on the grounds. From 1 p.m. to 6 p.m., I would do interviews during the afternoon matches for the same Amex radio network.

Since my expenses only allocated $250 a night for hotel, (and this was New York!) Patricia and I followed our ESPN routine of paying the difference to stay in upscale accommodations—The Carlyle Hotel for the first few years and the Waldorf Towers during my last year on the job.

Another perk was that we had family in the area—Patricia's daughter Celeste and her children lived in the city and my son Brendan and his family in nearby Rye—not that there was much time to see them with my wacky hours!

The show with Nick was a kick. All ad-lib, we would get his comments on the matches already played, get his picks for the night matches, have a "Q and A" with the fans gathered around our stage, and occasionally do interviews with tennis figures. Then I would race over to the stadium in time to start match commentary on the Arthur Ashe Stadium court.

This was the men's era dominated by Federer, when he won five U.S. Opens in a row before stumbling against Juan Martin del Potro in 2009. Patricia and I would see Roger at the Carlyle—an elegant, quiet hotel uptown on Madison Avenue—and one morning I arranged with his agent, Tony Godsick, (then of IMG) to meet with him and have him sign a photo for a woman friend of ours in Switzerland who was a huge fan. He was on his way into breakfast to join his wife Mirka and their twin daughters, but in his gracious style asked about our friend and included her name on the picture he signed.

My time on the USTA world-feed gig saw teenager Maria Sharapova win her second Grand Slam, the brilliant Justine Henin close out her career with a victory in 2007, Serena Williams win yet another title, and Kim Clijsters come out of retirement to win two in a row.

Our coverage of the women's play included the nasty incident involving Serena in her 2008 semifinal against Clijsters. On a big point late in the match, a woman line-judge called a foot fault on Serena, who went ballistic. With TV microphones capturing her rant, she castigated the official, shaking her racket in front of the woman's face. The call came on match point against, and the point penalty assessed by the chair umpire handed the match to Kim, who went to win the Open in the final over Caroline Wozniacki.

It was as ugly a scene as I have ever seen on a tennis court.

Serena is the women's game's biggest star and box-office attraction. Any thoughts of suspending her, or not allowing her to play in 2009 never surfaced. Instead, she received only a pocket-change fine.

To her credit, but not soon enough, Serena offered an apology (no doubt with help from her agent and PR advice) and said she "would learn from the mistake and be a better person as a result."

• • •

All good things come to an end, and after the 2010 tournament, Brian Williams called me to say they were not going to renew me—that budgets were tight and they wanted to spread the money around to the other announcers and production people. I knew that I was the highest paid announcer, and I liked and respected the others, but I'm not sure that money was the only reason involved… might have been something I said—either on the air or off the air. But that's show biz! It was a good run, and I still had my NBC commitments ahead of me—more ski-racing, equestrian events and more Olympics!

CHAPTER 60

Ski Racing and Porno??

Along with the World Cup races I have covered in Europe, Japan, and the U.S. over the years, and the five Winter Olympics already described, I have called ten World Alpine Ski Championships—on either CBS or NBC. Until the 2007 event in Are, Sweden, our broadcast crew had always traveled to the venues—ski towns in Italy, Austria, Switzerland, and Colorado. But the championships in Sweden were brought to you from…Saratoga Springs, New York!

In a money-saving effort, NBC decided Todd Brooker and I could make it sound like we were on the scene in Are (without saying we were), and the only announcer who had been sent to Sweden, reporter Steve Porino, would give the impression we were all there—although the viewer would only see Steve…occasionally.

Now this ploy was not without precedent, and in fact there is more of that nickel-and-dime approach to sports coverage now than there isn't. Much of the sports programming that goes to air "on tape" as opposed to live is described by announcers sitting in a studio somewhere in the U.S. calling the play from a television screen just as the viewer at home is seeing it. That saves "T&E" (not T&A, but we'll get to that!) travel and entertainment expenses incurred by the announcers and some production people.

The same approach is even more popular in Europe, where the announcers in various countries are calling events taking place all over the world. This is rarely done with team sports where a full view by the announcers of the field of play is necessary, but it works reasonably well for tennis, golf, boxing, and other individual sports—like ski-racing.

Of course much is lost in terms of the announcers not being able to interact with athletes, coaches etc., pick up personal stories, react to weather conditions, and generally transmit the vibe we get from being there. And it's disingenuous to say that the audience is equally well-served either way. It's all about saving money.

Why Saratoga Springs for the World Championships in Are, Sweden? Well, there is a very good production house there, Carr-Hughes Productions and they were able to successfully bid for the job of producing the program for NBC. The irony turned out to be that was there was much more snow in Saratoga Springs that February week than there was in usually snowbound Sweden! Todd and I drove through three feet of new, unplowed white-stuff to get to the studio from our hotel at 6 a.m. on one of the days we were calling races, while in Are, the sun was shining and snow barely covered the ski runs.

The next two World Championships, 2009 in Val d'Isère, France and 2011 in Garmisch-Partenkirchen, Germany were also covered in the same fashion—but not in a snow-town like Saratoga where at least it was winter, but rather from Los Angeles, which never has winter!

The Worlds were broadcast in full, live, daily at 6 a.m. Pacific Time and then replayed in the afternoon on Universal Sports, a cable network in which NBC has a financial interest and which had the rights to the Championships and a schedule of World Cup races as well. In 2008 I had been asked by NBC to help launch their involvement with Universal Sports by being the play-by-play man on a few of the more important races on the World Cup, including the men's downhills at Wengen and Kitzbühel.

So there I was in L.A., staying at a hotel in Universal City, and driving with analyst Steve Porino each morning at 4:30 a.m. to Glendale where the studio was located. Our contracts to do these races had an unusual paragraph, asking us to waive any objections to performing at a studio where "adult" TV programming was also produced and offering fair warning that nudity—both male and female—may be observed occasionally in the areas of the Universal Sports studios and control rooms.

Talk about "T&A: ski-racing, brought to you live from a porn-palace!!"

I am not making this up. Credentials were required to enter the building, ID was checked at the parking lot entrance, and the best parking spots were reserved with name plates for the "stars," whose names would only be recognizable to folks who subscribe to certain pay-per-view channels.

At 4:30 in the morning, it was a creepy experience to say the least, but did provide a few laughs, and the occasional glimpse of bare flesh in bathrobes flashing by in the hallways.

Todd Brooker and I were joined by Christin Cooper for the World Championships, taking place in Val d'Isère, France, but broadcast by us from Glendale, California. Coop came in for the NBC shows that were taped to be aired on the weekends. Needless to say, it was a first for Christin as well to be calling ski-races from a basement in a porn factory. And it was certainly our last. Gratefully, Universal Sports moved its operations to another studio that was a major upgrade to say the least—the Four Seasons hotel in Westlake Village, near Thousand Oaks.

So for the 2010 World Cup season, leading to the Vancouver Olympics I did a handful of races with Todd, Christin, and Steve from a studio that had been built in the hotel by the son of the owner. Staying at the Four Seasons, a luxury venue for sure, and taking the elevator down to the lobby level, stopping to grab a coffee and then strolling to the studio made the early morning hours more palatable. But still, there was the incongruity of calling live races taking place in European ski villages from a hotel in sunny California where the nearest snow was four hours away in the Sierras.

For the 2011 World Championships, we had a two-week stay at the Four Seasons, calling the races live for Universal Sports and making taped calls for the NBC weekend shows. That stay afforded us time to get into the L.A. lifestyle—trips to the beach, dinners in Malibu, sunbathing by the pool and while Christin got some beach-jogging in, Todd was going on two-hour bike rides in the surrounding hills.

Maybe it wasn't so bad after all!

CHAPTER 61

Beijing Smog and Peking Duck

The 2008 Summer Olympics were historic in many ways. It was the first time the Games were held in China, the first time pollution and protests got more attention than the athletes and the first time a stadium was named after Chinese food.

Well okay, the last "first" is a bit of a stretch, but in fact the stadium built for the opening and closing ceremonies and track and field events was called the "Bird's Nest," which happens to also be the name of a soup seen on many Chinese restaurant menus.

Not that Wikipedia took note, but it was also the first time Tim Ryan had been to China. Having covered equestrian in 2000 and 2004, I was expecting to be with the horses at the Beijing Games. Actually, the equestrian events were to take place not in Beijing, but in Hong Kong, utilizing a racetrack facility that had ample grounds to accommodate jumping, dressage and the three-day eventing. But just as I was getting stoked about spending three weeks in one of the glamor cities of the world, NBC's Molly Solomon called to ask if I minded being switched to the rowing events. Well actually, rowing *and* flatwater canoeing—not to be confused with whitewater canoeing—and I would not just be covering rowing and canoeing, but also flatwater *kayaking*!

My experience with covering these disparate water sports was limited to a one-time, one-day local TV show calling canoe races on Lake Ontario during my Toronto days at CFTO more than forty years earlier. My knowledge of the sport was limited to paddling cedar-strip canoes on a lake in Canada and competing with friends in summers at the annual Stoney Lake Regatta north of Toronto.

Molly was unmoved.

Beijing, 2008: Tim on air with Yaz Farooq.

"You can do it Tim. I know you will do the research, and we love the way you call ski races."

Thanks Molly.

Well it was only January—I had more than six months to prepare. My expert was to be former U.S. Olympian coxswain Yasmin Farooq, known as "Yaz" who had worked the Athens Games for NBC. Yaz was the coach of the Stanford women's rowing team, and I arranged to meet with her in Palo Alto while I was there covering a women's tennis tournament for ESPN. We hit it off immediately, and her husband Roger, a sports cameraman, would become our statistician and spotter in Beijing.

Yaz recommended websites for research where I could also watch online-video coverage of important international rowing events leading up to the Olympics.

Canoeing and kayaking were another matter. There was far less available online and my analyst, Joe Jacobi was actually a former Gold Medal-winning whitewater paddler whom NBC asked to double up on the flatwater events with me.

Needless to say, I didn't arrive in Beijing with a huge amount of confidence about my assignment. In June, I had driven to Lucerne from our Swiss house to watch (in pouring rain) an important international rowing event featuring most of the Beijing Olympians, and in July, while back in the U.S. I spent a day with the U.S. team in Princeton, New Jersey. As for the flatwater folks, I just had to wing it—most of them came from eastern European countries along with a couple of contenders from Canada in the kayaking.

Our hotel in Beijing was within walking distance of the Bird's Nest Stadium, and my spacious room had a great picture-window view of it, albeit a very smoggy view. The pollution was no joke. It hung over the city as a yellowish haze and only on a couple of days did a breeze diminish it somewhat. Chinese authorities had closed all of the coal-fired factories in the vicinity before and during the Games, and had enforced alternate-day driving rules—license plates with odd last-numbers one day, even ones the next.

Nothing helped.

Fortunately, our rowing/paddling venue was outside of Beijing—a forty-minute van drive each day to a beautifully designed water park where the air was at least slightly better than in the city.

All things considered, our coverage went well. Only the men's and women's eights would make the main network coverage, the rest of our races were consigned to cable coverage. The U.S. women's eights won gold and Michele Guerrette won silver in the single sculls, while the American men's eights scored a bronze.

A novelty of the competition featured the American twin-brothers Tyler and Cameron Winklevoss from Connecticut who were racing together in the double sculls, while at the same time launching a lawsuit against Facebook founder Mark Zuckerberg. The USA team allowed us to interview them provided we did not bring up the Facebook story. Being as they were not contenders for a medal in Beijing, we politely declined the interview.

Over the next three weeks in Beijing, Yaz, Roger and I sampled the local cuisine in the neighborhood around our hotel. Across a small park there was a modest place to eat, that like many other restaurants had made an attempt to westernize their name signs with an English translation from their Mandarin characters. Some of the results were amusing: "Wonderful Smoke" or "Happy Fish." But our local family served up very good food, albeit with very bad Chinese wine. Of course all of the visitors wanted to find the best Peking duck in the city that made it famous. Our hotel concierge sent us to a huge, brightly lit establishment where the service was rushed and pushy, but the duck was very Peking, the lacquered glaze enhancing the meat folded into thin pancakes with scallions and hoisin sauce.

We thought we must have tasted the best duck in town, but later in the Games we trumped the big glamour spot by venturing into a dingy back-alley cafe in one of Beijing's crumbling *hutongs*—old neighborhoods with labyrinthian streets and simple courtyards containing tiny houses and shops.

I had seen an article in *The New York Times* reporting on must-do restaurants at the Beijing Olympics. This one was called Li Qun (with no signage in English!) but after being left by our taxi outside a *hutong* and directed by the waving hand of the driver, we wandered down a winding street and came across a line of folks obviously waiting to get into an eating establishment. I had made a reservation for a group of six. Without confidence, I pushed my way to the front of the line, noting a wall lined with photos of famous customers—including Bill Clinton! To my surprise, the owner had my booking and steered us past seated customers in the cramped dining room, past a 1960s soda machine, through a section of the tiny kitchen, down a hallway where a rack of lacquered ducks were hanging on the wall, and into a back room. There was one sizable round table, with an incongruous chandelier hanging over a well-worn but clean tablecloth.

We had a private dining room. And, a view of the kitchen—which was not exactly a pretty sight.

Nevertheless... I think we went through three roast ducks between the six of us, and our vote was unanimous. This place deserves its acclaim for serving the best damn duck in Beijing! And while the capital city's "official" name has ping-ponged back and forth over the decades, the duck's name has resolutely remained: Peking.

The schedule of rowing and flatwater didn't leave much time for sightseeing, but on our one day off, we did the obligatory trips—a cab to the Forbidden City and Tiananmen Square, both dominated by a huge portrait of Chairman Mao, and of course the Great Wall. From Beijing, there are two tourist entrances to the Wall. We went to the closest one, which naturally attracts the biggest crowds of eager tourists. From a parking area, one had to navigate up a rocky road past a long row of hawkers of everything from flags to fish then take an elevator or a winding stairway to actually get up on the Wall. A five- or ten-minute walk along the wall enables the tourist to get some spectacular views of the verdant valleys and mountains through which the wall meanders. Of course camera-phones are constantly clicking at a great rate.

In the midst of the camera chatter I decided I would use my iPhone to call Patricia back in the U.S. (I had no idea what that would cost, but what the hell…) On the first ring, she answered.

"Guess, where I am? I am calling you from the Great Wall of China!"

Patricia replied, "I can't believe it, I was just trying to call you and couldn't make the international connection. But of course I didn't know where in Beijing you were!"

Like two excited teenagers, we enjoyed our Great Wall Moment.

CHAPTER 62

Christmas in Klammer's Austria

The years following the Beijing Olympics continued my nice part-time rhythm of "sports I like to do in nice places." I had the delights of Lexington, Kentucky in April for NBC's coverage of the Rolex Horse Championships, spending May, June, and July with Patricia at our house in Switzerland and coming back to New York in August for the long days and late nights of the U.S. Open.

The men's final in 2009 included the upset victory by young Juan Martin del Potro over Federer, stopping Roger's five-year U.S. Open title streak. The dramatic five-set win also featured a rare outburst of profanity from the classy Federer while berating the chair umpire who had allowed a point to be challenged by Del Potro.

Frustrated and infuriated by the lengthy discussion between the umpire and the Argentine, the normally calm Federer let loose with two of the more colorful expletives—which made their way into the TV microphones. In my commentary, I allowed as how, "Roger is human after all!"

The ski season brought the World Cup races in Colorado, leading up to the 2010 Winter Olympics in Vancouver, Canada. Once I knew that NBC was planning on me being there to call the Olympic alpine races for the sixth time, I gave my first thoughts to retirement. I would be seventy-one in May of 2010 and I couldn't be sure of further employment. I had been a contract player all of my fifty-year career and there were no guarantees that my handful of events each year would continue to be offered to me. Maybe saying farewell at an Olympic Games in the country of my birth would be a nice way to finish up.

But for now, our plan was to spend Christmas 2009 in Austria.

My great friend, ski-racer Franz Klammer, had raved about Christmas in his home city of Vienna, describing the city's decorative lights and the Christmas "markets" that dot the city from the beginning of Advent into early January.

"Tim, you must go," Franz would exhort each March when we would be together with other ski legends for the American Ski Classic, a fundraiser for the Vail Valley Foundation charities.

"You and Patricia will never forget it. It is very special."

So we made plans to travel by train, overnighting from our house in Switzerland to Vienna spending two nights there, and then training to Salzburg for Christmas Eve and Day. I booked us into the Hotel Bristol in Vienna and the Goldener Hirsch in Salzburg. I bought first-class tickets for a sleeping-compartment on the train from Lausanne to Vienna. We were expecting at least a semi-luxurious accommodation—after all this was a Swiss train and we were taking one of their nightly runs to Vienna. Surely it will be a lovely, modern train with comfortable sleeping arrangements.

Well, no. It was an old train and the cramped compartment's beds were like sleeping on boards. We had a tiny sink, with toilets at the end of the coach. So much for an Orient Express-type overnight trip.

When we arrived in Vienna, it was gray and cold. The last time we had been there, in January of 1998, we had stayed at the fabulous Hotel Imperial and had dinner one night at the then highly regarded Restaurant Corso in the nearby Hotel Bristol. Like many of the stately hotels in Europe—and in the U.S.—when it comes time to renovate, it most often turns into an update. The glories of the golden age—antique furniture, sumptuous bathrooms, and chandeliers—are replaced with modern amenities. Our room was quite lovely, but not special, and the Corso was now not only ugly-modern, but the food was even more so.

All was forgiven when we walked through the inner ring of the city. The Christmas lights Franz had raved about were indeed fabulous. Buildings and lampposts were done up in Christmas decorations like none we had ever seen, topping even New York's Rockefeller Center. A short tram ride to the Vienna city hall put us in the hearts of the market area, where the lighting was even more spectacular and dozens of small "pop-up" shops turned the huge garden area into a bazaar of Austrian kitsch, children's rides, and of course music.

This was the Vienna we had come to know and love from our previous trip a decade earlier. We had been there during the ball season, the month of January just after the Christmas festivities are over. A close friend of ours in Sun Valley, Frederic Boloix, had studied music in Vienna and had friends in the Vienna Philharmonic. Frederic put together a schedule of concerts for five consecutive nights, including tickets for one of the many balls taking place in January—ours turned out to be the Hunter's Ball, held at the stunningly beautiful Hofburg Palace. Many of the guests came dressed in Hunter's attire—men in loden shorts, knee socks, and jackets, the women in lovely ball gowns. It was a scene out of a film, and of course, we danced to a live orchestra playing Strauss waltzes!

The other nights we saw Mozart's *Magic Flute* at the Opera House, the famed Vienna Philharmonic Orchestra in their hall, the Vienna Symphony at their venue and a memorable chamber music evening in a lovely Vienna palace. We were seated in proper chairs, just three or four rows from the stage where the famed Alban Berg Quartet was playing an evening of works by Beethoven.

Our Christmas trip in 2009 also included music when we arrived in Salzburg. Christmas Eve we went to a Mozart dinner concert in the stunning Barocksaal, an opulent dining room that is part of a 17th-century restaurant, the Stiftskeller St. Peter. The singers and musicians were dressed in period costumes, and the decorations in the hall were magnificent.

Unfortunately, it rained. And rained. A planned sleigh ride on the outskirts of Salzburg turned out to be a bus ride to another, slightly more elevated village but which wasn't high enough to have the rain be snow. With lack of rain gear, protected only by blankets, we were soon wet blankets ourselves.

So much for a snowy Yuletide in the Austrian Alps. Our sogginess was only partly assuaged by a nice Christmas dinner in the dining room of the Goldener Hirsch.

But Franz was certainly right about Vienna's spectacular Christmas markets, and we were able to tell him so, since he and his wife Eva joined us for dinner at a neighborhood restaurant in Vienna owned by a friend of his. Our taxi driver dropped us at the door, and we knew we were at the right place because the door was festooned with pictures of Klammer—the ski hero still known in Austria as "the Kaiser."

The train ride back—during the day—from Salzburg to our Swiss home was a little more pleasant than the one on the way to Vienna—seven hours later, we got to sleep in our own bed!

CHAPTER 63

Homecoming in My Homeland

The U.S. ski team was heading to Vancouver's 2010 Olympic Games with great medal chances. Lindsey Vonn was leading the overall World Cup standing ahead of her friendly rival Maria Höfl-Riesch of Germany. Vonn had won ten races going into the Games that season, dominating the speed events. Julia Mancuso had injury problems during the World Cup year, but was known as a big event skier. For the men, Bode Miller was an unknown quantity having had a brutal season on the tour, and was bothered with nagging injuries and a questionable attitude. Among other things, he had trained outside the team and was traveling and sleeping in his own fancy bus instead of in the team hotels. Ted Ligety was the best hope for the men, leading the Tour in the giant slalom standings en route to Vancouver.

We had come back to the U.S. not long after Christmas in Austria and I was now revved up for the Vancouver Games, my ninth Olympics, and probably my last. London's 2012 Summer Games would be the final Olympics in NBC's deal with the IOC, and my contract ran only through events in 2010. That would include two equestrian events and two World Cup ski races. And I still had the U.S. Open Tennis in New York for the USTA on my work schedule as well.

Retirement would have to wait. But before I knew for sure that NBC was going to sign me for another go-around—to include the Winter Games in Vancouver—I had thought that if I was going to be invited, it would be an ideal time to announce my retirement. My fiftieth year in broadcasting and a farewell in my native country. But when my agent Sandy Montag told me that Dick Ebersol not only wanted me there, but expected me to continue covering alpine ski events and be involved in the final Games of the existing NBC Olympics contract: London 2012. Well…okay, I'll hang around!

The alpine ski events at the Vancouver Games were to be held in Whistler, a vast ski resort two hours drive from the city where all of the indoor events would take place. Weather in southern British Columbia, influenced by the humid winds from the Pacific Ocean had been a concern from the time Vancouver won the Olympic bid. Those of us who had been at the Nagano Games in 1998 assumed it would be similar—wet, and even warmer. Rain was common during the ski season in February—even at altitudes that would normally have snow. In fact snow had to be trucked to the nearby Freestyle ski venue, and then heavily salted to improve firmness. Conditions at the alpine venue were very sketchy and a little different each day. Todd and I did a feature on the conditions, lower on the mountain on a run adjacent to the racecourse. I was standing in slush, and our camera crew followed Todd down the hill as he sliced his way through the wet snow and with an exaggerated hockey-stop—sprayed me from head to toe.

While the program of races was not badly affected, the quality of racing was, even though the favorites prevailed in the medal count led by the Norwegian Aksel Lund Svindal who won three. Bode Miller bounced back from the bad memories of the Torino Games also winning three—including a gold in the combined event.

Lindsey Vonn fulfilled her dream of Olympic gold in the downhill, adding a bronze in the super-G, and her teammate Julia Mancuso scored silvers in the downhill behind Vonn and in the super combined. The Americans cemented their reputation for being big-event skiers, although Ted Ligety suffered disappointment with a ninth in his best event, the giant slalom.

The bad race conditions created some controversy within our NBC ranks, when in the women's giant slalom race—where Mancuso was defending Olympic champion—the bad weather shortened the intervals between racers, and in a fluky circumstance, Vonn was racing just before Mancuso. Lindsey fell on the course, getting tangled up in the netting. The race officials didn't realize she was still struggling to get up, and started Mancuso from the top. Julia, with an excellent run going, was waved off the course as she approached the fallen Vonn, and had to endure a re-run after all the other racers had completed the course.

Our producer John McGuinness came onto our headsets at the end of the race to tell us Ebersol wanted us to include in our taped race-call a calculus as to whether Mancuso—who had finished 8th, might have won a medal based on her time to the point where she was waved off the course in the first run.

Christin Cooper and I thought that was a dumb idea and just an effort to create a story featuring the American woman. There was no way to know what may have happened to Mancuso on the bottom part of the course—even in good conditions a small mistake or a fall could occur. No doubt her re-run time was affected by the fact that thirty or so racers had roughed up the track before Mancuso

Tim and his long-time ski-racing analyst, Christin Cooper.

came down again. It was a tough break for Julia, and she did well to finish top-ten and then go on to add a silver medal in the super combined event.

Yes, we did what the Boss demanded, but felt our "revised" coverage was way too contrived and demeaned the experts (us) who would have described the events in a more knowledgeable way. But hey, at least Chairman Ebersol was paying attention to our work!

Meanwhile, on the one day we had off from covering the races, our crew hit the one sunny day at the Games and we all had a brilliant day of skiing the higher slopes and taking the spectacular gondola ride across from Whistler to its neighboring mountain Blackcomb.

Our hotel was right in the heart of Whistler and the atmosphere every evening in the village was energizing. Locals and visitors were ignoring the wet weather and dancing in the streets. Todd Brooker and I were content to tangle with rib-eyes in the Hy's of Canada Steakhouse. (Highly recommended in all of Canada's major cities!)

When we left Whistler, I didn't know it would be my last Winter Olympics, but it turned out to be and so in retrospect I'm glad it was in my native land.

And of course those Games ended with the incredible gold medal hockey game won by Canada over the U.S. on Sidney Crosby's late goal.

I did know that I would be going to London in two years' time for the 2012 Summer Games and started planning to suggest where our hotel location should be for the rowing events. The historic town of Eton was the venue of rowing, very near Windsor Castle and even with England's propensity for rain, it would be an improvement on the pollution of Beijing!

CHAPTER 64

Ski Racers Are Special

My diminishing work-life had settled into a comfortable pattern of ski races and equestrian events in early spring and late fall in the U.S., and in the non-Olympic years, summers spent at our house in Switzerland with travels from there to England, Ireland (to visit my sister Mary Jo), France, and Italy to see friends and to explore in those countries places we hadn't been to before.

As I wrote earlier, NBC had us now calling the bi-annual World Alpine Ski Championships from the studios in Thousand Oaks, California. In February of 2011, the races were being held in Garmisch-Partenkirchen, Germany, a lovely but low-lying ski-town in the Bavarian Alps. Todd and Christin knew it well, but I had never been there. Our on-hill reporter Steve Porino was actually on-site for his bits, but we were doing our race commentary in sunnier climes back in the U.S.

The weather in Bavaria was foggy, wet and warm, making for less than spectacular racing. The big story became complaints during training runs—led by downhill favorite Lindsey Vonn—that the course was unsafe because of the poor weather conditions. The ski media immediately went to Vonn's friendly rival, the German Maria Riesch for comment, and she was put in the awkward position of defending her native country's climate and race preparation.

As it turned out neither Vonn nor Riesch won the speed events—Austria's Elisabeth Goergl won both the downhill and super-G!

Getting reports from Porino that the lousy weather, the uninspired skiing and the strained atmosphere made for a long two weeks in Bavaria, also made Todd, Christin and I just as happy to be in California! Of course at that point, I didn't know that Garmisch would be the last World Championships I would call from anywhere.

A month later I was in Vail, Colorado for the 28th annual American Ski Classic—not a World Cup event, but a charity fundraiser for the Vail Valley Foundation that features legends of the sport in friendly competition. I referred to this event earlier in the narrative, and my history with it is long and valued. Back in the early eighties I raced as a CBS Sports celebrity on a team with corporate types not long after former President Gerald Ford created the Classic in Beaver Creek (near Vail) where his family had a second home. A number of years later I was asked to host the televised version of the event and Todd Brooker and I have worked it for the last ten years or more.

The ASC has meant as much to me as broadcasting the major sports events I have been lucky enough to cover during this lengthy odyssey in toyland. Not because it is a highly watched program with critical acclaim attached to it, (it is neither!) but because I have come to realize how much the sport of ski-racing—one of more than thirty different sports I have lent my voice to—means to me.

A hockey player as a youngster, I didn't learn to ski until I was in my thirties and of course have never raced—except in the occasional celebrity-charity event. But being around young racers, men and women, at the peak of their powers in World Championships and Olympic Games and then to get to know and ski with them a few years later when they race in legends events, has made a great impact on me. Part of it is having learned what great people almost all of them are—fun-loving daredevils who come back from inevitable injuries, racing for their countries, not making the big bucks of the kind in bigger sports, willing to share their skills with novices on the snow, showing their passion for the great outdoors and a healthy lifestyle—not to mention their ability to party-down at gold medal levels!

To a degree, athletes from other individual sports like golf and tennis are able to stay close to their sport by competing on seniors circuits and gathering at the "Majors" and Hall of Fame ceremonies. But believe me, none approach the camaraderie and mutual respect demonstrated by ski-racers. It is an international family—a special club—sharing the secrets of matching themselves not just against each other, but against the mountains of the world. They are not always welcome guests of those mountains, which often scorn the skiers with icy slopes, blinding snow, gale-force winds, fog and flat-light—all the weapons Mother Nature can use to remind the racers they are mere mortals.

Of course there are bluebird sunny days, and powder to play in, and the thrill of victory in a sport where that elusive goal can be gained or lost by the length of a ski-tip, a thousandth of a second.

And when they share their memories of those times on the ski-tour, and joke about the results of their fun races at the American Ski Classic—it's a treat just to be a listener to the joyful banter.

I love them all, but my favorites over the years—some of whom I get to see in the off-season here and there include the great Austrian downhiller Franz Klammer, Americans Phil and Steve Mahre, Billy Kidd, "Moose" Barrows, Pam Fletcher, and Holly Flanders, Lisi Kirchler from Austria, Brigitte Oertli from Switzerland, and the three Norwegian brothers Stein, Jarle, and Edvin Halsnes—and their female counterpart Toril Forland— Bernhard Russi the great Swiss downhiller, Otto Tschudi, a Norwegian-American, Canadian Laurie Graham, Franz Weber, an Austrian import to the U.S. and so many more.

And each year, I could always plan to see Dr. Richard Steadman—he of the world-famed Steadman Clinic for Sports Medicine in Vail and his artist-wife Gay, whom Patricia and I are honored to call dear friends.

CHAPTER 65

Not All Horses
Are Created Equal

My equestrian world was a busy one in 2010, starting as usual with the Rolex Three-Day Event in Lexington, Kentucky in April. NBC carried it again, but had also signed up for the World Equestrian Games—held every four years—a world championship involving jumping, dressage, eventing, carriage driving, vaulting, endurance and more recently, the American sport of reining. All of which is more than you need to know unless you are a horse lover who cares about one or more of these competitions.

The telecasts were a bit of a nightmare. NBC carried four shows over two weekends—a big deal for the sport. It was only on the network because it was a time-buy, and that was made possible by the fact that it was the first time ever the event, "the WEG" as its known, had ever been held outside of Europe. My schedule was challenging. The night events during the week were carried by Universal Sports, which had limited production facilities. I, and my expert analyst Melanie Smith-Taylor, were paid extra to provide live commentary to Universal. But communications to them (and their studio to us) were virtually non-existent so things got pretty messy. We were covering preliminaries that would not see air on NBC, and without our usual support system we were winging it—all live!

The star of the whole World Games was appropriately, a horse. His name was Totilas, a Dutch Warmblood breed and a heavy favorite to win the dressage event. He was ridden by veteran Dutch rider Edward Gal. Totilas had dominated on the dressage circuit coming into the Games, and rumors were flying that he would be sold immediately after the WEG for as much as nine million dollars to a German syndicate to compete for that country at the London 2012 Olympics.

Even the most cynical viewer of dressage competitions who finds that horse-sport as boring as watching paint dry had to be captivated by Totilas's performance at the WEG. An incredible specimen of horse flesh, a haughty stallion of gleaming black color, Totilas simply demanded one's attention even when just walking into the competition ring.

Edward Gal and his mount dazzled the crowds in Lexington winning three gold medals without seemingly breaking a sweat—performing with an elegant, arrogant élan that broke all previous scoring records from the judges. It was a privilege for Melanie and me to have described his victories there.

All things considered, the NBC shows went relatively well, thanks to excellent production by Jim Carr and his Carr-Hughes crew with whom I had done all of the Rolex shows for several years. Unfortunately, due to heavy winds and some rain affecting our outdoor set, we had a few technical problems during our on-camera appearances. But overall I was happy to have had the chance to cover the first WEG ever to be held in the U.S. The Americans didn't fare too well except for sweeping the event they were naturally favored in—reining, (cowboys and cowgirls on Western quarter-horses) winning both team and individual golds. The only other medal wins were a silver in dressage, and a bronze in driving. The usually strong riders in the jumping competition were a bust, which was a bad omen for the Olympics in London just two years away.

CHAPTER 66

"Chateau Pour Le Loyer"

Before returning from Switzerland to the U.S. for the 2010 World Equestrian Games, Patricia and I had made a big—and sudden—decision to consider a larger house than our little one in Fechy. With a lease renewal coming due there, we started looking around in the same area for available rentals.

In a local paper, I came across an ad with one small black and white photo of what looked like a sizeable house with a courtyard and imposing stone wall. It was in the nearby village of Mont-sur-Rolle.

"Let's take a look for fun," was Patricia's request, even though the rent was more than double what we were paying in Fechy.

It took a little looking, but we found it without having to involve an agent. It *was* sizable—a 16th-century wine chateau that had originally been (we learned from the owner) a Cistercian monastery with its own vineyards. It even had a name: "Le Couvent de Germagny," which in English would be "Monastery of Germagny," (pronounced "jer-mon-yee).

Germagny was the name given to a large landholding owned by French royals in the 17th century prior to ultimately becoming part of the village of Mont-sur-Rolle, which overlooks the lakeside village of Rolle on the northern shore of Lake Geneva.

The entrance to the main part of the house was up a short stairway from the graveled courtyard. What had been the attached residence of the vigneron, or winemaker, was owned by another member of the family, a small piece of which was presently rented to another couple. The rest of the house would become ours—with a three-year lease at an exorbitant price. But it was magnificent. Much more than we needed. It was unfurnished, and would still be largely so, even with the meager belongings from our little house in Fechy.

In order to entice us, the landlord—widower of the woman's family who had owned "Le Couvent" since 1734—said he could bring up a few antiques from the basement "cave" where the family furnishings had been stored since he had moved to a nearby apartment after his wife's untimely death.

"We are seriously interested," we unwisely said, and were then told that a British family had also shown serious interest and he, the owner, would advise us by a fixed date which interested party he had chosen for the privilege of renting the property, which included a large beautiful stone-walled garden with adjacent vineyards.

Fechy, Switzerland: View from our house in the vines.

We left for the U.S. with mixed emotions about the wisdom of stepping up to such a huge house with a huge price, but enticed by the romance of its history and beauty.

When I got to Aspen for the World Cup races Thanksgiving weekend, an email came from the owner, Pierre Tacier, that he and his daughters had "selected" us to be their new tenants. We would move from our little house in Fechy on the first of July.

Being allowed only six months a year of residence in Switzerland, we got the most out of Le Couvent over the next three years. Now we had three spacious guest rooms for friends and family to visit, and lovely rooms on the main floor to use as offices and ample space in other rooms to entertain—all with gorgeous views of the lake, and the vineyard around us. From the master bedroom and from a balcony off a gorgeous, high-ceilinged *conservatoire*— Mont Blanc could be seen in all its glory across the lake in France.

NBC was now my only employer. My last year doing the world feed commentary was 2010 at the U.S. Open Tennis Championships, so the skiing and horse events—along with the Winter and Summer Olympic Games were my only gigs. Having made the big investment in the Swiss chateau, we were determined to enjoy our time there and make short trips within Europe.

Comcast had closed its deal to buy 51 percent of NBC Universal and had new management in place in 2010. The big cable company would ultimately buy the remaining 49 percent in 2014. Employees waited for shoes to drop. The sports department prepared for the departure of its boss, Dick Ebersol and some of his top staff. Ebersol was to produce his last Olympics in London with the new sports chairman Mark Lazarus literally looking over his shoulder.

The first clue I had that maybe things were winding down for me at NBC came when I inquired about the 2011 Rolex Kentucky event in April. I was told that another announcer had been assigned to it—Kenny Rice, an accomplished thoroughbred racing commentator who had worked the Beijing equestrian events—calling them from the New York NBC studios. Kenny had subsequently been the announcer for the reining events at the World Equestrian Games in Lexington when I hosted those shows and called the major events with Melanie Smith-Taylor.

My NBC arrangement included working through the 2012 London Games, and Molly Solomon had indicated I would again handle the rowing and canoe events as I had in Beijing. I assumed Kenny was earmarked for Equestrian in London and thus given the Lexington event. So Patricia and I planned to be in Europe in April instead of in Kentucky.

While visiting our friends the Duguids in England, we drove from their house near Oxford over to Eton which was to be the venue for the rowing.

Eton is a small village near Windsor Castle and its magnificent grounds. The village is an English landscape painting—driving through you think you are on the set of one of those English schoolboy films—young men dressed in morning attire: striped trousers, vests, white tie, black morning coats with schoolbooks in hand walking briskly through the village to nearby classes.

On the edge of the village is a road leading to an estuary of the Thames River where the most picturesque rowing venue imaginable lies. When we arrived, there were already several TV production trucks in place and cables were being laid to camera positions. There was a small office open nearby the start line and I was able to get a list of hotels in the area, with the admonition from the nice lady that many were already fully booked.

I was now totally psyched to be doing the rowing again—mainly because the setting at Eton was gorgeous, the village was charming, the pubs were cute and Windsor was minutes away. I fired off the list of hotels to Molly in hopes NBC would book the rowing crew in one of them.

The answer was no.

Yaz Farooq—my partner at the Beijing Games—and I would be staying at the Holiday Inn at Heathrow Airport—seven miles away, and with traffic on the two-lane roads, a nightmare to commute to and from during the Games.

Not long after scouting trip to Eton with our friends, and a brief trip from the UK to Ireland to see my sister Mary Jo, I received word from Molly Solomon that there had been a change in London assignments. She now needed me to switch back to the equestrian events. "But don't worry, you will still be going to London to call them—not to New York!"

So we would not be staying at Heathrow Airport. We would be in London Town. But, we would not cover the horse events from the venue in Greenwich Park—for monetary reasons we would be calling them from a monitor at the International Broadcast Center a few miles away!

Patricia was thrilled we would be in London. She frankly didn't give a damn where I was calling the events from! She immediately planned to find a health club near Canary Wharf where we would stay at a rather nice Marriott Hotel, from where she could take the Tube—London's subway system—to the museums and art galleries, and to visit old friends while I was commuting each day to the monolithic cavern of the IBC.

So I shifted my preparations from oars and paddles to saddles and bridles. At least we would have a shorter flight to jolly old England from Geneva, Switzerland than from Ketchum, Idaho.

But the London Games were still months away, and I found myself more and more thinking about the future, and my past....

CHAPTER 67

Musings While Sipping Swiss Wines

When I have been asked the question, "What would you have chosen to be if not what you chose? I have answered to intimates (or the less intimate, but simply curious): "A concert pianist—Artur Rubinstein."

I have an innate love of music. Of all kinds. I have never played an instrument. There was a piano in my family home when I was very young—I think my mother played a little, my oldest sister Mary Jo took lessons and later in life taught some. My father had a limited interest in music, but I do remember as a child that he would play "records" of the cabaret chanteuse Hildegarde, the pianist Jose Melis and an obscure nightclub singer Dorothy Shea who had a song my Dad loved titled, "Pure as the Driven Snow."

Whether stimulated by this limited exposure or by some reincarnated spirit, I recall that at the age of about six, I would play one of the classical records in the small family collection and with a wooden spoon in hand, direct the orchestra playing Beethoven, Mozart or whatever.

At the age of twelve, I remember trying out for a place at St. Michael's Choir School in Toronto, which was kind of Canada's Vienna Boys Choir. I was an alto by then. I did not make the cut. But at my all-boys Catholic high school, De La Salle "Oaklands," I was good enough to perform in Gilbert and Sullivan operettas. Not in a feature role however, just as a member of the sailor's chorus in the *Pirates of Penzance*, and as one of the maids in "Three Little Maids Are We" in "The Mikado." Yes, with crinoline skirts and curly wigs.

My penalty for cross-dressing was to take extra hits at football practice from my more macho teammates.

By the time I was a sophomore at Notre Dame, I had been introduced to jazz. A neighbor in my residence hall from Chicago by the name of Skip Bergeron had a collection of 33 rpm albums and shared his pleasures from the likes of Duke Ellington, Flip Phillips, Illinois Jacquet, Clifford Brown and other jazz stars of the era. By my junior year I was among a small group of jazz enthusiasts who convinced the university administration that Notre Dame should be the first college in the country to host a collegiate jazz festival.

1958: Tim introduces jazz great Stan Kenton at the first Notre Dame Jazz Festival.

It was a big success, and endures to this day at ND, having spawned more than 300 college jazz festivals featuring competition among student musicians and vocalists in groups and big bands. I was the MC at the first one, and the judges included Robert Berklee of the Berklee School of Music, Frank Holzfeind owner of the famed Chicago nightclub the Blue Note, Chuck Suber, editor of *Down Beat* magazine and bandleader Stan Kenton who exclaimed at the finale: "This is the greatest thing to ever happen to jazz!"

That was the beginning of a life-long love affair with jazz, and ultimately with music of all kinds. My stint as a jazz critic for the *Toronto Star* introduced me to many musicians and singers and my life in TV sports brought friendships with others who were sports fans—the likes of Joe Williams, Stan Getz, Mel Torme and in later years, Paul Desmond and Jack Jones—whom Frank Sinatra once described as "the greatest singer of popular music."

Other music mavens, like jazz writers Doug Ramsey and Ira Gitler remain friends to this day. Doug spent most of his working life as a TV news anchor and we worked together at WPIX-TV in 1970. Ira was also a hockey writer, and our paths crossed at that time as well. Jack Jones and I met at the tennis tournament in Palm Desert when I covered it one year, and have since become close friends.

Over the fifty-two years of my career travels I have heard some of the greatest living jazz musicians in some of the best jazz spots in the world—most of which are long gone. The famous strip along 52nd Street in New York saw the closing of several famous rooms before my arrival there, but Eddie Condon's was still there in 1969 and I got to hear trumpeter Roy Eldridge at that club before it closed. Of course I would go to the Village Vanguard, in New York's Greenwich Village and Baron's in Harlem, and when on the road, the London House in Chicago, Jazz Alley in D.C., El Matador in San Francisco, the Town Tavern in Toronto, Le Bilboquet in Paris, Ronnie Scott's Pizza Express and the Boisdale Club in London and many more around the world. I survived the smog from smokers but frequently drank too much in all of those musical saloons.

I have embraced many favorites: the Modern Jazz Quartet, the Count Basie band, and instrumentalists Chet Baker, Miles Davis, Paul Desmond, John Coltrane, Stan Getz, pianists Bill Evans, Marion McPartland and Hank Jones, Ray Brown on base, Gene Bertoncini and Jim Hall on guitar, drummers Shelley Manne and Chico Hamilton.

My favorite singers, along with Jack Jones and Mel Torme, include Anita O'Day, Peggy Lee, Blossom Dearie and of course, Sinatra. Gene Bertoncini, a fellow Notre Dame grad and a musician Tony Bennett has called the "best guitarist in jazz," is warm, witty, and with Jack Jones one of my dearest pals.

Why the Artur Rubinstein reference at the top this chapter? Well, I saw a PBS documentary about him a few years ago, and was envious of his passion, his obvious connection to his music and I thought: What a legacy he is leaving the world, as do many other great musicians.

He represented to me the kind of person who had a great and valuable gift that he would continue to share with mankind long after he had passed on. Somehow, I don't think describing the prowess of great athletes to their fans quite measures up to that.

• • •

My own musical career was limited to my high-school Gilbert and Sullivan appearances in the choruses, and a brief stint as a singer in a pop-duo called the "Two Tones" with a friend, Jimmy Nolan who actually went on to a successful professional career.

In fact, it was a long time between drinks. My next appearance on stage was forty-three years later, when for reasons still beyond me, I was asked to play the role of Michael in Brian Friel's play *Dancing at Lughnasa*. It was not on Broadway, or even off-Broadway, it was really way, way off Broadway—in Sun Valley, Idaho at the Community School Theater.

I was asked to play the part by David Blampied, a professional actor and director in Sun Valley, who ran the New Theatre Company. The play was set in Donegal, Ireland. If I said yes, I had to subject myself to learning not just an Irish accent, but a *Northern* Irish accent from a dialect coach imported from nearby Boise.

I said yes.

Actually it was a reading, rather than a full-on play, but it had a modest set and lights, and would be performed on a proper stage in a proper theater. Admission was ten bucks.

I was nervous about this, but I drew on my experience as a cross-dresser in operettas. I knew only two of the other cast members—David who convinced me my television voice was perfect for the part, and another real actor, Claudia McCain—who, if she hadn't chosen to live quietly in Sun Valley, could have been a major Broadway star.

When it came time to have what we in show biz call a read-through, I was actually quite nervous—especially about the dialect coach. When I entered the room at the school, I recognized David and Claudia, but the others were strangers to me except for one older, portly man who looked vaguely familiar. He was holding a copy of the script in his hands.

"Holy shit," I said silently, "That's Albert Finney!"

Finney is the British stage and film star who, it turned out was visiting his friend, another Brit actor David Hemmings, who had a vacation home in

DANCING AT LUGHNASA
by BRIAN FRIEL
★★★★★★★ ★★★★★★★ ★★★★★★

Director	David Blampied
Dialect Coach	Ann Klautsch
Technical Director	Justin Rowland
Stage Manager	Matt Gorby
Technical Assistants	Tony Jefferson
Voice Over	Sue Noel
Publicity	Rochelle Reed

CAST OF CHARACTERS

Michael	Tim Ryan
Chrissie	Cathy Reinheimer
Maggie	Patricia Conwell*
Aggie	Marilyn Teitge
Rose	Jonelle Anderson
Kate	Claudia McCain
Jack	David Blampied*
Gerry	Gordon Gammell

Setting: The home of the Mundy family, two miles outside the village of Ballybeg, County Donegal, Ireland

Time: 1936

~ There will be one 15 minute intermission ~

* Produced by special arrangement with Dramatist Play Service, Inc.

*Member of Actors' Equity Assn., the Union of Professional Actors and Stage Managers in the United States.

Sun Valley, Idaho, 1998: Tim's acting debut.

253

Idaho. Apparently the theater company thought there was a chance Finney might agree to play a part in *Dancing* since it was just a one-night show. He had offered to David to come to our read-through.

The very thought of him actually acting on the same stage with me frightened me to death. I was relieved to find out later that he wouldn't be in town on the show-date.

Meanwhile he read one of the parts, and offered comments to the rest of us as we read ours.

It was three or four weeks before the big night and I didn't feel my dialect sessions were going so well. But when the curtain went up and I read the opening monologue there were no sneers or chortles from the audience, which I guess meant none of them had relatives from Donegal.

I don't recall if there was a standing ovation and curtain calls.

The whole experience was great fun, and I gained enormous respect for the real actors who were on the stage with me. Patricia thought I did very well (of course she did!) and kept the program and her ticket stub as souvenirs.

Oddly enough, despite my triumph on stage that night, I was never again approached with acting offers....

CHAPTER 68

London Bridges Not Falling Down

More than anything else, security was the big issue leading to the 2012 Summer Olympics in London. The suicide bombings in London subways seven years earlier were still fresh in Britons' minds.

Slow ticket sales were also a concern. Oh—and traffic. And venues for the various sports—some old, some new. And of course, the English weather just a couple of weeks after Wimbledon—which always has rain.

As for security, yes there were military gun emplacements on the tops of high-rises, helicopters buzzing like mosquitos around the Olympic sites, and more London bobbies around than you could shake their sticks at—but now, many of them were actually armed.

But everything turned out, as the Brits would say in jargon of the day, "brilliant!"

There were empty seats at many of the events—including the big ones like track and field—but as the British athletes started winning medals at an alarming rate, sales picked up noticeably. As for traffic, yes, the Olympic lanes for athletes, media, and VIPs made some of London's narrow streets even narrower, but since many civil servants were given the two Olympic weeks off and other Londoners had escaped to the countryside, most of the city center was left for the ubiquitous black (and expensive) taxis.

The Underground, London's tube was a big hit with tourists, with cheerful volunteers wearing pink vests who were everywhere and very helpful. Their advice to newcomers and themselves was spelled out on T-shirts that sold like hotcakes: "KEEP CALM AND CARRY ON."

One could quibble about the production of the Opening Ceremony—especially after the sensational show at the previous Summer Games in Beijing—but despite some odd bits depicting social services in Britain, it was saved by the James Bond helicopter delivery of a fake Queen Elizabeth dropping into the Olympic Stadium, neatly segueing into the entrance of the real Queen to the Royal Box.

Of course leading up to the Games, Heathrow airport's arrivals hall was the primary concern for travelers. It is one of the worst in the world at getting customers from overnight flights through immigration and customs. By all accounts it maintained that reputation, but Patricia and I, traveling from our house in Switzerland, lucked out immensely by arriving at midnight when the arrivals hall was virtually empty. We skated through customs and there was no one in line at the Olympic Credentials desk so we sailed through that too.

The downside was that NBC transportation personnel had left for the night, and it cost us 100 pounds sterling for a taxi to our hotel on Canary Wharf—the far side of London from Heathrow. No, NBC did not reimburse!

One of the venue choices that had caused controversy for the London Olympic organizers was the equestrian grounds. They had chosen Greenwich Park over better-known, established sites in the English countryside. It meant taking over a public park with lovely gardens for several months and finding space to build temporary stables, media facilities, and create a kumping and dressage arena as well as constructing a cross-country course for the eventing competition.

Melanie and I had only one day to go over to the venue and see what we would be describing from a TV monitor in our little broom-closet at the IBC. The organizers had done a beautiful job, although the cross-country course was somewhat crammed in among the trees and walkways, making for a tight course for horses and riders.

Mel had brought her iPad with her and took pictures of the obstacles as we walked the course. Great idea, since we would only be seeing it on our monitor with no chance to look ahead to each jump. She gleefully sent it off to some of her horsey friends back home. One problem. We were not supposed to be on the course or take pictures until after the riders had walked it a day before the event—and that was several days away. Fortunately, nobody squealed.

Our broadcast schedule was friendly, the events were daytime only and we had most evenings free so Patricia and I were able to have dinner together—some nights alone, sometimes with London friends or NBC colleagues. There were many good restaurants right in the Canary Wharf area—all within walking distance, including an excellent Spanish one and a decent Italian one along the wharf abutting the Thames.

Better yet was the Boisdale Club—a membership club with a top-flight restaurant, a lively terrace for drinks, and live music every night with some of the UK's top jazz musicians. I had become an Honorary Member by telling them that I would frequently be bringing NBC folks over from the Marriott during the Games.

They were glad to have me—especially when Patricia and I brought Tom Brokaw along one evening. The great NBC News commentator is well-known even in England!

Of course I left way too much money at Boisdale. NBC's meager expense money—paid in advance during Olympic Games—was more suited to a bacon-and-eggs and hamburger menu than to real restaurant prices in the most expensive city in the world. But the evenings out from our mushroom cellar at the IBC were well worth it over the nearly three weeks in London.

The equestrian events were not kind to the U.S. team. Its riders failed to medal in any event—even the talented jumping team was shut out. The Brits did very well on their home court, winning five medals including two golds.

Unlike at the 2010 World Equestrian Games in Lexington, Kentucky, there was no particular horse star at Greenwich Park. The much-anticipated appearance by the sensational dressage horse Totilas never occurred. After his brilliant performance at the "WEG" in Kentucky two years earlier, the Dutch owners sold the horse for a reported nine million dollars to buyers in Germany where the stallion would have a German rider. That rider became ill while training for the London Games and apparently did not recover in time to compete.

Totilas stayed at his new home in Germany, presumably busy with other activities that were more lucrative to his new owners.

CHAPTER 69

Okay, What Now?

When we left London that August of 2012, I was expecting to be working the World Cup ski races in Aspen and Beaver Creek in the late fall as I had for the previous ten years. My deal with NBC was officially up, but since they already had the rights to the 2014 Sochi Winter Games, I thought they would ask me to stay for Sochi, and if so, I could plan a farewell (this time for real!) at the World Alpine Championships which were to be held in Vail the following year.

After all, I had felt content that if the 2010 Winter Olympics in Canada were to be my last event, fifty years in the biz with a send-off there would have been just fine. But now, with Vail on the horizon, I thought there was a good chance I could "do it my way" and tell NBC that I would be retiring after the Vail events.

Patricia and I headed over to Ireland from London to visit my sister Mary Jo, who had just had her eighty-fourth birthday and was still going strong. We flew to Dublin and decided to take a northerly route across to the west to see parts of Ireland neither Patricia nor I had been to. I booked country-house hotels for a night each in County Donegal and County Sligo, and then we spent three nights with Mary Jo in County Mayo. The wonderful Irish poet Seamus Heaney had just died, and the country was in mourning. Each village we went through had signs telling where one could sign a register with messages of condolence. It was quite an experience to see and feel the impact that Heaney had on his fellow Irishmen of all ages with his wit and wisdom.

To celebrate my sister's birthday, we made our annual stop for dinner at the Newport House, just a short distance from Mary Jo's home. It's a well-preserved 19th-century country house with a few rooms for folks who want to fish the adjacent river for salmon, and with a lovely Old World dining room and an excellent wine list.

On the way back to our Swiss house we made plans for visits to friends in Italy and France and for Christmas in Zermatt, a trip to Cape Town to spend time with the Duguids in January and be back in the U.S. in February for me to cover the 2013 World Alpines in Schladming Austria.

The only nagging thing was that unlike when Dick Ebersol was still in charge at NBC and knowing he was a fan of mine, I could expect that after the London Games he would have said, "On to the 2014 Winter Games in Russia." This time there was silence from the new brass. But we "kept calm and carried on" with the assumption that I would continue as the ski and horse guy at NBC.

Within weeks of the conclusion of the London Olympics came the call. It was Sam Flood, the newly named executive producer in the new NBC Sports regime. His message was that I would "not be needed" for the World Cups in the winter of 2013, nor for the Sochi Games. Another announcer, Dan Hicks—a rising star at the network, would be replacing me as the ski-racing voice in Russia, and so would do the World Cups and the Schladming World Championships in preparation for the 2014 Winter Olympics.

Testing the new waters, I asked Sam if I could continue doing the equestrian events—specifically the 2013 Rolex Kentucky the next April. He clearly hadn't even thought about that minor event on the NBC Sport calendar, and after a minute of flummoxed hesitation said, "Sure, that will be fine."

Of course I knew that the Rolex would be my last event for NBC, and told Flood that I would like to make my own announcement that I was "retiring from NBC Sports coverage of ski-racing," thus leaving the door open for other opportunities if they came along. I then emailed Dan Hicks and offered to chat with him about announcing ski-racing, (a sport new to him), tell him about his expert analysts Christin Cooper, Todd Brooker and Steve Porino, and assure him they would welcome him and give him all the help he needed to get started.

In my heart I knew I was done—or would be after the Rolex event in April of 2013. Gratefully the Vail Valley Foundation wanted me to return to do the American Ski Classic with Todd, which would keep me in the ski world at least through March of 2014.

So, fifty-three years after my start in TV sports (and news) at CFTO-TV in Toronto, a career covering more than thirty different sports in more than twenty different countries on four broadcast networks, two cable networks and syndication, a few things for Sirius satellite radio—I guess it's enough, unless… an offer comes along to do a sport I like, in a nice place, and on someone else's nickel….

CHAPTER 70

"Old Soldiers Never Die..."

Back in Switzerland, Patricia and I had a fabulous 2012 Christmas in Zermatt with perfect weather—snow falling, holiday lights illuminating the quaint streets, great skiing under the Matterhorn, fine drinks and dining at the splendid Monte Rosa hotel—the base camp for the first man to climb the Matterhorn, Edward Whymper in 1865.

In late January, we flew to Cape Town to spend ten days with the Duguids there, with a one-night stop in Amsterdam to see Patricia's niece and new baby. In March we went home to Sun Valley and then to Vail for the Ski Classic, and with the Rolex scheduled for the last week in April, we had planned a trip farther west to visit friends in Pebble Beach and Santa Barbara and then go to Mexico for two weeks. My sister Mary Jo had good friends in Miami who had a second home in San Miguel Allende and for several years had offered it to us for a vacation anytime we wanted.

While we were in Pebble Beach an email came from Lovee Arum: Call Bob.

Arum is like a bad penny, or a good one in my case—he just seems to turn up and complicate my life with something good. This time he wanted me to make a one-off comeback to my TV boxing career. In Macao. In a week.

"We leave next Sunday for Hong Kong, overnight there, then to Macao. You and George Foreman and Larry Merchant—boxing icons!! Gathering together in a reunion to televise a fight with the two-time Olympic champion from China. I just signed him! He's gonna be HUGE! There are 300 million people watching TV in China. Lovee's coming—bring Patricia—we'll have a ball! We leave from LAX next Sunday—you're in Pebble Beach? Going to

Santa Barbara? Perfect! Plane leaves Sunday at 2:50. Whaa? You're going to Mexico? When? Perfect! We get back to L.A. the following Sunday, you make your flight, works great! Call my guys they'll book your tickets."

Click.

I have paraphrased that pitch from Bob, but it captures the essence of that greatest of pitchmen, and as usual I said yes.

Some things (and people) never change. Arum was now eighty-one— still the boss of Top Rank, although his stepson Todd DuBoef was running things day-to-day and handling all the arena productions of the big fights.

We cut short our visit in Santa Barbara and joined the boxing party on Cathay Pacific Airlines to Hong Kong. Two nights seeing that fascinating city for the first time, then an hour ferry-boat ride to Macao, the former Portuguese colony now part of China.

The fight would be at the Cotai Arena, attached to the Venetian Hotel and Casino, a sister property of the Venetian in Las Vegas. The Venetian is one of two American-owned casino-resort properties in Macao, the other being the Wynn Macao, named, as is his huge resort in Las Vegas for my long-time friend and Sun Valley skier Steve Wynn. The main event would feature the Chinese Olympic champion Zou Shiming, making his professional debut. After he won gold at the 2008 Beijing Olympics, the Chinese government convinced—meaning paid—Zou to remain "amateur" so he could represent his country at the London Games, where at the age of thirty-two, he won gold again. Arum then signed him up and assigned the excellent trainer Freddy Roach to mold an amateur into a pro.

In his debut on our telecast on HBO the Chinese didn't dazzle against an eighteen-year-old Mexican, but his whirlwind style and hand-speed earned him a four-round decision. Larry, George, and I called the fight along with two earlier title fights on the card—the first time I had called boxing matches since Arum had hauled me back from the French Open tennis tournament in Paris to announce that title fight in New York in 2006.

While Macao looks like Las Vegas-Far East, with its tiny city-center the only remaining vestige of its Portuguese history, it's become a mecca for mainland Chinese who pour in by the thousands to play the slots and leave money at the craps and black-jack tables. But with new tax laws and corruption investigations, the Chinese government is now making things harder for the gamblers and the casino owners.

Having a Chinese boxing star—a sports hero in his country of 1.3 billion people—gives the Venetian another attraction to draw people to its casino and a potentially enormous TV audience for Arum's Top Rank to tap into.

After a night in L.A. to recover from the long flight from Hong Kong, Patricia and I flew overnight to León, Mexico where a driver in a rickety taxi was waiting at 6 a.m. to drive us to San Miguel de Allende. Having never been there before, we didn't know what to expect in terms of the environment or our accommodations.

My sister's friends, Andrew Oerke and his wife Anitra had sent us a link to some videos that showed the town—the best-preserved city from Spanish colonial days in Mexico—as an architecturally beautiful place set in an arid mountain valley with a population of artists, writers, and musicians from all parts of the world—in addition to talented locals. It was all of the above. Andrew joined us for the first week in their charming home—Anitra was in Miami where she had a real-estate business. Both of them were marine scientists and Andrew was also an award-winning poet. It was our great good fortune to have him with us to share their love for this special place. Each evening we would sit on the rooftop terrace, margaritas in hand, and Andrew would point out the flocks of black cranes returning from the mountain tops to the lake below, and read some of his poems to us before dinners out at one of the many excellent restaurants in the town.

It was an idyllic stay for which Patricia and I will be ever-grateful—saddened in retrospect when we later learned that our new friend Andrew, eighty-two, had died suddenly only days after leaving us in San Miguel to return to Miami.

Patricia, a gifted photographer, put together an Apple book of some wonderful pictures she had taken during our two weeks there, and sent a copy to Anitra as a memorial to Andrew.

Our seemingly endless road trip took us back through Houston to Lexington to do what was indeed my final show for NBC, the 2013 Rolex Kentucky Equestrian Championship. For several years we had stayed at a cute little hotel in downtown Lexington called the Gratz Park Inn that had an excellent restaurant called Jonathan's, featuring a sophisticated southern cuisine. Right next to the hotel is an authentic French bistro, Le Deauville, and nearby a world-class restaurant called Dudley's. Yes, we dined well! And it was just a fifteen-minute drive to the Horse Park each day of the competition—a scenic drive that offered frequent glimpses of gorgeous thoroughbreds grazing on the Kentucky bluegrass along the roadside.

Knowing it was my last go-round for NBC, I was glad that Carr-Hughes Productions was the team I was doing my farewell show with. Jim Carr and I had a long history together since he also freelanced with NBC on the ski events I had covered for many years, and so we knew each other well and had a great trust of each other. His partner in the company, Bob Hughes, was also a great guy and I always looked forward to working with them.

I never ceased to be amazed how Jim directed the cross-country phase of the three-day event because there would most often be three horse-and-rider combinations on the course at any one time. No one in the U.S. has the skill Jim has to know how to "cut" the cameras to keep the continuity of the competition. I relied on him totally when we did voiceovers of the cross country—knowing he would cue me to the right horse and rider every time.

The champion for 2013 was Andrew Nicholson from New Zealand, holding off the challenge of British super-star William Fox-Pitt, who had won the event in 2010 and 2012.

When our live coverage of the jumping portion, which had decided the champion was over, I signed off with the usual, "And so for Melanie Smith-Taylor, I'm Tim Ryan saying so long from Lexington, Kentucky!" Minutes later, Jim Carr and I toasted each other with a glass of champagne—and a hug.

That itinerary—Sun Valley to Pebble Beach, to Santa Barbara, to Los Angeles, to Hong Kong, to Macao, to Los Angeles, to Mexico to Lexington, to New York to Switzerland gave us pause—pause to maybe think about slowing down and downsizing and maybe actually retiring to a nice warm place in the U.S.

But sure enough, even before we left from Macao, Bob Arum had said he wanted me to return there in July for another telecast featuring his Chinese champion. Of course, we went. This time staying on the Kowloon side of Hong Kong at the famed Peninsula Hotel, and had a great walking tour of the exotic city with a local friend of Patricia's sister Verna.

Zou Shiming won his fight again, and we flew back directly to our house in Mont-sur-Rolle and enjoyed being there during what would be our last grape harvest, and planning a "last hurrah" family Christmas in Sun Valley. I had put our house in Ketchum on the market.

For the first time in my career, I was looking ahead to an empty calendar.

CHAPTER 71

"A" For Alaska,
"Z" For Zimbabwe

While "A" is alphabetically distantly removed from "Z," Alaska—Americas's vast and wild wilderness state actually has much in common with my beloved Zimbabwe.

Both have spectacular terrain and both have a plethora of fabulous wildlife. Zimbabwe's natural assets are land-locked, except for its northern border with Zambia where the Zambezi River and Lake Kariba separate the former countries of Northern and Southern Rhodesia. Alaska is of course virtually surrounded on three sides by the Pacific Ocean and the Bering Sea. But what they also have in common is the sense of awe they bring to visitors—most of whom can't wait to return again and again.

I have deliberately left Alaska until the end of this narrative because a special place there, the Kachemak Bay Wilderness Lodge and its owners, the McBride family, still hold a special place in my heart. My late wife Lee and I made two trips there, the first in 1983 when CBS had sent Gil Clancy and me to cover a lightweight fight in Anchorage featuring the colorful Puerto Rican star, Hector "Macho" Camacho. The local fight promoter gave the McBrides a rave review, and since we couldn't be sure we would ever be back in Alaska, we decided to stay an extra few days and book into their lodge, a short flight away by chartered aircraft.

It was love at first sight—for both the land and sea-scape and for Michael and Diane McBride, whose zeal to brave the wilds and winter weather of Alaska to create a magical oasis reminded us of our many friends in Zimbabwe who had shown the same passion and love for the wild in building their safari camps.

Michael and I became good friends and stayed in close touch. Not too many years later, with Lee in the early stages of Alzheimer's, I called Mike to say we were coming back. While Lee was now unable to fully comprehend all of the joys of returning to Kachemak, Mike and Diane's sensitive hospitality provided another happy experience for us. It was to be Lee's last trip away from home.

Sometime later, after Lee had succumbed to the cruel disease, Patricia and I were visiting our families in New York. Michael was there from Alaska to speak at the Explorer's Club, of which he is an esteemed member. He invited us to attend, and then insisted to Patti that she must come soon to see the McBride lodge in Alaska.

And so I was able to share the beautiful tranquility of Kachemak Bay with Patricia, which was very meaningful to me. Mike flew us in his Piper Cub from the lodge to nearby Loon Lake, where the McBrides have a private cabin for guests, and we had an idyllic couple of nights there under the looming magnificence of a huge glacier. The next day, we paddled a canoe on the lake and listened to the call of loons as they fished nearby. In a chartered eight-person antique aircraft with a wooden fuselage, we flew over ice-fields and wilderness land, spotting elk and mountain sheep.

Alaska…Zimbabwe. Kindred spirits, continents apart.

CHAPTER 72

Encounters: Good and Bad...

All the years and millions of miles of international travel naturally provided airline anecdotes. None was as dramatic as our crash-landing in the Namib Desert recounted earlier in this narrative, but some were more amusing for sure. The some that stand out in my memory involve famous people.

On a flight to South Africa for one of Top Rank's fights there during my CBS days, my seat-mate in first class overnight London to Johannesburg was golfer Gary Player. I recognized him as he sat down, but he did not recognize me—no surprise. We exchanged pleasant greetings, but I resisted conversation knowing as nice a man as he is, he would probably be grateful for silence.

After dinner was served, Gary politely made a request of me. We were in the first rows of seats with a "bulkhead" in front of us. I was in the window seat, Gary in the aisle. Would I mind if he stretched out on the floor in front of us to sleep?

In those days you could remove the arm-rests between the first-class seats. Gary said I would be welcome to stretch out across the two seats and he would sleep on the floor. This of course led to some inevitable conversation—Gary responded to my quizzical look by telling me that as a child growing up on a ranch in South Africa, he often played with children of the family's black servants and had learned from them that sleeping on a hard surface, i.e. the ground, was good for one's back and that of course since he had played golf from a young age, he believed it had helped him avoid back problems.

So down he went to the floor, a blanket over him, while I enjoyed the comfort of two cushioned seats.

· · ·

A far less pleasant experience on a trip from the U.S. to Europe found me again in a first-class bulkhead window seat, and being joined by a portly, familiar-looking man with a large briefcase and a gravelly, basso-profundo voice. Henry Kissinger.

Distinctly lacking Gary Player's charm and politesse, he sat down without a word, placed his briefcase on the arm-rest between us and as soon as we were airborne, opened it and took out most of its contents labeled "Council on Foreign Relations," spread them on his tray-table, leaving a thick stack on the arm-rest—and leaving no room for my arm, let alone any papers of mine!

When our meals came—and he had to move his papers, I made sure to slide some of my homework material into my space on the armrest and offered an innocuous, "Where are you headed?" to charming Henry.

"Moscow," he grunted, and went back to his reading. That was the extent of our conversation. Not being a huge fan of him or his politics, I was grateful.

Henry did not ask to sleep on the floor in front of us. Which would not have been a pretty sight.

· · ·

A far more pleasant experience involved the actress Diane Keaton, only a few years after her hit Woody Allen film *Annie Hall.*

She and I were both seated in first class en route from New York to Paris. I had not noticed her during the flight—and oddly enough—she hadn't noticed me! When we landed, I could see an attractive lady getting some extra attention from the flight attendants as we were waiting to leave the plane. It was Annie—I mean Diane!—being helped with her topcoat, (it was wintertime and a cold blast of air came in from the jet-way). I was right behind her as we disembarked. At the end of the ramp a mob of paparazzi—light bulbs flashing—blocked the way as the passengers were trying to get through. I was now alongside Ms. Keaton and she looked frightened.

"Excuse me," I said, "I will help you get through if you like—pull your coat collar up and hold onto my arm."

She looked at me, smiled and said, "Thank you!"

I made like I was her escort and the two of us pushed through the maze of cameras and microphones until we got to immigration where she was met by officials. "Thanks again," said Annie—I mean Diane—and off she went.

. . .

A less enchanting famous lady, Barbra Streisand, provided a far less pleasant encounter back in 1992. It was at the U.S. Open Tennis Championships, during which she was linked with Andre Agassi. One evening when I was hosting the highlights show for CBS, there was a knock at the door of the small office in the bowels of the Louis Armstrong Stadium adjacent to our studio. A handful of our TV crew was in the office while matches were underway on the court just yards away. Our receptionist opened the door, and a man who turned out to be the music producer David Foster asked if we minded if he brought in Barbra Streisand to stay for a few minutes, since she was being hounded by spectators and paparazzi while she was waiting for the Andre Agassi match to begin. You may recall that Barbra referred to her new "friend" as the "zen master."

The receptionist explained this was the CBS studio, we were on and off the air and that she would have to check with the announcer Tim Ryan. She did, and I said okay. Foster ushered in Streisand and a couple of more people with them into our tiny space. Without a word of greeting, Barbra made herself at home on the one sofa in the room. No introductions were made by Foster. When they were told the Agassi match was about to begin, the group got up and left, as the old expression goes, "without even as much as a fare-thee-well," not even a thank-you, or a smile from the prima donna.

. . .

A zanier encounter occurred years earlier at the bar of the Berkshire Hotel on East 52nd Street in Manhattan. I had just a had a cocktail-hour drink there with my cousin Pat, in town from his Toronto home. From there I was headed to a Knicks playoff game at Madison Square Garden.

In the lobby lounge I recognized the actor Bill Murray a couple of bar-stools down from me. He was, as the Brits say, "in his cups." It was pouring rain outside. Murray got up to leave and headed to a bicycle standing near the door. The bartender called over to him that it was a, "Heavy rain out there, Bill, I'll get you a cab."

Murray answered that he was just going to ride his bike to his apartment nearby. He didn't look or sound like that was a viable prospect. I introduced myself and told Bill I had a limo coming shortly to take me to the Garden and I would happily drop him off at his apartment.

"It's rush hour, and dumping rain. You'll drown out there!" I said, leaving out the possibility that in his shape, he would more likely fall off his bike and be hit by a speeding taxi.

"You're going to the game? Wish I had a ticket," said Bill

"Come on with me." I said, "I'm sure I can get you a seat with me in the CBS box. You can come back here tomorrow and pick up your bike. The bartender will take care if it for you. And you can get a cab to your place after the game."

Anything to keep him from getting on his bike.

So my new friend Bill and I went to the Garden and it turned out there was an empty available seat in the box. Murray nursed only one beer through the entire game and we had a great time. We shared a cab uptown afterwards, Bill gave me his New York phone number, but ever since our fun night at the Knicks game, I have only seen him in the movies.

• • •

Way back in my California Seals hockey days, April of 1969 to be precise, our Coliseum arena hosted its first big boxing match—a heavyweight championship match between Jimmy Ellis and Jerry Quarry for the vacant WBA title. Ellis was a former sparring partner for then Cassius Clay and Quarry was the current "white hope."

The fight brought the national sporting media to Oakland, and the night of the fightI found myself in the food line in the press hospitality suite with a man I recognized from photographs on book covers, the esteemed author/ screen-writer Budd Schulberg (*What Makes Sammy Run*, *On the Waterfront*). I introduced myself to him as the PR man and broadcaster for the Seals hockey team. He introduced me to the man he was with to watch the fight— Elia Kazan, the brilliant film director.

It was a huge thrill. Both were very pleasant and it turned out that Budd and I would see each other frequently over the years at big boxing matches around the world and at favored New York saloons like P.J. Clarke's and Elaine's.

• • •

Ah yes…Donald Trump. I was going to leave my encounters with him out of the book but since his

New York, 1997:
The Donald finds the camera.

latest grab of the spotlight—running for president of the U.S.—it's hard to leave him out. "The Donald" as admirers and cynics alike have come to call him, introduced himself to me back in the eighties when I was covering the U.S. Open Tennis Championships for CBS.

Already an established real-estate entrepreneur in New York, mainly by putting his name on buildings he built, bought, or leased, Trump took every public opportunity to become a celebrity. He showed up at all of New York's sports events and at the big boxing matches in Las Vegas—somehow always finding a way to get attention. At the U. S. Open he had bought a box right at courtside in the old Louis Armstrong stadium where the big matches were played. He had a front-row seat adjacent to the court entrance used by the CBS-TV personnel. One night, as I was going onto the court to interview the winner of a match, he leaned over the railing, loudly called my name and waved at me, "Hey, Tim, how are ya!"

I had never met "the Donald," but simply by my acknowledging his greeting, he had now shown the audience around him that he was acquainted with a well-known sports-TV guy. Over ensuing years when he was at an event I was covering he would be sure to say "Hi Tim," especially if our cameras were near.

There was an upside to this for me. After he had acquired the TV rights to the Miss Universe and Miss USA contests in the 1990s, and I had become a partner in the aforementioned Diamond Sports, I saw an opportunity to pitch him our electronic voting system to use in judging his beauty contests.

Now that I was "one of his good friends," getting an appointment to see him at his Fifth Avenue Trump Tower office was easy. He was polite, friendly, and interested but not to the point of leasing our product.

Gratefully, I didn't make it into his book, *The Art of the Deal!*

• • •

Far and away the most rewarding encounter occurred a number of years ago when Patricia and I joined dear San Francisco friends Linda and Ron Colnett in San Jose, California at a fundraiser for schools in Tibet. The event featured an appearance by the Dalai Lama. We had paid for our tickets in advance and were expecting to be seated at the same table as our friends in the large banquet room of the hotel where the luncheon was held.

As we approached our numbered table near the speaker's podium and checked the place cards, we saw that our friends were not among the eight names on the hand-printed cards. Our names were, and on the place card next to ours was…Dalai Lama!

There were about five hundred people attending the luncheon and presumably many were more important than we were. We assumed, and never learned for sure, that there must have been some lottery, or just random seating that brought us such good luck, but sure enough, after his remarks from the adjacent stage the world famous Tibetan monk was escorted to his place right next to Patricia. As we stood to greet him, Patti quickly shared with the holy man that we were thrilled to meet him, particularly since it was our birthday that very day, May 16. "Both?" he asked with his famous broad smile, and spread his arms around us. "Yes, we have the same birthday, your holiness."

Best encounter ever.

CHAPTER 73

Closing the Circle

Back in the U.S. from the boxing gig in Macao, it was time to think about what lay ahead for us. Knowing that the game was over, I was done with NBC, not interested in pursuing another full-time job in sports-TV, and so my focus changed to life as a retiree. Ideally, I would still find a few things in TV or related activity—after-dinner speeches, corporate hosting, and also explore book-reading for money.

Patricia and I could now seriously plan our living arrangements. We had been looking to make a move from Idaho to warmer climes, and give Patti a chance to sleep better at lower altitudes. (In Ketchum we were at 6,000 feet). But on our return from Switzerland, it was all about Christmas and doing our best to gather as many kids and grandkids as we could for one last great Yuletide together in Sun Valley.

Having two families between us which included seventeen grandchildren had for several years inevitably compromised getting them all to Sun Valley Christmases. And 2013 was no different. Travel costs, lodging, weather-cancelled flights, and in-law logistics all conspired against us having thirty people at the table for turkey.

Still, we had my son Brendan with three kids, son Kevin with four of his own, and two more from his wife Tracey's first marriage. Skiing was good, Christmas dinner for fifteen of us was catered—to keep everyone out of the kitchen—and Patricia did her usual "Queen of Christmas" performance with a fabulous job of decorating the tree and much of the house.

Before leaving Switzerland we had decided that we would not renew the lease on our lovely domaine in the vines of Mont-sur-Rolle. Our part-time life in Suisse over eight years had been wonderful, but we were ready to be back in the U.S. full time.

With three months left on the lease, we made sure to visit our friends in France and Italy, and hosted our American pals Mike and Jan Quinn at Le Couvent for a weekend in May. And before the snow left the Alps I convinced Patricia we should take the train to Zurich, connect to the narrow-gauge railway up to Kleine-Scheidegg and stay two nights at the 19th-century Hotel Bellevue des Alpes.

While covering the World Cup Lauberhorn men's downhill race at Wengen over the years, I had always wanted to spend a night or two there. I knew it was unlikely I would ever be back, and it would make for an idyllic farewell to Switzerland. Patti agreed. We would not take our skis, just enjoy the hotel, the alpine air, and the spectacular views.

On the downhill side of the tracks at Kleine-Scheidegg—adjacent to one of the long turns on the Lauberhorn ski run are a few small, low-lying wooden buildings and an incongruous Indian teepee housing a beer-bar and a somnolent St.Bernard, complete with a small wine cask hanging from his collar. He is the resident photo-dog.

On the opposite, uphill side of the tracks, the gracious five-story Hotel Bellevue des Alpes stands as a sentinel at the base of the ominous sheet of black rock rising behind it—the Eiger, the most famous and mysterious mountain face in the Jungfrau range of the Swiss Alps.

We found the rooms as cozy and charming as we had hoped for and the dining room better than we expected. The outdoor terrace overlooked a steep pitch into a broad valley below. On the sunny afternoon we arrived, skiers were enjoying pristine conditions from the Eiger down to the villages of Wengen and Grindelwald.

As we sat outside with a glass of wine before dinner, an amazing thing happened. What had been a pleasant breeze across the terrace gradually picked up a startling force. The ubiquitous black mountain ravens that inhabit the high alpine altitudes suddenly appeared by the dozens over the slope below the hotel—swooping, and diving in an almost frantic display.

While the sun still shone, the wind began to whip up the fresh light snow from the valley below, and gradually the snow actually defied gravity and cascaded upward toward the blue sky. This remarkable display went on for an hour or more with the birds beating about as the wind continued to scoop up snow and hurl it skyward and darkness started to cover the nearby mountain peaks.

As the evening went on we were grateful for the warmth of the hotel dining room, but the howling of the wind became more insistent and by the time we were in bed, the windows were rattling and the wind was whistling through cracks in the wooden walls of the more than 100-year-old building.

Remarkably, there was no snow falling, and after a noisy night we awoke to a calm and beautiful sunny morning. It had been a major wind storm— apparently not uncommon in this region, but the hotel staff rated it as one of the most severe in many years.

Breakfast was filled with conversation among the guests about the storm, which apparently even caused parts of the old hotel to sway, as in an earthquake!

We spent the morning walking down a snow-packed road alongside the railroad tracks, watching happy skiers enjoying another bluebird day in paradise and peering at the magnificent Eiger that apparently had slept peacefully through the tumultuous "night of the wind."

After an exit through the gift shop we boarded our train back to Mont-sur-Rolle, grateful we had made our pilgrimage to the Hotel Bellevue-des Alpes.

We left Switzerland July 2, 2014, after a teary farewell to our favorite restaurant owners down the road in Rolle, Gabrielle and Veronique, the French couple from Brittany, whom we promised to return to for hugs and *moules frites*.

Back in the U.S. Patricia and I decided we had found our climate, our town, and our new house in St. Helena, California, in the heart of the Napa Valley. Yes, once again in the vines! When the Sun Valley house sold in September we were on our way to a new life. And for me, an ironic return to the San Francisco Bay area to which I had emigrated from Canada forty-eight years earlier.

My career in TV's Toy Department had been a great run, filled with hits and misses, good decisions and bad ones, successes and failures. But at the end of the day, it had been a career that gave me the chance to see much of the world, learn more about it than I could in any classroom, and to appreciate the gifts I had from family, friends and colleagues who shared the adventure with me.

ACKNOWLEDGEMENTS

Terry Casey: My brother-in-law who loved my sister Cindy well, and their children Megan and Ryan.

Paddy Sampson (Deceased): who got me in front of a TV camera on CBC.

Johnny Esaw: (Deceased) Who gave me my first job at CFTO-TV in Toronto.

Barry Van Gerbig: Who brought me to the U.S. with the NHL expansion.

Jack Price (Deceased): Who got me to New York.

Dick Corbett: My ND classmate who loaned me the down payment on our first house.

Mark Mulvoy: Friend in need, indeed.

Dawn Vicars: Lee's guardian angel in Santa Barbara.

Don Hodge: My best friend in Sun Valley who gave me great support during dark times.

Scotty Connal (Deceased): Who took a chance on me at NBC.

Barry Frank and Sandy Montag of IMG: My agents who never gave up on me.

Neal Pilson: Who appreciated me at CBS.

Terry O'Neil: Who made me the CBS winter-sports guy.

Rick Gentile: Who paired me with John McEnroe, Mary Carillo and Al McGuire at CBS.

Ed Goren: A prince at CBS who gave me a shot at FOX.

Dick Ebersol: Who brought me back to NBC.

Tom Brokaw: Who gave me good counsel.

All of my colleagues in production over the years at NBC, CBS, ESPN and USTA with special mention to David Dinkins Jr., George Finkel, Bob Mansbach, Mike Burks, Mike Arnold, George Veras, Bob Stenner, John

McGuinness, Andy Rosenberg, Bob Fishman, Chuck Milton, Ted Nathanson (Deceased), Suzanne Smith, Mark Shapiro, Jed Drake, Harold Hecht, Brian Williams (USTA TV) and many, many more.

All of the announcers and expert analysts recognized in this book, with special mention of Gil Clancy, Matt Millen, Al McGuire, Mary Carillo, Christin Cooper and Todd Brooker.

Bill Potts, NBC alumnus—my cheerleader!

Olivia Anne Barker for her typing and her thumb-drive!

Fiona Hallowell, my wise and patient editor.